The Bamboo Chest

An Adventure in Healing the Trauma of War

2nd Edition

by
Cork Graham

RIGEL MEDIA NONFICTION

Copyright © 2000 by Cork Graham

Paperback published 2004

Second Edition published 2011

www.corkgraham.com

All rights reserved.

No part of this publication can be reproduced or transmitted in any form or by any means, electronic or mechanical, without permission in writing from Cork Graham.

ISBN: 0-9703580-5-9

Library of Congress Control Number: 002090380

Disclaimer: Neither the publisher nor the author of this book accept any responsibility for any techniques whatsoever described within this book or attached or inferred materials. It is the responsibility of the reader to seek further training for any types of mental health techniques described in this book.

"Cork Graham is a wise and intelligent writer whose story is sure to please any reader interested in memoir and adventure."

— **Maxine Chernoff, author of *A Boy In Winter***

"I'll look for it on the best seller list."

— **Charlton Heston**

"Your innocence and honesty have been very engaging, refreshing compared to those so-called outdoor experts who write as if they know or have done, but whose sincerity and, more importantly, authenticity (key to me and ISE) seems hollow. Thank you for allowing me to experience your adventure, in a well-written book. I eagerly look forward to the other installments. Yours is a rare tale, told with a rare form of excellence."

— **John Kirk, Director of Communications, International Sportsmen's Exposition (ISE)**

"The Masai sent their youth out to slay a lion not for the end result of a dead predator (though it was an added bonus) but so they would have to face themselves. They returned from the hunt adults, with a knowledge of their own mortality and abilities, and a respect for the precious gift of life. Cork Graham has found his share of lions and lived to tell, in a unique and enriching style. Worthy of any Masai's campfire!"

— **Kurt Bickel, Senior Editor, *Spearfishing Magazine***

"Stranger than fiction"

– *The Guardian*

"Masterful job of keeping the reader's attention"

– New York Times

"Electrifying"

– The Sunday Times

Visit The Bamboo Chest website on the Internet to see full color photographs and maps associated with this book.

Books by Cork Graham

Non-Fiction

MAKE THEM PAY: How to Recruit, Train, and Integrate a Civil Defense Force Against a Much Larger Invader

Fiction

THE PANMUNJOM PROTOCOL

For the latest list of past, present, and future books by Cork Graham visit http://www.corkgraham.com/author.html

Cover Photos

All cover photos copyright by Cork Graham, except for the AP/ Wide World photo. Full screen/color photos at www.bamboochest.com

Left Top: Beach on Grand Pirate Island where Cork Graham was forced to sit bound.

Left Middle: Cork Graham back from a day of waterskiing and almost being swallowed by a python on the Saigon River, 1972.

Left Bottom: Richard Knight oversees the tinkering on the day of departure. Pi is seated in the tropical drink ornament while Ti hangs over the stern and fiddles with the motor.

Right Top: Front page of the *San Francisco Chronicle*, with permission.

Right Middle: Entrance to Bach Dang #3 Political Prison.

Right Bottom: Thai PBR gunboat patrolling up the Maekong River, highlands of Laos in the background.

In Memoriam

To my cousin, **Capitan Jose Ricardo Valencia Torres**, Fuerzas Especiales, Ecuador, a highly decorated veteran of the 1995 war against Peru, receiving the *Cruz de Guerra*. On December 3, 1999, at approximately 1200 hours, he jumped out of the transport plane and his chute didn't open. He was part of a jump team preparing for the annual December 6th Founder's Day celebration in Quito. Because of our mutual love of adventure, that hardly anyone else in the family could understand, he was the closest to me in my family in Ecuador. As it was reported, he had dropped right through the roof of the barracks at Cayambe, after free-falling 12,000 feet. It was a horribly sad Christmas that year, as he is dearly missed. And to his mother, my **Aunt Mercedes**, who loved him so and joined him in Heaven soon thereafter.

To my **Aunt Frances Delaplain**, Miss Washington 1954 from Spokane, Frances Mildred Graham, who, over the years, helped a number of veterans entering Santa Maria Community College. She passed away November 14, 1998, in Santa Maria, California. I enjoyed her spirituality and the time we shared on this physical plane; I took a great strength from her belief that I should graduate from photojournalism to writing.

Dedications

To my parents, **Fred Sr.** and **Maritza**, for without them I'd never have had such a wild life opportunity.

To **Kay, Jerry,** and **Lynnie,** my extended family in Nebraska and South Dakota, *on the Res,* who reminded me my nickname is Cork.

To Bob, Wick, Paul and in special rememberance of Bob Hyp (who passed away much too young—Semper Fi), who debriefed me at the Pentagon's Joint Casualty Resolution Center (JCRC) upon my release.

Especially to my dear love, **Robin,** for her editing, advice and inspiration.

To all of you who helped me get the hell out of the Socialist Republic of Vietnam in 1984. Thank you!

Foreword

Fame can truly be that proverbial double-edged sword, especially when it borders on infamy. It gets you invited to private parties and events, and even introductions and meetings you never thought possible. The other side of fame is that it can get you recognized when you least want to be recognized, either for personal or professional reasons.

After getting my teenaged face plastered on the front page of newspapers around the world from 1983 to 1985, I did my best to sink back into the woodwork so that I could more efficiently ply my trade as a photojournalist. I got so good at letting the publicized events of my life fade into the shadows that whenever I actually had to explain that part of my life, too many who had either forgotten the story, or didn't pay attention to the news during 1983 and 1984, thought I was coming up with tall tales about having been the photographer invited on a hunt for Captain Kidd's treasure buried on an island in the forbidden area of west Vietnam. "How old are you?" they'd always ask, as if they thought I was talking about an adventure that happened during the Vietnam War, not seven years after the war had ended. Now, I'm once again confronted with the potential ramifications of my past.

When I was released from the Vietnam prison in 1984, I told everyone that we had not found the treasure. I did so for a variety of reasons, the main one being that Richard Knight and the two Thais were still imprisoned in Vietnam, and Hanoi had told everyone that there was no treasure. Ironically, upon his release, even with the two Thais still in prison, Knight admitted to finding the buried treasure. This was in his memoir written with the aid of author Glenys Roberts. But, he said he had found it during his first attempt out of Malaysia in 1982, which was ludicrous, unless you understand the mind of a treasure hunter: his story could possibly have garnered the further investors he needed, and at the same time, would not anger the Vietnamese government as much as telling the truth. Though a poor gambler, Knight always liked to hedge his bets.

By 1985, I was in Central America and so focused on getting my photojournalism career back on track, that Vietnam was the last thing on my mind, other than learning they were the source for American-made arms and ammunition, left behind by the US government in 1975, and then being smuggled into El Salvador to arm the communist insurgents in an attempt delude the press and the American public that the FMLN (Farabundo Marti National Liberation front) of El Salvador was totally a people's front, and had no support from the outside.

Not even a year after my arrival in El Salvador, I witnessed an atrocity committed by the FMLN (that not one bureau chief at the Camino Real would report) and so, accepted recruitment by my friend Sam, yes, the same one you'll read about in the book. As one of the youngest (if not the youngest) United States' paramilitary officers in Latin America, I received a number of very expensive trainings, not the least of which was counter-insurgency schooling by the US Navy SEALs military advisors at the Punta Ruca Naval Base in El Salvador, and sniper training by the 7th Special Forces Group at nearby CEMFA, the Salvadoran Army's main training center, just down the road from La Union.

The original copy of ***The Bamboo Chest*** was published as a paperback in 2004, and became a bestseller soon thereafter, reaching #2 on Amazon's International Top Seller list for three weeks. When I originally wrote the book, I wasn't too keen on letting everyone know the complete truth about the treasure. I'd been hassled by a number of treasure hunters over the years and felt that they were simply Johnny-come-latelies and frankly, didn't put in the time to find any treasure, nor put up the risk. Also, that training that I used to keep alive in Central America was the training I had so needed during the treasure hunt with Knight back in 1983. As I had told my Vietnamese interrogators, had I actually been with the CIA at that time, I wouldn't have been caught in the first place—after fighting counterinsurgency wars against Raul Castro's boys in Central America and South America for four years, I had become well-versed in airborne and waterborne covert insertion.

When the first edition of ***The Bamboo Chest*** was published in 2004, I had an interest in returning to Southeast Asia in order to *do it right*. Cambodia still had that Wild West quality to it and anything could be got on the blackmarket. Though Vietnam had improved its navy, the team I could have put together would still have easily bypassed their defenses, and no less embarrassingly to Vietnam, than a bumbling middle-aged Brit and teenaged Yank had done in 1983. That idea went by the wayside, as a covert retrieval of the treasure became pointless: in 1983, the treasure would have been kept safe from the Socialist Republic of Vietnam in a Philippine bank. Because of new post-Cold War agreements between the Philippines and Vietnam, that is no longer the case. As time went by, and I lost interest in the treasure I'd already put a year of my life into, I shelved the idea, only going back to it whenever contacted by the all too frequent armchair treasure hunter who had read the first edition of this book and wanted to know more. This is something I dread once again with the present world economy and the average reader's thinking that finding treasure is easy money. The last one to contact me, and the most entertaining, had an Order of the British Empire (OBE), an affinity for the heydays of communism, and many professional connections within the higher echelons of Vietnam's never-ceases-to-amaze corrupt government. Captain Kidd's treasure haunts everyone...I leave it to you whether Kidd's gold can get a hold on you. And please, as I told bestselling author Tomasz Michniewicz, who flew all the way from his homeland of Poland to San Francisco in order to interview me for his next book on the psychology of treasure hunters, "My days of treasure hunting were pretty much over the day I walked off that freedom bird at Don Muang Airport in Thailand."

    As for Knight, after you've read the adventure, it shouldn't be a surprise what happened to him...

Cork Graham, 2011

Don't Go There - 8/9/98

Voice 1 - Night in the bush in the drivin' rain
Heard the rockets burst then the screamin' pain
Feelin' pretty good 'cause I'm still whole
My body's intact but not my soul
Choir - Don't go there is what my Mama said
You're gonna get hurt, wind up dead
But I had to go, stand and fight 'cause
I didn't listen, I died that night
Voice 2 - My tour was over, I was done
The battles fought, but the war not won
I caught that bird, took me to the World
See my home, see my girl
Choir - Don't go there is what my Mama said
You're gonna get hurt, wind up dead
But I had to go, stand and fight
'cause I didn't listen, I died one night
Solo
Voice 3 - John Wayne told me to be a man
Defend my country the best I can
My home had changed, my girl didn't care
Made fun of my clothes, ridiculed my hair
Choir - Don't go there is what my Mama said
You're gonna get hurt, wind up dead
But I had to go, stand and fight
'cause I didn't listen, I died one night
Voice 4 - Nights at home in the drivin' rain
I hear rockets burst and the screamin' pain
Feelin' pretty good 'cause I'm still whole
My body's intact but not my soul.
— Written by S.L.Ponciroli USN, Danang '68-'69

Part One

Thailand

Chapter 1

"I guess it was bound to happen."— Dickey Chapelle, combat photojournalist, Chu Lai, 1965, as she lay dying from a severed carotid artery, after stepping on a landmine.

Beginnings

Kien Giang Provincial Prison, Socialist Republic of Vietnam,

July 1983

      It is the second morning after a night of beatings and the prison guards have been sloppy. Normally they use rubber hoses, but last night someone brought in a stick, and I think they dislocated a rib from my spine. It's hard to breath. I fidget on my wooden stool trying to find some salvation from the pain, but it hurts so damn much every time I take a deep breath.

      I try to distract myself by glancing at light coming in through the barred window; then at the high ceiling of this crumbling concrete leftover of French Imperialism. A metal-against-metal clicking disrupts my scan and brings my attention to the guard who grins suggestively as he fingers the bolt of his loaded AK-47. I roll my eyes and then anxiously slide my gaze over the stained, crudely simple table that centers the room, the dull gleam of the metal thermos and thimble cups arrayed in a semi-circle on top.

      Normally I'm offered tea at the beginning of interrogations—friend or foe, everyone gets tea in Vietnam—but today, I'm offered none as the three man judge and jury go at each other in Vietnamese. The one I call Frogface, because of his wide upper-lip, breaks off and looks sternly at me. "Why do you keep moving in your seat?" he asks.

      "You know full well why I'm fidgeting!" I answer.

      "Remember what I said, Mr. Gra-ham, if you are insolent you will be punished!"

      "What do you call last night?!"

"I do not know what you are talking about," he says and turns his attention back to the other two seated at the table.

How can I not want to share at least a little of my pain? I want to jump up from my seat and ram my fist right through his glasses. I sure don't want to be stingy at this moment. I want to give and give, all that they had given me last night! But the pain I'm already suffering reminds me that this is only a smattering of possibilities they have to offer. I draw a trembled breath, and sink deeper into my seat.

This isn't supposed to be happening!

The war has been over for more than eight years, and I'm only a fresh out of high school photojournalist on his first big story, but yet, I'm feeling like I'm being set up, that this is just a warm up for all that I had read about the experiences of American POWs during the war. This is an American flashback I don't want to experience!

I let out a sigh and repeat what I'd been telling them since my capture: "I told you, I'm a photojournalist freelancing for the AP, you know— Associated Press."

"Again, Mr. Gra-ham. If you tell the truth, you will be taken to Hanoi, the world press will record your admission of spying; and then you will be released. . .If you continue lying, you will be taken out and shot! And no one will even know you were in Vietnam. Your country does not know you are here. Your family. No one—"

"But, I've been telling you for the last week that—"

Frogface slaps the top of the table, and yells, "Again, tell us why you are here—and do not lie!"

* * *

San Francisco International Airport, four months earlier

Ever since we lived in Vietnam, my father has hated both CIA operatives and journalists. Spooks were always drunks to him, and suspect of authenticity—a lot of embassy staff liked to brag that they were *dirty-shirts*[1], especially when they were drinking and needing a story to tell. As for the rag-tag of journalists he dealt with in Saigon as a contractor; they were self-righteous assholes who thought they could manipulate his feelings to some guilt about being there, and somehow get him to cleanse his soul. Far-fetched ideas, considering what he knew was being reported back in the States. Vietnam was never so easy to put down in words.

No wonder he was dismayed when, out of the blue, I told him that I was going to Thailand to cover the war between the Khmer Rouge and the invading forces that renamed Cambodia, Kampuchea.

My freedom flight wasn't due to leave for another twenty minutes. I offered to wait by myself, but my father said, "Nonsense!"

I looked at my father, the ex-Korean War Marine, who had been such a terror in my childhood, the man whose robustness had intimidated me the way large animals do some people. But, now as I sat next to him, I only saw an overweight older man who was searching through his well-educated mind for reasons I shouldn't have skipped out on college, much less used my college fund to run off to Thailand with a half-cocked idea. He worked himself into a seat, took a heavy breath, and slicked his gray hair back with the palm of his hand.

Carrying my own extra twenty pounds that had made me so insecure in high school, I sat myself down for the unbearable quiet I knew would envelope us again as it had on our drive to the airport. He sought refuge in a copy of *Time* magazine, extracted from his briefcase. He never went anywhere without that briefcase, as though it held some mystical power that I'd been trying to decipher all my life. He removed his driving glasses and began reading.

I unfolded a Sunday edition of the *San Francisco Chronicle*, and with a rustle of newspaper erected my own wall between my father and me. Like tribes on opposite sides of a river, we had long ago built forts without ever bothering to first ask if the other was friend or foe.

"Looks like the Marines are staying in Beirut," my father said, without looking up from his magazine.

"Yeah, looks like Reagan really wants to make a point."

My father nodded and returned to his magazine. I withdrew back into my newspaper. As I turned the page, I could barely control my anticipation as I read that the springtime border fighting between the Khmer Rouge and the Vietnamese had flared. Looking at the photo of a Khmer Rouge riding a bicycle next to a T-55 tank, I said, "I could take that shot!"

"What did you say, Freddy?" My father lowered his magazine.

"Nothing, Dad." Dreams of the Pulitzer Prize, or the Robert Capa Award given to photographers for exceptional achievements under hazardous conditions, danced through my mind. A great comfort for me while being so reminded of the giant rift I'd always felt between my father and me.

Though my family name came to me from the David Graham who arrived in South Carolina from Scotland and County Antrim, Ireland in 1774, and whose sons fought redcoats at the battle of Kings Mountain;

my grandmother's line on my dad's side were immigrants who came from Hamburg and the German area of Switzerland in the late 1800s. Like many a good carpenter and construction worker, my grandmother's father, Great-Grandfather Äbischer, worked hard pounding nails, and laying brick (more brick than wood as Chicago was terrified of wood ever since the Great Fire), and in the evening he'd unwind by having his daily mug of lager. Not something to worry about, until he decided to clean the handgun he kept for home protection while having his drink. That particular evening, he was slightly drunk on beer, and definitely tired from a long workday; and worse, he didn't even check to see if the chamber was empty. My great-grandmother, who had been preparing the family's dinner, must have been lined up perfectly with the muzzle when it suddenly went off. It killed her instantly. When great-grandfather realized what he had done, he felt he couldn't live without his love, put the revolver to his own head, and cheated his children of a remaining parent. Nineteen-eighteen was a bad year for the Äbischers, especially my grandmother, who was fourteen and observed the whole ugly scene.

My great-uncle Fred, a teenager and the eldest of the siblings, had to raise his three sisters pretty much by himself, and while he did, my grandmother sought solace—the closest she could find to therapy—through the Christian Science religion. My grandmother was always very spiritual. She loved to quote the Bible to me and my brother. I enjoyed it, but, somehow I never felt I could ever connect with her on a deeply emotional level, the way I did with my Step-grandfather, Ed Thompson, the man who had instilled in me my love of fishing and the outdoors. Grandma seemed to be so much higher into the heavens, too far for me to reach on my mortal feet. Even as a child it seemed to me that even though my grandmother was kind and said sweet things, there was an emotional part of her that just wasn't available, which taught my father to be emotionally unavailable and disconnected from his own sons.

"Freddy, I still can't understand why you're doing this. Do you have any contacts? Anything?" my father asked, wrenching me back from my thoughts about our family history.

Mr. Logic, he was so out of character! Such emotion, such anguish! I'd never seen either from him before. When I first told them my plans, my parents seemed only mildly attentive, as though I was still the little child they once knew, full of fantasies best kept private. A sudden sadness sunk me deeper into my seat, as I truly realized how much we *really* never communicated. It hit harder than the normal enlightening realizations of before, as though it really meant something, as though in that moment I knew that all my father had learned and wanted to share with me would die with him, and I'd be left only with the dismay that I had never known him at all.

I had to think of something fast: people to contact, members of the foreign correspondents community who would welcome me into their brotherhood. I loved that term, *foreign correspondent*. It conjured up nights spent covering jungle operations, days photographing military coups and turmoil, risking life for truth, and joining in amorous bliss with beautiful women of intrigue at foreign embassies. Just like in the movie that mesmerized me only a few weeks before— *The Year of Living Dangerously*!

Chance offered me the quick answer: my eyes at that very moment landed on an article in the pink entertainment section of the *San Francisco Chronicle/Examiner*. I gazed at it like a fortuneteller into a crystal ball. It was an article about a photojournalist living in Bangkok, an Australian about whom a TV-movie had just been made.

"No, I don't have anybody set up right now. But there is this guy I read about, John Everingham. They just made a movie about his life as a photojournalist, starring Michael Landon. See? That's him." I pointed to the tow-headed man in his early thirties, standing next to Michael Landon and two Asian women.

My father shook his head. "Son, why don't I just give you the name of an old business associate of mine? His name is Bill Hwa. He bought the AMTRACO²office in Bangkok at the end of the war when they went bankrupt. He's a good man. You probably don't remember him, but he visited us a few times in Saigon."

Dad reached for his briefcase. Instinctively, I reached for my newly purchased briefcase. He pulled out a small, black telephone book. I pulled out a similar black notebook in which to enter the name of my father's friend.

"Wa, with a W?" I asked while drawing my thumb down the alphabetical tabs.

"No, it's H-W-A." He said and slowly closed his briefcase. His crinkled forehead betrayed a rising concern. "Why are you doing this, son?"

I had never felt totally at home in the United States because he had kept me overseas too long and that time away from the land of my nationality, my identity, had only caused me to resent him and blame him for my feelings of displacement. Yearning always to feel more American, I was poorly repatriated, and what Dr. Ruth Hill Useem coined, a [Third Culture Kid (TCK)](), and quickly becoming an Adult Third Culture Kid (ATCK). I was an American without ever knowing what it meant to be American.

Instead of being truthful, and because of not having yet had the opportunity to read the vast amount of research done on TCKs, I offered the other part of the answer, the canned response from so many other authors who turned to writing in order to connect with those they felt they couldn't otherwise. "I want to be a writer, Dad," I said. "I want to be like Jack London and Ernest Hemingway. They wrote so well because they had exciting lives. You always told me when I was a kid about how you met Hemingway in Cuba. You talked about it as though it was worth talking about, right up there with the time you saw John Steinbeck in Saigon."

"I never should have told you that story." He pursed his lips and sighed. Once again we hid behind our reading materials. After a moment, he couldn't hold it back any longer. "So, what you're saying is you have no magazine or newspaper backing you? Only one contact whom you've never met?!"

I nodded.

"Do you even have any leads?" His face had turned beet-red.

"When I arrive in Bangkok I'll go to the border of Thailand and Cambodia to cover the fighting. Also, I can check out the Colonel Bo Gritz story in Nakhon Phanom on the Lao border."

I had planned my return to Southeast Asia for almost two years, ever since junior year at Carlmont High School. There was that time I was in the library reading a book about Vietnam and came across a black and white photo of two men, an ARVN soldier and Errol Flynn's son, Sean. I was stunned by his daring look and how much I wanted to be like the Sean in that photo: a wild, devil-maycare grin, a US Army helmet on his head, a Nikon around his neck. And the article on the front page of just about every newspaper in the Bay Area that fall, well, that was the last push: Colonel Bo Gritz was going back into Laos to find American MIAs, and I was going to be right there next to him! Me and my cameras!

"You can get killed, you know!" It was hard to tell whether my father was just furious, or concerned, but there was something very liberating in holding my ground.

Names ran through my mind: Sean Flynn, Dana Stone, Robert Capa, Larry Burrows, Kent Potter, Keizaburo Shimamoto, Henri Huet, Kyochi Sawada, Ollie Noonan, Dickey Chappelle, Bernard B. Fall, François Scully. And their demise: landmines, helicopters shot out of the sky, disappearances in the jungles of Indochina. My mind froze on the full-color image of mud and brotherhood immortalized by Burrows at the DMZ in 1966—a head-bandaged black Marine reaching for his wounded white buddy. That those names are only a tiny number of photojournalists killed in Vietnam, and percentage-wise combat photographers are killed and wounded more often than combatants, was not lost on me. But, I had only read their names in books. I had only seen their work on photo gallery walls. There was no harsh reality that I could remember of Vietnam that would keep me from doing something really stupid.

I flashed back a *c'est la vie* look. "I can get run over by a car here, but you stopped holding my hand and leading me across the street long ago. I'll be okay." My ignorant confidence of youth and the vividness of dreams about my future would be the shields to protect me from all harm.

A voice over the intercom announced my flight. On most other trips, I would wait until the last minute to be seated. Not this time. I jumped out of my seat and grabbed my carry-on baggage.

"We've got a little more time. We can wait."

"I think I'd better board now, Dad."

Dad's look told me I had driven my blade deep. I didn't want to hurt him, but I had to be true to my own life choices. And from a very young age, I knew my choice would not be the path of safety, or least resistance.

"Okay." He took a quick breath and pushed himself up out of his seat. Without a word we walked to the gate.

As we shook hands, he said, "I think what you're doing is wrong, son. But I want you to know we love you and you'll always have a place to come back to."

I stiffened and challenged, "I'm not coming back until I'm successful."

Dad smiled, unsuccessfully masking his worry. My jaw clenched in answer to what I considered his last slight. I wanted to slap him the way he had me, when as a child I'd done something to anger him. The words now, as many times before, revolved through my mind—*he already envisions my failure! He's telling me he'll catch me if I fall. But I'm going to stand on my own two legs. Thank you very much!*

My father turned and walked away. He never looked back as he approached the security checkpoint, though part of me hoped otherwise. I turned sullenly toward the gate, wondering why he frequently made me feel so uncomfortable. When my brother and I were children, he'd make us smile at night by reading J.M. Roberts' *The History of the World*, and J.R.R. Tolkien's *The Hobbit* to us and tucking us into bed. In high school, though, I fantasized about putting a bullet through his head, and the memory of those thoughts almost made me cry. I didn't want to hate him but I didn't know how to stop. Our relationship had escalated from low-level conflict into full-scale war. Over what, I did not know.

At the gate the flight attendant accepted my boarding pass. Long and covered, the ramp wound its way towards the 747 like a tunnel descending into the dragon's cavern. As I crossed the threshold I recalled with disdain one of my father's favorite defeatist sayings: "Never send a boy to do a man's job."

Chapter 2

"No bird soars too high, if he soars with his owns wings."— William Blake

Introductions

In my large suitcase were the essentials of a combat photojournalist: two pairs of tigerstripe fatigues; a Marine Ka-bar knife; a Gerber Mark II stiletto; an Army surplus canteen; and a kevlar vest festooned with pockets of every size. I had purchased the bulletproof photojournalist's vest, on top of everything else in that bag, for a little more than $500 from a manufacturer in Florida, a guy who thought that I was on my way to Central America, like every other journalist looking for the latest *bang-bang*. Only upon landing did the realization hit me that I could be suspected of being a mercenary, or at least a drug runner. I was scared shitless, but took a deep breath, smiled, and offered an air of confidence to the customs officer as I heaved my suitcase onto the table.

"Passport," barked the khaki officer, extending his open hand sharply. A customs official at his side made a snide-sounding remark in Thai that I supposed was about me. I tried calming my nerves by assuming that the hour was late, and the customs officer was thinking to himself that his time would be better spent sipping a beer with his buddies, instead of dealing with some teen-aged American.

"Where are you staying in Bangkok?" His eyes locked on mine as he looked up from my passport.

"The Nana Hotel," I answered, and wondered if it was my emotions soaking my shirt, or just the heat. Taking a quick look around, I noticed that an American and his Thai wife, waiting in the line next to mine, were also soaked around the armpits and back. I relaxed a bit and licked the sweat off my upper lip, while my mind raced forward to the Nana and its air-conditioned lobby, that right now seemed like my favorite flavored ice cream. If I didn't get out of there soon, though, I was in danger of passing out from the heat and the fear.

Leafing through my passport, the officer found my Thai visa. "Reason for visit?"

"Business." I smiled, filled with a new feeling of confidence offered by the statement.

He looked up disinterested. "Anything to declare?"

"No." I hoped my expression of innocence was believable. Thank God he didn't take my pulse right after he asked me.

He stamped my passport, handed it back, and waved me through. "Welcome to Thailand."

Outside, a yelling throng of taxi drivers were jumping like puppies for a full nipple. They were careful not to cross the line of the customs gate. The heat and stress had definitely taken it out of me as the world now looked and felt like the deck of a ship on rough seas. Much more of this and I was going to launch my last airline meal at the crowd.

"I have best price!" shouted one of them, grabbing for my luggage. I swiped his hand away and shook my head.

"I have nicest car!" shouted another, putting his hand on my shoulder as though he was confiding words of wisdom to a friend. "American. Drive in comfort."

The least pushy of the drivers with the best command of the English language got my business. He was a stout man who reminded me of my Dad. "Where you want go?"

I told him, offering my luggage, but guarding my camera case. A Thai man jumped in next to the driver and waved back at me after I got in. "You don't mind my friend come along?" asked the driver as he closed his door and started the engine.

I shook my head.

"You don't want go Nana," said the taxi driver as we pulled away from the mass of tourists and taxi drivers spilling off the sidewalk.

"Nana no goot," said the passenger as I returned my attention to the front. "They charge too much and their girl no vely pletty. My hotel bettah. Vely pletty gurl. Cheap. Cheap. Maybe you like boys? Have that too." This was my reminder of how Thais switch between Ls and Rs in their own language, seemingly with a devil-may-care attitude. It didn't take too long to become at ease with it.

So accustomed to the army of sexual adventurers who invaded Bangkok weekly, the driver and his friend were both under the impression that this could be the only reason I was here. They offered to procure some of the best Thai stick in Thailand. I told them that I didn't even smoke cigarettes, that I was really tired from my flight, and sex was the last thing on my mind. Hit by a sudden rush of paranoia, I berated myself under a hushed breath. *You stupid fool! They could kill you and dump you in a hole and nobody'd know!* I wished for the imagined protection of my Marine Ka-bar knife and Gerber stiletto, hidden in my luggage.

"No—no, that's okay. I already have a *reservation* at the Nana. I'm expected."

"Oh, my friend, I guarantee you goot time." He turned his head to show off a gold-toothed grin. It was a gesture that instead of instilling the sense of rapport I'm sure he wanted, only conjured up mental images of thugs, murderers, and pirates. Though having lived in Southeast Asia most of my life, I now felt completely like a guppy in a puddle, gasping for air. Even the sense of safety I'd had as a child here was gone. That I was so inexperienced and out of my element was no more apparent than right then. "Come my hotel I buy drink. You have great time," he said.

YOUNG AMERICAN FOUND DEAD IN BANGKOK CANAL—MULTIPLE STAB WOUNDS! The imaginary newspaper headline shot shivers through me. "I'd love to have a drink, but I have to report to my boss when I get to the hotel." For dramatic emphasis, I raised my forearm like a GI in a movie, checking for *Zulu* time. "Shit! And I'm already an hour late because of that damn plane. Could we hurry up and get to the hotel? My boss is a real hard ass."

"Okay, okay. My friend, no problem. We almost there."

I sat back and anticipated hoods lunging through the car door, and cold-cocking me. The Thais laughed and looked at me like I was nuts. Instead, the lights of a large, familiar hotel appeared in the window.

"Nana," the driver said.

"Great!" I let out my stopped breath, and exited the cab.

"I could have taken you much better place. More girls, less price."

"Thanks." I picked up my bags from the pavement and was engulfed by the fluorescent lighting from the Nana's lobby.

From age four to age twelve, I lived in Southeast Asia with my family. For summer vacations, we would travel to Spokane, Washington and Santa Maria, California to visit my grandparents and aunt. Other years, restricted by finances, we visited nearby countries, which often translated to the Philippines and Thailand. The Nana was the hotel where we always stayed when we arrived in Bangkok. Most Americans with any past connection to the United States government, or military, stayed at the Nana.

I expected it to be just as I had last seen it in 1977. But, the only remnants left from my childhood visits to the brightly lit Nana lobby were the small concrete pond and waterfall, and the US Air Force Squadron and other U.S. military shields left over from the war: wood and painted brass, hanging along the front of the hotel desk. I smiled at the surroundings with the feeling that I had stepped back fifteen years. Several attractively dressed Thai women sitting around the edge of the pond were unmistakably staring at me as I spoke with the clerk about my reservation. I noticed them during my scan of the surroundings while I waited for the desk clerk to finish checking me in. They offered smiles and grins I politely returned. Considering this was the place my father thought wholesome enough to bring his wife and children to, I thought nothing more of their attentions than simply those of hotel employees whiling away their time off by chatting amongst themselves about the latest hotel guests. The memorabilia kept my eyes in the past, not seeing what I would have seen were I much older during the 1960s and '70s.

When the bellhop took my luggage, I followed him towards the elevator, past the waterfall and the Thai women. Two fetching girls latched onto my stolen glance. One was very thin with long black hair. The other buxom, with a perm. They rushed over to me.

"You want company, American boy?" the slim one propositioned.

"He no boy. He man. That why he want date me," teased the other.

"U-uh. No thanks."

"Why? You no want me?" The slim model pouted, arms akimbo, and then slipped into a smile. "We always here." The elevator doors closed too slowly and I was lifted away to my floor.

By the time the bellboy deposited my luggage on the hotel bed, my head was spinning: from terrified for my life to having two sexy Thai women dash to my side, offering to not only take me to bed, but also—unbeknownst to them—bring me forth, past my virginity. All in one night! The excitement! The surprise! I hadn't even left Bangkok yet! This was what I'd been looking for. I thumbed through my wallet for a couple dollars. I could only imagine what the next day would bring. Closing his fingers over the tip, the bellboy bared a lecherous grin. "Is there anything else I can get you?"

I smiled and shook my head, remembering that tomorrow I would have to begin my search for Everingham. "No more excitement for today," I said as jet lag finally overwhelmed my evening's rush of endorphins.

* * *

Surprisingly, contacting John Everingham was as easy as picking up the phone, calling information for the local press club, which in Thailand is the FCCT[3], and getting the number through them. To say that I was tickled to be meeting this legend within a day of my arrival in

Bangkok would have been an understatement. With my camera bag slung over my shoulder like a security blanket, proof that I was a photographer, I arrived at Everingham's house late in the morning, that moment in the tropics between hanging fog and poaching sun. When I walked past the large metal gate of Everingham's home, the immediate impression that hit me was how grand the grounds were, reminding me of a Victorian palace, just like in *The King and I*. The estate seemed like a royal court, not belonging to a king, but definitely a count, or a duke, with a fish pond covered by giant Victoria lily pads, and two large houses. Certainly not what I expected from someone living on photojournalist wages. But then I remembered that one of my father's reasons for living in Southeast Asia was how far the American dollar could stretch.

A petite woman in black slacks, thongs, and a collarless shirt answered my knock. She was thin in the way of many Asian women. Long, jet-black hair. A smooth, almost ageless face. Keo smiled, and I recognized her from her picture in the entertainment section of the *San Francisco Chronicle*. A Thai returning on the plane I arrived in had mentioned that he knew their story and said she was a Lao princess. By her beauty alone, it was easy to see why John had risked his life to have her alongside him.

"You must be Fred," she said in perfect English, her voice mesmerizingly soft and comforting, with just enough jubilance to keep it interesting.

"Yes."

She raised an eyebrow. "You're the young man without any experience?"

Crestfallen, I shook my head and answered, "No, I don't have any experience."

Her smile broadened. "John's very excited to meet you. You've got a lot of courage coming all this way to follow your dreams."

She pointed me in the direction of a tiny Japanese house with white paper walls, and said, "Good luck!"

The house's unique, fragile-looking paper walls baffled me. Amazingly, it had survived the monsoons well. I walked alone past that small paper house to a glass-walled bungalow. And through the door, I laid eyes on the man I had read about in the *Chronicle*. He was with someone, looking over an array of slides on an expansive drafting table. Trim and tanned with a freediver's chest, not to mention his sun-bleached Beatle's hairstyle and sarong, made John Everingham out of place in the city: he belonged in Bali with a surfboard under his arm. He couldn't have been more than thirty-five. With a broad smile, he opened the door and introduced himself.

"Nice to meet you!" I returned, suddenly aware that my wide grin made me look like an idiot fan. Everingham represented everything I had come to idolize, and I felt like a seeker about to have an audience with the journalist's Buddha, under the correspondent's Bodhi tree.

Hunched over a typewriter, sat the man who had just been at the desk with Everingham. He, too, was wearing the same Bali surfer garb, although he was a few years older. "This is my friend, Ron Watkins." John pointed to the barrel-chested man with the wavy, gray hair, his concentration almost unbreakable. "He's a good mate. A bit like you, I guess; taken by the romance of journalism and looking for his big break."

Watkins glanced up from his work, offered a wave, and said, in an accent lilting between nasal Western Australia, and a refined Oxford, "How're you doing there, Fred?"

"Great. You?"

"Excellent!" He fell back into his seated slump, into what must have been focused hell, his eyes scanning his typed words, his mind chasing fleeting words that would accurately describe his observations and experiences. I felt relieved that I was starting out as a photojournalist and not a journalist, a prisoner of the well-crafted word. Watkin's own personal prison would keep him in perpetual servitude until one day, according to Everingham, the never-attained success as a journalist—and probably an extreme case of mid-life crisis—would cause him to take his own life at the end of a rope.

"Fred, it'll just take me a minute to finish off these captions and I'll be with you." Everingham walked over, sat down at his own desk and resumed typing a letter. Not one to miss out on an opportunity to see what foreign correspondents adorn their offices with, I scanned the room. Photos of Thailand and Southeast Asia covered the walls. On the other side of Watkins, an eight-by-ten inch black and white shot of a World War II British bomber crew. There was a startling resemblance of one of the crew to Watkins. My attention was drawn to the man held prisoner by his typewriter. He was older than Everingham, but I had assumed by only a *few* years. I was flabbergasted. *Is journalism the real fountain of youth?* The other pictures on the wall were of the Thai and Lao hill tribes, their clothes spectacularly colorful, like those I remembered from my father's stacks of *National Geographic*. Crimson reds. Burnt oranges. Saffron yellows. Bone whites. Coal blacks. Silvers. Smiling Hmong and Montagnard (properly called Degar). Photos of orange-and-maroon-robed monks. Golden temples and bamboo-shack villages glowing in the orange evening twilight. My insides lifted with the lightness of a child's skip. I was elated that I had found Everingham.

He led me past a glass partition to the adjoining room, and then took his place atop a stool on the other side of a light-table that took up most of this elongated, much smaller room. The dark red, cherry wood of the frames holding the glass partition caused me to stop and draw my hand along the grain. It felt amazingly smooth, warming me. Continuing on, I took the other bar stool, while Everingham got up for a moment and moved around pulling negatives from a wall of cabinets, deciding on which developed strip to work with first. He turned to the light-table and began mounting slides by cutting them up and inserting them into their plastic mounts. It was something I had never seen, something that Kodak did for me behind the closed doors of the photo lab. *So that's what they do*, I mused.

"Do you develop and cut up your film like this at home?" he asked.

"No," I answered, not wanting to admit to him, or even myself, that I had purchased my camera equipment only a week before I left California, or that I didn't even understand how the damned thing worked yet.

He studied me for second. "Have you ever even developed your own film, Fred?"

"I always went to Fotomat. You know. One of those next day deals..."

"Can you tell me anything, Fred? That you've taken pictures for the high school yearbook?"

"I grew up in Vietnam," I said quickly, as though it meant anything to anybody other than myself.

He raised his eyebrows and donated a fraternal smile. "Crazy times, huh?"

"Yeah."

"All you had to do then was run down to the nearest US airbase and hop a chopper," he said wistfully, as though thinking of the journalists' *good old days.*

I shifted my balance on the stool. "Do you know much about Colonel Gritz and the MIAs?"

"Yeah. He's a crazy bastard. Watch out for him. Now listen, Fred. I'll give you a little advice about camera work." I wanted to listen, but I was so taken by the romance of photojournalism, the technical part took me back to high school, and being tutored by my father when I was flunking biology. Just like back then, I steeled myself to keep the tidal wave of facts from dimming my enthusiasm. ". . . Nikon has the best lenses, but you've got to watch out for the damned fungus which gets on the lenses and into the electronics. The best way to protect your camera is with silica gel. Ever used it?"

"No."

"Another thing you've got to remember is that editors pretty much buy only slides."

My insides seemed to pour out of me and run all over the floor. I almost wanted to cry for having wasted $200 on color print film in California!

Everingham grinned when I confessed my error. "Well, you can use the black and white you brought to at least get started. But, you'll have to pick up chrome[4] to shoot for the magazines. . . Now, when you get your film, the best thing to do is put it in the refrigerator to keep it cool." He reached over and opened his. Pointing at the mound of film surrounded by frost, he asked, "Like this refrigerator."

I admired the small unit, perfect for also helping a college student keep beer cold in a tiny dorm room.

"Costs a lot to get good quality out here," he said. "I bought it with the money from that movie they made about my wife and me."

"<u>Love is Forever</u>?"

He nodded. "They say it played pretty well in the States. What did you think of it?"

"I actually didn't see it, but I read about it."

"Better you didn't see it." He shrugged. "It turned out like one of those damned 1950s B-movies about Communists. I mean, it was so Hollywood. But, what can you expect?"

"What was your story really like?"

He stopped and gauged me, and then said, "A bit of adventure. After the war the Pathet Lao let me stay in Laos. They knew how much I'd been opposed to the B-52 strikes carried out by the US. I was the only non-Communist journalist allowed to remain. I thought the new regime would be better, but it wasn't. Remember, Fred, as a journalist you can't let your own biases cloud things. Even after you learn that journalism and objectivity don't always walk hand in hand. We all have different eyes and ears, and they don't catch everything."

I grinned as though I was in on the joke. I wasn't. It would take much more experience and another five years for me to understand that sombering joke. Yep, much more experience, the type filled with personal emotional pain, the kind only combat can offer you when you still think you can remain objective while people are getting shredded into little pieces around you.

"Well," he said, "the new regime started treating the people badly, so I did what I'd always done. I took my pictures and sent them out of the country to let the world know what was really happening. The Pathet Lao caught my runner at the border and found out about me. I'd been using a phony name with the pictures. They threw me in jail and accused me of being a spy for the CIA."

"And Keo was already your girlfriend?"

"Yes." He glanced out the window and caught a glimpse of her moving about the house. The soft light on his equally soft features and expression pleased the eye. It was a moment I wanted to capture right there, and name it *Man Loves Woman*. "She was scared for me. She thought they'd execute me for sure. The press corps made it pretty hot for the Pathet Lao. Eventually they released me, but I couldn't legally get Keo out. I told her I'd come back for her."

"What did you do?"

"I fine-tuned my scuba skills. Then I used what they call an octopus rig, two mouthpieces and regulators on a single rig, to smuggle Keo out by swimming under the Maekong[5] River. The papers loved the story. The rest, as they say, is history."

"That's amazing!" This was the kind of person I wanted to know. Back home an adventure was having too much to drink and throwing up, or smoking marijuana, or racing down the freeway with the risk of ending up in a head-on collision. But what Everingham revealed was *REAL*. This was an adventure that mattered. "How'd you get started? I mean did you grow up with an automatic drive to take pics?"

"I love traveling." John wearily put a hand to his cheek, looking like he had spent most of the night meeting a deadline. "For a while I was a hotel manager in New Guinea, then at sixteen when I'd saved enough money, I headed for Indochina. I picked up the languages pretty quick, and the TV crews covering the war always needed a translator. I got some soundman work, snapped some pictures, then one of them won a photo contest in the *San Francisco Examiner*. It was bloody easy in those days!"

"I want to do that. I want to be a combat photographer," I declared, sitting up proudly in my seat. Having such good rapport, I had a feeling that one of the reasons Everingham took a liking to me was that I reminded him of his own youthful hunger for adventure, though of course he had me beat by two years.

"Why do you want to do that, Fred? Don't you know you can get killed?" I was surprised by the question. For a moment I didn't know if I was talking to a famous adventurer and war photojournalist. . . or to my father.

"I think it's the best way to get into the business. It's the most dangerous work and the fewest people do it," I challenged.

"Fifty dollars a picture. Is that what your life is worth to you?"

"What?"

"That's what the wire services usually pay you. I've had friends shot in the hand, others who've lost their arms and legs, all for fifty dollars. It's not worth it."

"But you did it!" This was just too much. I was back in my parent's house, trying to keep from banging my head against the low-hanging lamp above the dining room table, as I argued with my father.

"So I did." He shrugged. "Doesn't mean you should. I was a damned fool. I shouldn't be alive. None of us should be alive. Take my advice. Go home. Go to college. Get some photos under your belt. Marry some girl, have a bunch of kids, and get a job where nobody shoots at you."

"I'm not going home."

"Fine with me. Who am I to tell you what to do? Listen, I don't mean to be lecturing you. Who knows? Maybe you'll become a great combat photographer, and have your face plastered all over *Paris Match*, like Natchwey and Capa. Look, I need to be getting back to work. I'm the half-owner of an Indian restaurant in town, Himali Cha-Cha, over on Charoen Krung. Give me a call and we'll have dinner." I thanked him for his time and the invitation, and then let myself out.

Outside Everingham's gate was a strange man. He was small, dirty and naked except for a soiled loincloth. His long, bushy black hair draped almost to the ground as he squatted to take a drink from a puddle of water in the street. An ideal photo subject.

Hastily removing my Canon F-1 from my camera bag and mounting a lens, I snapped away. Suddenly he looked up, like a deer sensing a puma. He turned his head and locked eyes with me, a wild look that many mistake as evil, or mad. Transfixed, I lowered my camera. He grinned and I recognized a fearlessness in his eyes that I'd seen only once before. Sean Flynn's eyes.

Chapter 3

"The compulsion to do good is an innate American trait. Only North Americans seem to believe that they always should, may and actually can choose somebody with whom to share their blessings. Ultimately this attitude leads to bombing people into the acceptance of gifts."— Ivan Illich

The Professionals

      In 1983, Bangkok was a large, sprawling cosmopolitan city in the middle of a much larger and more ancient marsh; a gigantic, vibrant opaque pool of the sacred and profane, not yet having transformed into the safe, tour guide-urbanized, wannabe-hippie traveller and adventurer's waypoint it has become nowadays. Huge Buddhist temples, glinting gold in the sun, reached toward the sky in pointed spires, only a few miles from the famed red light districts of Patpong and Soi Cowboy that maintained Bangkok's reputation as the most wide open city in Southeast Asia. Bridging the distance between these disparate worlds was the Bangkok street system: bustling commerce that jammed its streets with people and grid-locked its modern roads with cars, trucks and rickshaws. Air pollution was only a slight nuisance. It had not yet become the killer that would suffocate the populace of the 1990s, causing all kinds of respiratory ailments. It was a city in which a Buddhist monk in his burgundy red robe stood next to a mini-skirted bargirl on her way to work, in a long line of well-dressed business types waiting for the bus.

      My immediate concern was finding a new place to live inside this wide expanse of concrete and unlimited opportunity. The $3,000 I had brought with me across the Pacific would not last with long stays at expensive hotels like the Nana. Every free moment was spent as a final opportunity to enjoy its amenities. A man who so impressed me with how easily he communicated in Thai with the prostitutes at the Nana's pool, had become my friend and mentor to the ways of getting things done in Bangkok. Wolfgang was not like most of the other German ferang*s* who emigrated to Bangkok to nurture a large belly with lager, making you wonder if they were still able to prolong the necessary erection for that infamous Thai sex buffet. He kept in shape by swimming in the pool at the Nana, lifting weights with a friend in his neighborhood, and making sure to have sex at least twice a day. He took pride in his erotic workout schedule. To afford such a lifestyle, he kept bank accounts full by running a jewelry export business between Munich and Bangkok. There is an Asian saying that a man who runs a shop should have a smiling face, and Wolfgang did, coaxing me to open up and tell him of myself and my journalistic aspirations, though I suspected he thought I was wasting my time, which according to him would have been better used getting into the precious stones business.

"Just can't get the kind of stones you find in Asia anywhere else in the world," he told me during our first good chat. "And you can't beat the labor costs. When everything becomes too Western here, it'll be the same as anyplace, but for now this is the place to make a fortune. And have a great time doing it!"

Thanks to his Thai, and understanding of the culture, he had negotiated a cheap price on a sixth floor room for me the next day. It was nothing to brag about, being your average Southeast Asian air-conditioned apartment—queen-sized bed, adjoining bathroom, table, chair, wooden closet. But the view was magnificent! From my balcony, I would savor the view as a respite during searches for assignments and curious characters; I felt as though I had my own personal grand garden, populated by the magnificent spires of the great Buddhist temples, and the jungle off to the north. And when the wet monsoon winds stirred from the Indian Ocean they would feel like the cool breath of freedom from the oppressive heat.

After moving me in, Wolfgang invited me to my first roadside meal. "The food's very good and cheap. A lot of foreigners wanting to be journalists go there. Keeps the body and soul together during lean times. I think you'll become a regular."

* * *

Around the stall table that had been fashioned from rough-cut lumber and polished by the sweaty arms of many patrons, and spills of many meals, was a ring of journalists, representing just about every part of western Europe. You could tell who had come from money and who had not, and those who lived in the slum behind the line of food stalls on Soi 22. The French were tricky. Whether rich or not, they often rented bungalows in the slums because many of the bargirls from Soi Cowboy lived there, too. But, even then you could always tell who had money back home. They were the French who always made a scene with the waiter or cook because their meal wasn't just right. The French national who didn't live behind the food stalls was Jacqueline. She was twenty-five, with a striking resemblance to a brunette Catherine Deneuve.

Jacqueline lived across the street in an apartment that was not only air-conditioned all the time, but also had maid service. She had moved to Thailand after working in the Middle East for two years. She was also the one who seemed to know everything about photojournalism. But that was how most of the French journalists presented themselves: trying to outdo each other. Basically, I was surrounded by French who felt that France was the last defense for *d'arte de photojournalisme*, Germans who thought that only they could accurately do a photo essay or feature, and English who initially were just trying to get the hell out of England, and were now enjoying frequent writing assignments from local English-language papers because of a Third World misconception that everyone English is a William Shakespeare.

Within minutes I found myself in a heated conversation with Jacqueline because of our mutual passion for the art of photojournalism, and because she was much more direct than I in communicating our mutual attraction—she put her hand on my thigh when I first sat down and kept it there, sliding it up and down, smiling every time I blushed and squirmed in my seat to indicate she was indeed turning me on.

She was a wealth of information, and she made sure I knew that between drags and repeated re-lightings of her Gauloises: the MIA story was old news; drug smuggling was a more worthy story; I needed more cameras—Leicas; I needed to wear black, so that I wouldn't stand out so much. "And be sure you keep your lens pointed toward your body to protect it, and from being singled out by snipers looking for a giveaway flash," she said, and then offered to buy me another Singha. Later, by one of her French cohorts, I would be told that she was just a tourist who had read a lot of books on the subject: she'd never even been to the Middle East. And that part about keeping your lens facing you so that you can protect the lens? That was pure *merde*! In reality, if it's so dangerous that you have to protect your lens, you're either being sized for a body bag, or you'd better have that camera's viewfinder up to your eye so that you can get the shot.

It wasn't long after I sat down that I was overcome by an urge to either excuse myself from the table or at least the conversation with my chain-smoking black widow—either she had been taught by her mother that the only way to seduce a man was to treat him like a child, or she was just on a power trip. I turned my attention to one of the Brits, John Carlisle, a man in his early twenties with a skinny frame and close-cropped hair. He resembled the stereotypical heroin addict I was warned about in the Singapore American School health classes I attended as a child. His blonde Fu Manchu mustache clinched the image, but there was more behind his macho appearance. With money saved from working as a hotel bellhop in London, he too had come to Southeast Asia to become a photojournalist.

"Why does trouble so often come in the form of a woman?" he asked and took a drag on his cigarette that stank of cattle dung.

"*Frédéric*," Jacqueline purred, "would you like to join me for a drink at my apartment?"

"No thanks."

"*Bonsoir, monsieur.*" For such a warm evening it was surprising to be hit by such a cold turn in her demeanor (She may as well have given me a Bronx cheer) as she said goodbye to everyone at the table and stepped out across the poorly-lit lane.

Carlisle returned to his tirade about women, specifically his ex-girlfriend. "Her name was Anne, or at least that's the name she used at the bar where I met her. Seeing her dancing up on the stage, wearing only a G-string, I fell in love. She took most of my money and ran away. When I was in Pakistan I was so low on cash I had to sell my camera to get a ticket back here. That fuckin' bloody cunt!"

He shrugged. "It got me doing some writing. Did a story on prostitution after she left. I've got it in my notebook here. Pretty good stuff. . .Tell me what you think."

I attempted to decipher it. Cursive was not one of his fortes. Very emotional, more appropriate to a solidly-written hate letter, full of facts and stats, more than any story I had read in a newspaper. "Do you have a paper that'll take it?"

He shook his head. "Not yet."

"What're you doing for money?"

"My mother is sending a few pounds. It should be here in a couple days. I just can't have anymore adventures until then."

"Have you done a lot of traveling?"

"Been through the Middle East and India. Met an Afghan guerrilla commander in Pakistan by the name of Masood.[7] He's very charismatic. Very friendly. He invited me to come see their war." I was interested, but reminded myself that my story must begin in Southeast Asia. I didn't want to find myself years down the road like so many of those around the table who envisioned themselves as journalists, but who were really just well-dressed vagabonds chasing fairies through the woods of life. Always easy to recognize, their faces were soured by the scowl of arrogance; always chasing after a story, but never published; never staying in a country longer than allowed on an initial visa; and finally unhappy, always unhappy.

"Did you go?" The image of Carlisle traveling by horse caravan through the Khyber Pass, while evading heavily armed Soviet Mi-24 Hinds, rushed blood faster through my veins.

"No, I turned him down."

His answer completely floored me. I was at once appalled and saddened that he hadn't jumped at the opportunity. But, I told myself, that was probably why he was in such a state.

"You can go if you want. I'll give you the commander's name and the tailor shop contact in Peshawar."

"Intriguing." I was sure he was not even aware of how tempted I was. "But I'll start here, thanks." Carlisle was an amiable sort. "I was planning to hit the Bangkok news offices tomorrow. Want to come along?"

"Sure." We spent the night drinking Singha beers, celebrating as though we had already accepted our offer letters from *Time*, *News-week*, Reuters, and UPI.

* * *

NO JOURNALISTS WANTED was the imaginary sign on the front door of every one of those offices we hit the next morning. Carlisle wanted to go home for the rest of the day. Reflecting, I reminded myself that in order to succeed, I must not fall into the same quagmire he had led himself into.

"There's only Denis Gray at the AP left. Everingham recommended him. Want to go?" I asked.

"Nah. I'll come along, but he's your lead. You should talk to him."

At the AP office, I asked for Denis Gray and was led to his desk surrounded by a large, wood-framed, glass cubicle. I was impressed by how much Gray appeared the picture-perfect foreign correspondent: tall, stout, with well-trimmed brown hair and mustache, wearing a multicolored Hawaiian shirt. He definitely had the credentials. Born Zdenik Mecir, in Pilsen, Czechoslovakia, Denis D. Gray had been an adventurer since childhood. When the Communists overtook his birthplace, his parents escaped to the United States with the help of the CIA. Gray was a refugee at the age of seven. Because of his family's roaming, he had travelled most of the world and had become skilled in a number of languages by the time he entered Yale. Paying for college through the Army ROTC, he ended up in Vietnam after graduation, assigned to military intelligence and was active up in the DMZ, the Central Highlands, Saigon and the Cambodia border. Coming back disillusioned from his military experience in Vietnam, he returned to his love of writing, getting a job with the Associated Press (AP) in New York. Within two years he was back in Indochina, covering Cambodia and then the fall of Vientiane, Laos. Yep, Denis D. Gray sure had the credentials.

"There aren't any assignments. The best way to get into AP is to work for an office in the States and then ask for a foreign desk assignment," he said as I balanced myself on a wobbly chair beside his desk that seemed too big for his office, even though the desk itself wasn't big at all. I almost fell off when he suggested I go back to California and work for AP there first for a couple years. Fortunately, he added, "But there is a list of photos and stories we need."

"Where's the open assignment list?"

"It's right next to the door. Here, I'll show you." I followed after him with the humility of a novitiate.

"Here's something that might interest you." He pointed to the words *Killing Fields* chalked up on the board. "That's a movie being made just north of Bangkok. It's about Cambodia, when Pol Pot and the Khmer Rouge took over." Sam Waterston was playing Sydney Schanberg in that movie. Gray remembered Schanberg from Cambodia, and did not enjoy his abrasive personality—which was much like the character played by Waterston. Schanberg was a journalist who considered the *New York Times* the center of the world, much in the same way the New York publishing industry thinks the rest of the world revolves around them. "And there's also some actor by the name of Spaulding Gray. They've really got a tight clamp on it. No journalists are getting in. Almost like Cambodia and Vietnam."

Carlisle had told me the night before that the film company was headquartered over at the Rama Hotel, and they were looking for every Caucasian they could find to be extras! According to him, they were paying forty-five dollars a day. Carlisle was anticipating getting a job because that day's pay under the present exchange of twenty-two baht to the dollar would pay his rent for a whole month. I pulled a small notebook out of my camera bag and copied the movie's name down. "Great! I'll get right on it."

"Do you have a press pass?"

I shook my head.

"It won't matter if you don't have one for the movie set," he said. "But, you'll need a press pass to get past security in most places, like government and military sites. The Thai authorities won't issue credentials unless you have a press pass. Have you got a letter of introduction from a newspaper back home? You have something like that? Even from your hometown paper?"

I spun away from the door, hit by the journalist's Catch-22. "No! I don't have a damn thing. I just want to be a photojournalist, but how can I get any experience if nobody lets me start?"

Returning to the door and barely controlling my rage, I felt a hand on my shoulder. "Listen, Fred." Gray's face wrinkled with concern. "So you don't have a press pass. So what? You can still go out and get pictures. If you think they're interesting, bring them in and we'll develop them for you. No charge. If you have anything we like, we'll buy it."

* * *

"Are you doing anything tomorrow night, around six?" I yelled over the noise of the tuk-tuk[8] Carlisle and I shared on our way back to Soi 22.

He shook his head.

"Gray told me that the Prime Minister of Japan is speaking at the Foreign Correspondents Club of Thailand. Do you want to go?"

He pulled a cigarette out of the pack he carried in his shirt pocket, and while searching around in his trouser pockets for a lighter, said, "It'd be a good chance to meet just about every foreign correspondent in Bangkok."

"That's what I was thinking." I smiled.

Carlisle shrugged. "Okay. Drop by my place around five."

* * *

If cleanliness is next to godliness, then the slums of Soi 22 were as far from heaven as possible. A petite Thai woman opened the door just a crack when I knocked at five that afternoon. "Is John Carlisle here?"

"John not heah." She was about to close the door. Blocking it with my foot, I said, "I'm supposed to meet him."

She smiled nervously, then relaxed. "Oh you Fred. Friend of John's. He be back soon. Come in. . . wait."

Carlisle's room was not much larger than the queen-sized bed at its center. A rattan chair, which seemed an afterthought, was squeezed into the corner. I sat in it and sunk into turbid thoughts that without an assignment I would soon end up in a place like this.

The woman's legs drew my attention, keeping me from drowning in my own muddied thoughts. They were shapely, extending from a baggy pair of shorts which probably belonged to John, and a tank top which hung easily on her shoulders tanned very brown by a lot of sun. When I noticed the pink scars that covered her knee and calf, she reacted by trying to cover them with her arms as she curled up on the bed.

Attractive in the way of many Asian women, her skin and eyes almond and exotic, she looked to be about nineteen or twenty. She very self-consciously put a hand to her chest and said, "My name Anne."

"No shit!" Caught off guard, I stared. *Could this be the woman Carlisle had written about?! The heroin addict?* I was then alarmed when she crossed her arms, but she was too slow in keeping me from noticing the needle marks up her arm.

"I do something wrong," she admitted out of the blue, looking up at the ceiling as if she was talking to it and not me. "But John forgive me."

The door opened, and in came Carlisle, right into the spider-like arms of Anne. She gave him a kiss and just before letting herself out she said, "I go take walk now to store." She kissed him again and left, but not before giving me the look of a sad puppy that had just pissed on the carpet.

"Are you ready to go?" I wanted to get away from that place with Carlisle to someplace sane, a place not so dark and depressing.

"I've been thinking, Fred. Maybe you should go to the club on your own."

"What?!"

"We're not making much headway in our job search. Besides, I just got a job as an extra in the *Killing Fields*. Why don't you go over to the Rama Hotel? That's where they've got their offices. They're looking for foreigners to dress up as Marines."

"But what about getting assignments? We've got to be persistent."

"Bloody hell, Fred, you are such a Californian!"
"What do you mean by that?"
"You're just so bloody optimistic!"

It was hard to tell which hurt worse; that he had called me a Californian with such disdain, or that he was bailing out on me. *Too optimistic?* That was the only part of myself that was keeping me going! A thought occurred to me: considering Carlisle's own pessimism, which was so culturally based, there was a very practical reason all my ancestors did everything they could to get the hell out of Europe. I recoiled inside as I realized I, too, would have been raised on the bottom rung of an unbudging class system had my ancestors not followed a dream.

"I wish you luck, but Anne's just come back. We've got things to talk about."

"Wake up! She stole your money!"

Carlisle's face went blank, but his eyes bulged and his pupils bounced around like he was suffocating. "She apologized. And besides, I love her. We can work things out. She needs me. She got into an accident in Pattaya. She was on a scooter and went over the handlebars." Surely John knew that prostitutes worked their trade in Pattaya by prowling the streets on mopeds. And once they found a client, they'd have the customer hop on the back and then drive them to their hotel for a little *bang-bang*. Evidently, Anne's moped must have been too much for her.

"She ripped you off and you're still going to help her? How stupid can you be?"

"You're such a Californian! You just don't understand."

"No, I don't." Like a drill sergeant, my fists on my hips, I faced him. "This woman breaks your heart, steals your money, then when she gets in trouble, you take her back. That's friggin' crazy! Get your ass in gear and let's get the hell out of here!"

"Fred, let me ask you this. Imagine the Communists come streaming into Thailand. Which way would you go? Toward the fighting, or toward the airport to catch the next flight out?"

I didn't answer; I was too furious. He nodded. "You'd run towards the fighting even though you might get killed. You'd do it because you love the idea of being a photojournalist. It's in your heart. You were born for this. I'd be on the next flight out."

* * *

Considering it was the Japanese Prime Minister at the podium in the FCCT, I was surprised that the only security I passed was the uniformed lobby guard at the mall entrance. Or maybe, that was who the smartly-dressed Japanese were, standing off to the side in the corner as the Prime Minister gave a speech about the latest direction of his country.

Half an hour passed as I finished my Cuba Libre. Humor-coated questions referring to Japan's involvement with Thailand during World War II drew a reaction from the attendees, such as, "In the future, will Japan once again bring military assistance as part of its economic aid to Thailand?" The lack of seriousness, only added to my initial feeling that this press conference was an excuse for the press corps to collect for drinks. But I was told by Everingham that everyone got together here every Friday, so maybe tonight's collecting around the water hole was an excuse for the Prime Minister to get his points across. The Prime Minister barely suppressed a slight smile and finished off with his last answer to questions. "The future will be different from the past," he assured the audience.

Correspondents seated at the dining tables gathered around the bar. Tall Denis Gray from the AP office stood out amongst the rest of the patrons collected on wobbly feet and stools. "How's the job hunting?" he asked.

"Same. Nothing."

"Just got to keep plugging," was his final comment.

A giant caught my eye. He was Russian and surprisingly stood even taller than Gray. He worked for TASS, the Soviet news agency. Except for thick, brown eyebrows that almost touched, he had a clean-cut look.

"Does TASS need any journalists?" I asked.

He looked down at me and smiled enigmatically. "TASS doesn't hire outside."

I smiled and gave him a wide berth for the rest of the night, sure that he was the eyes and ears of the KGB in Thailand.

I recognized a journalist from Reuters standing close by, so I ambled over to him by the bar glowing under the bright spotlights. He was a likable fellow in his late fifties, with curly gray hair and a short, plump frame. He reminded me of Friar Tuck. "Where's your friend?" asked the friar.

"He had an important appointment." It sounded better than confiding that he was screwing someone who had screwed him.

"How's the search going?"

"Not too well," I said, surprised the friar didn't already know by the drawn look on my face.

"Have you met Jim Wolf? He's from AFP."

Upon the friar's tapping on his shoulder, Jim Wolf, a man in his mid-thirties, spun around from his conversation with another journalist and shook hands with me. Physically trim, with short, wavy, dark hair, Wolf sported wire-rimmed glasses, and reminded me of an older version of my younger brother, Frankie. *Maybe meeting him is a good omen.*

"AFP?"

"Agence France Press," said Wolf.

"How'd you get a job with them?"

"Signed up for it at the main office in Paris."

"Is it pretty tough to get a job out here without signing up at the main office?" I asked.

"Sometimes. Looking for something?

"Yes," I said. *As if I didn't need the work!* "You looking for any photo work?"

He shook his head. "I've got somebody in Bangkok I use. You tried any of the other agencies?"

"Yep, all of them."

I thanked Wolf and the friar for their time, downed the last of my Cuba Libre, and walked out of the club. Thousands of miles from home on a crazy quest, and there was no light at the end of the tunnel to illuminate that special opportunity that I was sure would change my life, really make me. I sunk even further under weighty thoughts about the incredulous reactions of my high school chums to my plans, the cold look of betrayal from my mother the day I left, and the last stumbling attempts of my father to reach me after years of hostility.

Even with a heavy feeling in the pit of my stomach, I smiled at the security guard on my walk past him into the night. Suddenly he saluted. He had done the same upon my entrance hours before. But this time, because of my renewed optimism and conviction towards my goals, I returned a sharper salute than the sharpest I had ever given in my short career as a midshipman in the Naval ROTC.

Chapter 4

"He is a barbarian, and thinks that the customs of his tribe and island are the laws of nature."— George Bernard Shaw

Looking for the Good Soldier

"They say you're looking for a monk. Is this true?"
"Monk?!" I guffawed, "No way! I'm looking for the Hmong." So much for these guys saying they understood me. With the twenty-something monk, who had himself been a journalist for the *LA Times* after graduating from university in the States, and me in the room were Lam and Ton, two tax men who had saved me from a mass of rickshaw drivers surrounding me when I arrived in Nakhon Phanom the night before. Their offer to play tour guide for me around their home town seemed too good to turn down. Considering how poorly we were communicating, I wondered if it was such a good idea to have them take me anywhere.

The monk stopped laughing, and then spoke to Lam. They broke into laughter again and Lam said," Meo!" Sounded like the meow of a cat.

"You see," The monk said as he motioned for silence in this living room of a house that he shared with another representative from UNICEF[2], "They call themselves Hmong, but Thais call them Meo. It's like saying 'nigger'."

I nodded gravely, having travelled all the way up to what had been one of the busiest towns in the north, when the USAF based the covert 56th Special Operations Wing's A26s and O2s there to put a dent in Hanoi and the Pathet Laos' objectives. Nakhon Phanom (NKP), affectionately referred to as "Naked Fanny" by American servicemen stationed there until 1975, was now once again in the news as headquarters for Lt. Colonel Gritz's forays after MIAs in Laos. I had jumped on a bus yesterday in the hopes of finding contacts today who would get me into Laos with resistance fighters from the local Lao refugee camp. And maybe in the process even find out what happened to Gritz.

"Yes," said the monk. "It's the only name they know in Thailand, sorry to say. By the way, there aren't any Hmong in the camps here. They're up toward Chiang Mai. There are only lowland Lao here. You want to go to Ban Vinai. That's where they keep the Hmong, the hill people."

In desperation, I wanted to run screaming into the dry rice fields outside. "Do you know whether there are any people still here from Colonel Gritz's group, who were led into Laos by the Hmong?"

"Colonel Gritz?! Sorry, his group is gone. Sad story there. The Thai people are right behind your efforts to get your missing prisoners, but because of the tense situation between us and the Vietnamese, we had to bring charges against him. You understand don't you?"

"How long ago?"

"I'm not sure. Maybe a month or so. If you'd like, I can have Lam take you by his house?"

"Sure."

He led us out, and then embraced my hand in his two, as he said, "Good luck."

"Don't worry my friend," Lam said, and smiled. "I make you happy. Show many sights." Lam epitomized Thailand. Always friendly, always trying to please, it was how they remained devoid of overt occupation while every other country in Southeast Asia fell under the sword of the Imperial Japanese Army during World War II. Lam's enthusiasm re-ignited mine as we got back on his motorcycle. I wanted to drive this time. He acquiesced to my request by handing me the keys, and got on the back instead. If I was going to come up here for a fact finding trip that was offering me no leads, I was at least going to have fun finding nothing.

When we arrived at Colonel Bo Gritz's safe house, it was not much to look at, just like the adventure that I thought was going to be the story for me to make a name for myself as a go-get-'em photojournalist. First of all, Colonel James G. "Bo" Gritz was actually a lieutenant colonel, and was nowhere near the An Lo Valley in 1966, a very nasty Army Special Forces battle that he took credit for participating in. If I'd been reading *Soldier of Fortune* magazine that spring, instead of just the national newspapers that preferred to report the sensationalism of Gritz's MIA hunt-that-wasn't, I would have had a much more complete picture of Gritz before I left California. Not too many people in the press corps were checking these facts back then it seemed. (Is this the same "Bo" Gritz who ended up selling land to survivalists in Idaho, and playing hero during FBI-versus-militia group stand-offs? Yep.) Then there were the POW rescue operations: Velvet Hammer, Grand Eagle, Lazarus Omega, Operation Broken-wing. All of them ended in a jumbled mess of scam artists, piddled-away money from the ever-grieving families of MIAs, fuck-up MIA hunters getting taken prisoner by supposedly allied opium smugglers, and even the involvement of Hollywood—Clint Eastwood donated $30,000, and Captain Kirk of the Starship Enterprise purchased the movie rights to Gritz's life for $10,000 (William Shatner would have been more accurate by rewriting the script to *Animal House*, and setting the opening scene in western Laos and northeastern Thailand).

I needed a place to think about what to do next. My good luck that had greeted me when I first arrived in Thailand was apparently running away. I backed the motorcycle out of the driveway of Gritz's safe house, pulled out onto the heavily pot-holed dirt road, and went down the road to the river. On the steep bank of the Maekong was a seat formed from the top of the one long slide of dry gravel stretching down to the river's edge. Resting for a moment under a large tree, I gazed across the coffee-and-milk expanse. I visualized sneaking across that Lao border one night with a group of guerrillas. My thoughts played with the idea of crossing the line between courage and stupidity, that line between light and dark. A Thai PBR gunboat, patrolling for refugees, easily cut its way up the deceivingly slow current. Mounting a 200mm zoom on my Canon F1, I sighted through the viewfinder and found the PBR out of focus. The top half of the focus ring was to the right and the bottom half to the left. As the boat drew closer, I aligned the two halves of the circle. Checking the light meter to the right of the frame, I calculated that the dark, olive-drab color of the vessel would cause too much of a contrast against the light-brown of the water. I dedicated the metering to the boat, letting the sky and water wash out a bit. First exposure, great! Second, great. Third, right on!

* * *

"So what do you think, Denis?" Using the soft light filtering through from the overcast skies outside the AP bureau office, he studied the negatives. I smiled, finally having something to show.

"Well, Fred. They're properly exposed and framed." Almost always having a pleasant Buddha smile under his auburn mustache, it was hard to tell if Denis Gray was coming from any point other than one of good intention. "But, there really isn't anything I can buy. Something I couldn't easily get from one of my staff photographers."

Crestfallen, I urged him to expound. "There just has to be a bit more. I need pictures that no one else can get."

"So if I were to get into the base and actually ride along with them on the boat, those would be attractive?"

He nodded. "If you get something I can use, just bring them in here. I'll get them developed for you again." This is a common offer afforded anyone with a camera. But, in Gray's words it was a special hand-up for me.

"Great!" I said, though my enthusiasm was quickly losing its luster. My hopes of beating the odds seemed about to become even more insurmountable. I was no longer homesick for California. Any thoughts of going home now conjured up more of a feeling of apprehension than anticipation. For me to return home now would be no less than suicide— the spirit first and most assuredly the body right after.

* * *

A full bowl of noodles is always the perfect tonic to whatever ails the mind, body and spirit in Thailand, so I had beat it back to my neighborhood for some of the best in Bangkok after that dismal review at AP. And while enjoying, I met a man who would figure into my future for many years.

"Mind if I share this table with you?. . You speak English?" the American said.

"What?. . Oh yeah, sure. Have a seat."
He offered his hand as he sat. "Sam."

"Try the soup. It's not bad."

The waiter arrived and then the thirty-something-looking man sitting opposite me, who with his surfer-like tan, physique, and haircut, looking like he had just arrived from Hawaii, broke into Thai as though it was his first language.

Stunned, I just stared. He turned to me just as the waiter was about to leave. "Singha?"

"Uh, yeah, sure. A beer would be good. . . Thanks." We shared a grin for no reason other than I was just some young kid in awe of him for his language skills, and feeling a little sheepish about having told him what was good. As if he didn't know.

"So where are you from?" he asked as the waiter rushed back with a couple bottles of beer.

"California. And you?"

"All over, but the last time I was Stateside was in San Diego. But that was a long time ago. I hear you're a photojournalist."

"And who told you that?"
"Scuttlebutt."
Suspicious and disturbing.

"Small neighborhood, you know." He grinned.
"Yeah, I guess."
"Nothing to worry about."
"Oh yeah?"
He laughed. "I tried photojournalism for a while after I got out of the war." The fluorescent light above flashed on his large gold ring and made it stand out on his tanned finger. I found it disturbing not only because it was big, but because it was on his wedding ring finger. I realized at that moment that it was not a wedding ring, but a commemorative ring.
"Wild ring."
"Thanks. Had it made by a guy here in Bangkok. Too bad the old guy kicked. He was a great jeweler."
"How long ago did you get it?" Sam's demeanor put me at ease now.
"About '71, I guess. About the time I got out." He offered his fist to display a ring displaying a South Vietnamese flag against a black enamel background. It would easily have seemed gaudy had it not been so simply made.
"I was in Vietnam in 1971," I offered.
"How old *are* you? And I was thinking you were a straight shooter."
"I lived there because of my father," I said, annoyed because it was the same type of skepticism that I received from know-it-alls back home who automatically assumed that the only reason American children lived overseas was because their parents were in the military. "We lived in Saigon, he worked out of Tan Son Nhut."
"Didn't get a chance to visit Saigon," he said, between impatient looks back to the kitchen as the snail-paced cook ladled broth over his noodles. "Spent most of my time in the Mekong Delta."
When his soup finally arrived, he wolfed it down, ignoring the large plume of steam. "You want to go with me over to Lucy's Tiger Den?" he asked after he burped and reached for a toothpick. "You might find a story over there. At least you will be entertained by some wannabe mercenaries."
"Sure," I smiled, trying to sound nonchalant. "I'll go over there with you."
So, we paid our bill and headed over to the infamous Lucy's Tiger Den.

Chapter 5

"The cannon thunders... limbs fly in all directions...one can hear the groans of victims and the howling of those performing the sacrifice... it's Humanity in search of happiness."— Charles Baudelaire

Chasing Dragons

P 2101482Z JUL 83

FM AMEMBASSY BANGKOK

TO SECSTATE WASHDC

"Mr. Graham reportedly arrived in Thailand approximately three months ago in order to look for work as a freelance press photographer. He contacted many local newsmen about jobs and eventually did succeed in taking photographs of Lao resistance activities and submitted them to local news organizations."

    Chester was my friend. I don't remember much about him other than he was one of my best friends at the Singapore American School. He was from Texas, and the first one who taught me that I didn't really know how to deal with death.

    Chester sported straight hair the color of dark straw. Chubby like me, he enjoyed life and was not one to look down on you the way some people did. He wasn't like those who thought they were better than the rest, because one or both of their parents worked at the US Embassy. Most families in Singapore were blue-collar American, Australian, New Zealanders, and Canadian, some left-over Brits, dependents of oil men from places like Louisiana, Texas, Oklahoma, Alberta, and Perth, stationed at the island nation's refineries and working in the Thai Gulf or other oil-rich areas of Southeast Asia, like Borneo and Sumatra, for such companies as Halliburton, Brown & Root, and Exxon. My football team, the Robray Raiders,[10] was named after the Oakland Raiders, but kept in green and white jerseys, pads and helmets by the Robray Offshore Drilling Company. If it wasn't football, it was the Singapore American Club, where most American ex-pats collected on weekends for the pool, barbecues, and the best Sunday brunch on the whole island, where the waffles melted in your mouth, cinnamon-dusted and rich from butter and cake mix.

Chester and I used to have lunch together often, with football being the main topic of conversation, ranging from the last week's game to the cutest cheerleaders. We also used to spend afternoons and weekends launching Estes model rockets into the air. There was a large field in front of the Ulu Pandan Singapore American School that was perfect for our own private NASA launch pad. It was a pretty impressive school, I thought that even then: a white castle that could have easily come out of some Asimov science-fiction novel.

In that field in front of the Singapore American School, local farmers would graze their goats. Many times, while setting up our launch pad, I had to make my way around the dung pellets left by the herd. Those little pellets so resembled nuggets of chocolate cereal that, to this day, I can't stomach the idea of eating Coco Puffs. And I most definitely hated playing football in that field. Just the thought of getting tackled and rolling around in those pellets! It brought a whole new meaning to dingle berries.

Sometimes we'd stay out all afternoon shooting rockets into the azure sky. If we stayed out long enough for our parents to worry, we often went for broke and tried our luck walking through the Chinese graveyard, a small plot in a tiny creek valley below the school. There were gravestones all over the place with red Chinese characters on grave markers that had been molded out of concrete, some painted a pasty, lime-green, others in the color widely recognized in Asia as the color of the dead—white. Our parents would know we had been playing in that graveyard by the streaks of light chalk on our school uniforms: blue slacks, white dress shirts. Chester's mother and mine were a superstitious lot, so we got grounded a lot for our night forays into the land of the dead. Why did we love to stay up late looking to see if there were really ghosts in Singapore? Because we still had a healthy inquisitiveness.

One night, we thought we had hit the jackpot: we heard voices; we heard shuffling, and clanking of keys! And we thought it was all over for us as we watched the two dark figures coming towards us. They tried to jump us. In our wild imaginations cultivated on kung fu vampire movies produced by the Shaw Brothers in Hong Kong, we thought they were spooks, or worse, VAMPIRES! One had Chester by the wrist, but I kicked him in the balls. While he yowled and covered his crotch, I grabbed Chester and led him on a cross-country race for our lives.

They chased us for a long time, but Chester, who had calmed down enough to realize that they weren't bloodsucking ghouls at all, but guards, pulled me to a stop once we had run far enough away from them to hear their heated Mandarin fade. "Let's let them run past," he whispered. "I'm fed up with running."

I didn't know then that Chester had a heart problem. For that matter, I don't think Chester really did either. I'm sure he would have confided in me. We had an honest kind of a friendship that could stand up to whatever monsters the truth might bring out. We moved a bit off the trail we had been following to the last line of graves.

"Over here," he whispered. Crawling on hands and knees, and out of breath long enough for me to lose the edge of my excitement and sink into worry, he made his way to a large concrete tomb. We hid on the other side of that dead man's cradle, and I asked, "Are you okay?"

Barely able to close his mouth to put his fingers to his lips, he shushed me. He almost didn't soften his breathing in time to keep quiet as the guards headed in our direction. I thought they had us for sure. They stopped just five feet from us. I was totally amazed that they couldn't see us in our white shirts. But they didn't. We stayed as motionless as the stones around us for the fifteen minutes it took for them to lose interest and finally walk away.

On the way home, after picking up our rockets and tools back at the goat field, I asked Chester, "Why were you so out of breath?"

"The doctor told my mother it has something to do with my heart," he answered.

"Well, what did he say?"

"Not much. Just that I've got a hole in my heart." I didn't know what hit me more: that he had a hole in his heart; or that he had said it so apathetically.

We were more careful after that. We would trek across Singapore only in the daytime from then on. And we never went to the graveyard again after dark. But, like the old saying, boys will be boys, Chester couldn't give up playing tag football during lunch.

I was up on the second floor balcony that looked out onto the small field where we students used to play soccer or tag football. Its boundary lined the base of the school, and divided it from the main goat field by an entrance road. It was Louis Scavone who came running up the stairs and yelled, "Look! That's Chester!"

I dashed over to Louis, wondering what all the commotion was about. I followed his pointed finger out to the field below. I couldn't see Chester at all. All I did see was a large crowd collected on the green. A teacher was yelling at the circle to keep back and give them air. Soon, the school nurse came shooting out from below our balcony, a medical bag in her hand, a stethoscope whipping around her neck. The scene of a nurse running for the helipad that always plays during the credits of the TV show *MASH* flashed through my mind.

Five minutes later, a classmate trudged up the stairs to tell us that Chester was dead. *Dead?! How could he be dead?!* Questions looped constantly through my thoughts all that week, affecting my ability to concentrate during my classes. At one point, I felt foolish and guilty that I had felt such anger at him for doing something as stupid as playing football when the doctor had told him not to exert himself. *Jesus Christ! It would only have been a few more days before he was to have open-heart surgery, the hole would be sealed, and he'd have been able to play as hard as he wanted.* A week after Chester had been pronounced DOTF (dead on the field), our teacher told the class that we would be collecting money for a card and flowers to send to his parents.

That night, I went to my parents. They had just come home from a business dinner. They were unwinding from my father trying to impress a prospective customer with Kohler's line of electric generators, boat engines, and plumbing fixtures. Dad was, after all, the one who had created the Asia/Pacific Rim presence of Kohler International, headquartering it in our house's third bedroom in 1972, and then taking it all the way to a high-rise office by the time we left Singapore in 1977. Dad was tired when he removed his tie that night. Mom moved around removing her jewelry, looking very classy in her black dress.

I was at a loss for words to ask for the money. It was always so easy to ask for money when I wanted to buy a toy. Maybe it was easy because my parents were late in getting my brother and I started on an allowance based on merit, assigning chores such as making our beds and taking out the garbage. As for getting a job in Singapore, that was out of the question because I didn't have a work visa. It didn't make sense to me, or to my parents, to perform household chores. Maids were inexpensive and part of the culture. By cleaning, cooking, and babysitting for others, they could send their children to school in England or Europe, or even a Singapore University. In Singapore, a maid cost $150 a month (Singapore dollars.) The exchange rate then was two Singapore dollars to the American dollar. And our *amah*[11] did almost everything for my mother: house cleaning, making of beds, laundry, cooking, and taking out the garbage. There were some wives of ex-pats[12] who felt that they had finally hit the big time, and hired two maids to cover all the chores. These were the wives we'd hear about who quickly became bored with fidelity. They were the ones that I'd overhear mothers at the Singapore American Club gossiping about, and telling their own husbands to stay the hell away from these "wives," or else.

So, I took a deep breath and said, "Dad, I need some money."

When he asked why, I wanted to just state matter-of-factly that my friend Chester had died, and that we were making a gesture of condolence toward his parents. But, I had a habit of laughing whenever I was nervous, and what came out was laughter as I said, "My friend Chester died last week."

A look of confusion and concern overcame my mother and father. My laughter quickly sank. And when it bottomed out, I slipped even further into a pool of tears. I sobbed so much, embarrassed because my father would always become frustrated whenever I cried, telling me to stop, that big boys didn't cry.

That night, though, he didn't say anything other than words of comfort. I thanked my parents when they gave me the money, and quickly escaped to my room, not really wanting to share my most deep and confusing pain with anyone other than myself.

* * *

Not only were there adventurers of all types at Lucy's Tiger Den, especially the wannabes Sam had joked about, but I learned that Sam had been a mercenary ever since he returned to the States, got fed up with the anti-Vietnam veteran mess, and headed off to Africa in the early 1970s. I told him I wanted to sneak into Laos with the resistance. When he came by my place a couple days after our introduction, he asked, "Still want to go to Laos?"

All he had to do was ask those words, and in five minutes I was out the door with my ALICE[1] packed with my cameras and some clothes for a week's romp in the highlands. Sam said that he knew a Hmong guerrilla who was interested in drawing more attention to *yellow rain*. According to just about everyone in the press corps at that time, yellow rain was the next best story after the American MIAs. There were reports of the second citizens of Laos, the Hmong and Mien, coming out of Laos with burns and respiratory ailments. Those were the lucky ones. Some described a full hit by the poison gas as turning a whole village into a mass of chemically burnt and choking people. The name yellow rain came about because of the yellow color of the mist that appeared when bombs were dropped. Those who said that this was just a hoax created by anti-Communist forces in Laos against the Pathet Lao, explained it away as simply bee droppings. In Laos, the reactions to yellow rain were severe: vomiting, bloody diarrhea and death for those who didn't die immediately. As a final measure, the mycotoxins acted like the AIDS virus, destroying the immune system.

Sam drove while I sat in the passenger seat of his white CJ-5. The jeep was not a comfortable ride, even though it had a fine selection of tunes with which to enjoy the long drive through the middle of Thailand, a plain of trees and bone-dry rice fields waiting for the monsoon rains that would rejuvenate the land from June to October. I was along to get some pictures of the villages that had been wiped out by the chemical agents. Sam promised me that I'd be able to get further than anyone else had been able to in the last few months. Pathet Lao forces had been embarrassed by Bo Gritz's incursions and weren't about to have them happen again. He said that it would have been much more dangerous for me had I been along five months before, when Colonel Gritz had been limelighted by the press.

I adjusted my black Ray-Bans and watched the countryside flashing past. I should have been terrified at what I was about to do, but every time the fright worked its way around in my stomach and slowly up my throat, I concentrated on Eric Clapton's voice blasting at me over Sam's custom stereo system. I thought, like so many times before, when I heard the song *Cocaine*, Clapton was telling me, "It's alright, it's alright, it's alright, okay!"—the actual words are, "She don't lie, she don't lie, she don't like cocaine."

Sam broke out in a laugh as he heard me sing the incorrect lyrics. I wondered what he was laughing at. He didn't explain when I pressed him. Instead he rested his hand on my shoulder for a couple seconds and said, "Don't worry, man. You'll be alright. . ."

* * *

The refugee camp was lit by a red-orange sun when we arrived. It lay nestled at the base of a collection of mountains, one of which reminded me of a large, great white shark tooth. Ban Vinai, the refugee camp for hill tribe people, was surrounded by a collection of ramshackle homes. We pulled up a hill, into a collection of homes just short of the camp. The homes surrounded a small courtyard, some skinny trees and small wooden huts, the grounds half-covered in chickens.

A man slipping on slacks and a dress shirt came rushing out of what I assumed to be the main house, because of its size. He tried scattering the chickens and waved us over, and then, as though guiding a chopper into an LZ[14], his arms waving parallel back and forth, he brought us into a skidding stop just short of the big house. "How are you, Samuel?" he asked as we jumped out of Sam's jeep.

"This is Fred." Sam said.

We shook hands and nodded to each other. "You're hungry, I'm sure."

"Excuse me," I asked. "How do you say your name again?"
The Hmong said, "Xiong"

I said "See-ong."

Xiong and Sam grinned and Xiong said, "That will do." Xiong then yelled out in Hmong, his language that I couldn't even correlate to anything I had ever heard, except that it had the intonations of a cat's meow. I was reminded of the Buddhist monk back in Nakhon Phanom, who said that the Hmong were labelled pejoratively by everyone else, except themselves, as Miao, or Meo. Even the Chinese character for this people, who originated from an area in China, close to Tibet, supposedly represents a cat. In Thai and Lao, the word *meo* actually means cat.

A woman walked into the courtyard from the same house from which Xiong had earlier appeared. Unlike Xiong who was so modernly dressed, this woman who seemed old enough to be his grandmother, wore a traditional dress of silver coins that made the music of tropical rain as she moved over to Xiong. Like Xiong, her face was very round. "Auntie just returned from a celebration," Xiong said. "If you had been here earlier, we could have all gone."

She stopped to adjust her sash and the black and white turban that hid her gray hair, which, because of how full the headdress was, I assumed to be long and thick. She walked over to the chickens who had calmed down enough after our screeching stop in the jeep, to be back to pecking at the hard, bleached ground for a morsel. It took only a second for Xiong's aunt to reach down and clutch a young rooster in her hands.

"We eat well tonight, my friends!" Xiong clapped and then said something to his aunt, who giggled. We all followed her into the big house.

Barely through the door, Xiong stopped. He gestured down toward someone who was no more than a pair of bare feet, the rest of his body and identity hidden by the wall on the right side of the doorway. "This is my brother," Xiong said.

Peeking my head in through the doorway, I saw that the feet were connected to a boy who laughed at me as our eyes met. I laughed too, because it must have seemed funny to him to see only a head stick out from the edge of the doorway. I waved and said hello. He waved the way children do when they're excited to see a long-lost relative. His reaction was amazing, because as I studied him for a second, I realized he wasn't a boy, but a teenager. Xiong said something about his brother, Lor, being very brave, and that he had been in battle with the Pathet Lao at least three times that year. His laugh that turned into a grin reminded me of that picture of Sean Flynn. I liked Lor immediately.

"*Ko mu dashi?*" Lor asked.

"He's asking how you are," Sam said. Before I had a chance to say anything to Sam to translate, he said, "*Wa shi!*" Sam then told me that

Lor's question actually translated to mean, *where are you going*, and that the customary answer he gave was, *going to play*. *Going to play*, I thought. *Yep, that's exactly what we're going to do.*

"Ah, Samuel, you're very smart. You speak our language so well!" Xiong said. I felt out of place because I couldn't speak a word of it. I often couldn't speak with anyone because they spoke only Thai, or they only wanted to speak English. This not speaking the local language was really frustrating to me.

Sam must have read my mind, because he smiled at me and said, "You can't make up for twelve years of practice in a few months."

I nodded and told him I agreed.

"You scared?" Xiong asked. I was shocked that it showed so clearly. "No worry! We go across all the time. Thai Army Special Forces, all the time. Sometimes your Special Forces go, too. Like your LA freeway! Go boat, come back, just like tour bus. Ha-ha!" Xiong held his sides.

Surprised by his statement about incursions by American Special Forces, I pushed him for more information, but he turned serious and tight-lipped about it, returning his attention and the conversation to a hushed chat with Sam. Looking away from our conversation that had so quickly started and ended, I moved further into Xiong's home. At the far corner of the one-room house, Xiong's aunt busily plucked the rooster after having deftly wrung its neck. She had by this time already gone behind a sheet hanging from a line of twine, and changed out of her good celebration clothes into a long skirt and blouse. All the colors in her skirt that stopped just above her feet reminded me of a colorful Chinese dragon.

Xiong's aunt dipped the rooster in a pot of boiling water and resumed her plucking. When she was done, she gutted it and laid out its entrails, methodically, as though she were reading them. She then discarded the offal into a plastic bag that hung from a nail on the central post, a length of timber that held up the middle of the house. There were nine more posts that kept the corners and the other half of the house from falling down. In many indigenous homes, the floor was a set of bamboo or wood floor joists, covered with planks. This Hmong home had a dirt floor. The corner and center posts went straight into the bare ground. Wood and bamboo slats made up the roof and walls. Rays of light made their way through wall slats that had been nailed up horizontally. A thought about effective simplicity hit me as I watched Auntie squatting, her body moving like a small swing as she moved between plucking the chicken, and adding wood to the small fire that was right on the floor and bounded by four clay bricks. She must have sensed me watching her because she turned, without standing, and smiled. I returned her smile and looked over at Lor, who motioned for me to sit with him.

He had traded his place in the corner for a seat on one of the two bamboo double beds that took up the other half of the house. Pushing aside a corner of the white mosquito netting that hung like a flimsy box from the ceiling, he impatiently waved again for me to come join him. I laughed and acquiesced. Setting my camera bag on the edge of the bed that had only a mat woven out of plastic as a mattress, I sat down and turned to Lor. He grinned and reached over to the edge of the bed that was against the wall. Lifting a mound of clothing, he exposed a long bundle, wrapped in an oily cloth that by its color and texture must have once been a white bath towel. Next to the bundle was a Chinese combat chest harness with three pouches for 30-round AK-47 magazines. Dragging it out by the two shoulder straps, he reached into one of the small pouches that could easily hold a grenade, but instead he used for holding an oiling rag and a small bottle of gun oil. Unwrapping the oily bath towel, he handed me the revealed AK-47. "Pathet Lao," he said and made the motion of snatching something in the air. The metal of the weapon was mahogany-colored, like steel that had rusted and had then been oiled, rusted and oiled again and again.

I nodded, grinned, and checked its weight. It was heavier than I imagined. When I handed it back to him, he brought it halfway up to his shoulder and mimicked the sound of a machine gun, and said, "kill Pathet Lao." He pointed at the automatic in his hand, then gave me a thumbs up with all the bright glee of a boy with a new toy, "Number one!"

I thought back to a book I'd read about Laos, Air America, the Central Intelligence Agency, and a man named Lair. In 1960, CIA "Colonel Billy" Lair landed in Laos and urged the Hmong and Mien hill tribes to aid the United States in their fight against Communism, namely to stop Hanoi's incursion into Laos. Ho Chi Minh was bringing troops and equipment into South Vietnam along trails and roads through Laos and Cambodia, a system nicknamed the Ho Chi Minh trail. From 1963 to 1973, the Hmong were trained and led by the Central Intelligence Agency. A hill tribe people much like the Chiricaua Apache that fought a fierce guerrilla war in the mountains of the American Southwest, they were very effective in hindering Ho Chi Minh's efforts to supply his troops in South Vietnam by ambushing North Vietnamese Army regulars, and South Vietnamese Vietcong, as they worked their way through southeastern Laos and eastern Cambodia. Under the US military advisory who were working *on the other side of the fence* (a term used by US personnel in Vietnam because the US and ARVN weren't supposed be in Laos or Cambodia), the Hmong and their CIA advisors became so effective against Ho Chi Minh that Uncle Ho put a price on the heads of the Hmong and any US advisors his soldiers could kill or capture. Hmong successes came at a price: by 1975, when South Vietnam fell to Hanoi, Cambodia fell to Pol Pot, and Laos was subjugated to a cloak-and-dagger oppression by the Pathet Lao that rivaled Ceausescu's Romania. Twenty-thousand Hmong guerrillas offered their lives for a victory against the Communists. The loss of the victory led to repercussions that to this day haunt Laos. One of the worst was that the United States, who had promised to save the Hmong if the Communists overran the country, basically left them to their own devices. There was no explanation given even after the sacrifice of Hmong lives, their stunning successes against the North Vietnamese, and the large number of American pilots they had rescued.

  Lor looked up from oiling his weapon and smiled, taking me out of my thoughts of history. I must have been deep in thought because he had a confused look on his face. He was such a nice kid, I was thinking to myself, that had he been able to speak English more effectively, or if I was more fluent in Hmong, we could have had the kind of friendship that I would normally have had back in school or in a club. But I thought again, as I studied the weapon of war that he held with the closeness a young teenager might have held a baseball bat, or a hockey stick back in the peace of the States. I thought about how the world could be so lacking in compassion and justice, and I felt the corners of my face sag, and that part of me that searches for the escape of joy, instead fell into a deep, dark well of sadness.

* * *

  The boat looked too small. Matter of fact, it looked so small I was wondering why there were eight armed Hmong sitting in it when it clearly should only hold two. Xiong, armed and dressed like the others in camouflage, waved me in. "Come, come," he said. The others followed suit and began waving me in, too. I reluctantly made my way into the boat, with quite a bit of effort because of the Hmong already packed in like sardines, all the way to the middle of the boat that would have been called a canoe had it been carved out of a long tree trunk, instead of nailed together out of cut lumber. Just before I sat down, I grabbed for the gunwale and felt the sharp pain of a sliver stab my palm. I sucked air and drew everyone's attention.

  Sam, who was shin deep in the water and holding the boat steady, said, "Don't be a puss." With all the lights out after moving from the cars that had brought us up from Ban Vinai and along the river, I could just barely pick out everyone, and so, too, barely caught the glow off Sam's wide grin.

Xiong laughed, and tried digging the sliver out with the point of a dull and rusty combat knife while one of his men lit my palm with a red-filtered flashlight, making me glad I'd gotten my tetanus booster. In frustration, he said, "Wait until we get to Laos. I'll get it out when we have morning light."

"What?" I yelped, while putting pressure to the area on the side of the sliver, relieving at least some of the pain that now made my hand throb.

Sam said something in Hmong to the guy on the stern, who then lowered the outboard into the water and yanked on the starter cord. The loudness of the motor made me wince. Sam cast off the line, and terror almost made me jump out of the boat right then and there. Xiong clasped my forearm and pulled me back down to sit beside him. "Don't worry, Sam will meet us on the other side, later. He will come in the next boat." I slipped off my ALICE pack that held all my camera equipment, and stuck it between my legs. In retrospect, I can only thank Lady Luck for having done so.

I didn't know about another boat, but knowing that Sam would be meeting us over on the other side didn't make me feel any better. I wanted him in the boat right next to me, armed to the teeth, ready to help me keep my skin with all the training he had honed over the years in Vietnam, Laos, and Rhodesia. Forget having my life in the hands of armed teenagers who should have been playing Pack-man and reading comic books, instead of fighting bullet-and-grenade for survival. Lor, who had turned quiet and had taken on an aura of seriousness I had not seen during our jovial dinner of chicken soup and rice, patted me on the back and gave me a thumbs up. The gesture was appreciated, but I needed much more, so I looked up at the thin crescent of the moon and slowly took a deep breath.

Sam moved up the bank and was joined by a group of other dark figures scrambling along the shore. They just seemed to melt into each other in the moonlight along the steep bank. We backed out and I tried my best to sit still, even though my heart was trying to pound its way out of my ears, and the sliver had now taken on a life of its own, with the sole purpose of driving deeper into my hand.

It was the dry season, but the motor didn't seem very effective in keeping the boat from being at the mercy of the current. I wanted to say, *I told you there's too many people in this boat!* But, I held myself in check against my pain and emotions. At least I felt protected by the darkness. I could see where the Maekong started and ended, and I could just barely see the dark mass of the mountains against the stars. A cloud here and there. Except for the motor, it was almost peaceful. Too peaceful. That quiet permitted dark images to churn through my mind, thoughts that would have chained me to the bank, well away from the boat that now carried me closer and closer to an uneasiness I had so far been able to evade through constant distraction. I unsuccessfully tried dodging thoughts about cobras that grew almost fifteen feet long, long enough to loom at eye level before striking, like out of some really scary Rudyard Kipling story. And what about Russell vipers? They could kill you in thirty minutes, an extremely painful death because their venom destroys your blood cells and dismantles your nervous system. The worst part about *russelli siamensis* is that they bring a whole new meaning to the word "attitude": at least a cobra will choose to escape given the chance. I hadn't yet read the chapter in my survival manual about insects and flora, but I could only imagine that they would be worse. I cursed myself for even reading that book recommended by a neighbor in Bangkok who actually went out and caught Russell vipers to create the antivenom. If that wasn't enough, every ambush scene from every John Wayne movie I ever saw replayed across that imaginary silver screen that separated Laos from me.

As for the Hmong, because of the poor light, I could only see the expressions of those closest to me, Xiong and Lor. There was a sense of security in that, if for no other reason than I had enjoyed myself in the openness of their family home, even with the language barrier that had forced Xiong's aunt and Lor to communicate in hand signals. I dipped my hand in the water, feeling the resistance of the cool current. A dryness in my mouth along with the hot, humid air made me thirsty for a cup of that water. I pulled a canteen from one of the three small pouches in my pack, and quenched the urge with a sip.

Minutes felt like hours, and I suddenly became aware that everyone else in the boat was crouching down except me. I realized that, sitting up, I must have looked like a mast on a ship. I thought of Denis Gray, who almost towered above my own six-foot frame, and wondered if he too drew such attention. I crouched over, and tried to make myself as small as a cicada on a tree. So the mast and the boat became one, looking more like a floating log with a shivering fat muskrat on top. A chill ran through my body as I could only imagine the thoughts of a Pathet Lao marksman on the other side thinking how easy it would be to line up his sights on my torso.

Ten minutes later the mass of trees on the Lao side of the river had taken shape, looking in the dark like a collection of giant, gray cauliflowers, the heavy foliage sometimes weighing into the water. I imagined that in the rainy season, there was just a straight transition from water to trees and bushes, no open bank.

A red light, about halfway up the tree line from the water, began blinking at us. It was hardly Morse code, and seemed more like just a signal to draw attention. "Our signal," Xiong said.

I looked over at Lor, who patted me on the back. I looked back at the signal and then it happened. It wasn't choreographed like in a movie. It started off with one burst of automatic fire, and then, as though the shock had worn off our bushwhackers, another joined in and then another. What was a silent mass of trees and bushes turned into a string of flashing lights. The tracers, the muzzle flashes, and the fireworks would have been a sight to admire had they not had but one purpose.

I think I was the first one over the side, not long after two of the guys in front had been either wounded or killed. The bullets chasing me into the water sounded like snapping metal strings on a guitar. The Hmong running the outboard kept the boat moving, which probably saved the lives of those who had bailed. I caught the action intermittently as I was repeatedly forced to the surface because my lungs burned for air. He was trying to turn back toward Thailand before I heard the unmistakable slapping thunk of a bullet hitting a man's chest. After he was hit, the boat began circling, almost masked by a sheet of water raining up into the sky instead of down. The machine gun fire was almost non-stop now, and I prepared to dive again as the lead and copper hail moved away from the boat and worked its way left and up and down the current. Amazingly, there was someone still alive in the boat, and when he tried to bail out, it overturned and looked like the back of a whale as it drifted aimlessly down the river.

Xiong was right on my heels, but I lost him after the first time I dove under the water to swim as far as I could away from the boat and commotion. Lor was caught in the boat for a few seconds longer than the both of us. He had snagged his ammo harness on something, most likely a nail, and it was too much for him to get over the side. He was right next to me when I came up for air the second time. It was hard to tell whether he got hit in the boat while freeing himself, or later on in the water. As I moved closer to him, I noticed he was having trouble keeping his head out of the water. He kept on splashing with one hand. His other hand was holding in his guts. I felt them squish against my arm as I swam up behind him and kept his head out of the water.

I cursed quietly to myself that I was dressed in the fatigues and jungle boots I had brought with me from California. A sudden rush of anger made me grimace and choke on accidently inhaled water. *LA freeway, my ass! Running across an LA freeway was more like it!* Had I been wearing sneakers and shorts, I could have kicked off the shoes and had more effect in propelling us toward Thailand. I was lucky enough to come across a flotation device—actually it was just a piece of foam that had been used as a seat on the boat—and I alternated between kicking and sidestroking us slowly, but ever so closer to safety. The drill was kick and stroke, choke, take a breather on the seat, and then hand it back to Lor to help him keep his chin above water. "It's going to be okay, man," I said over and over, maybe for me as much as for him.

    It wasn't until we were three-quarters of the way back to Thailand before I thought about my camera equipment. I recalled having it in my hand as I went over the side. But its weight and the boots, and the fatigues that acted like a water anchor, were too much for me. The cameras had been packed in a waterproof bag, but I had squeezed out any air that could have kept not only the cameras but me afloat. I grumbled to myself that one of the monster catfish that prowl the bottom of the river had probably swallowed my pack full of cameras. I then had my only laugh that night as I bet that some fisherman down in Cambodia or Vietnam would catch that catfish and pay off all his debts and retire off the sale of that safe and dry collection of camera equipment he would find after slitting open the fish's belly.

    A groan from Lor brought me back to the gravity of the situation and I again comforted him with whatever reassuring words I could muster. I was about to drown from exhaustion myself. As we came closer to the bank, I heard a car driving along the river. I thought it was weird that they were driving without any headlights on. But, in Third World countries, there are a lot of weird actions by people who think they're saving on materials such as the life of a light bulb filament, but instead are diminishing their chances of surviving, period. I yelled out, but could only manage a hoarse, "Help!"

    Surprise could hardly describe the elation I felt as the car stopped and I heard Sam's voice over our splashing in the water. Sam was in the pitch black under a tree, still wearing the NVGs[15] he had been navigating the road in the dark with. He had been driving with the headlights off, not only so that they wouldn't draw attention to themselves, but so that it would be easier for him to pick Lor and me out of the large mass of dark water.

    For the first time since we met, Sam actually got his nice clothes wet. He grabbed Lor under the arms and I locked my arms under Lor's knees. It was tough going up that bank, stumbling over mismatched rocks, through a low-hanging eave of branches and prickly leaves, but we got him up to the car. One of the guys who had been in the boat was already sitting in the passenger side of the front seat. He'd been beat up pretty badly, and had even broken his hand during the escape! Nonetheless, he got out and helped us get Lor into the back seat of the Toyota sedan. "Keep applying pressure," Sam said as he quickly got in and started the engine.

The road was way too pitted. I felt every bump, as though it were me and not Lor who had his guts spilling out of his stomach, every time we hit a hole in the dirt road. Sam tried his best to keep the ride smooth, even turning on the headlights to evade the potholes in the road. But by the time we arrived at the village, it was as though all of us in the car were wounded, as we empathized so much with that nice kid, Lor.

Xiong was horrified when he saw his younger brother. Having just shucked his wet clothes, he barked orders like a madman as he hopped around, pulling on a pair of jeans. "Quick! We must get the doctor! Get the doctor!"

Xiong said something in Hmong to one of his guerrillas who went off into the night on a dirtbike. He then helped us get his younger brother out of the car and onto a bed in his home. I thought his aunt was going to start crying right then and there. But, she held her hand to her mouth and motioned for us to get him in quickly and lay him on the bed. All through this time Lor was almost peaceful, except for the bouncing on the road. Sam said it was shock, and that he had lost a lot of blood. We had been a long time in getting back to Thailand after the ambush. Unsettling feelings ran through me as I thought that I should have kicked and stroked harder, even though I had given my all. I confessed this to Sam as I kept my vigil at Lor's side. "You did the best you could," Sam said. Somehow it wasn't enough.

The doctor, a tall, lanky, and very tired Brit with straw-like hair, arrived from the camp shortly and began working on Lor. He inserted an IV into Lor's arm and handed me the bag of plasma to keep elevated. Xiong, who stood next to me, had his arms folded over his chest and rocked back and forth on his heels. Lor was tough, the doctor said. The doctor took a bag of saline solution and did his best to wash away the bloody mess for a better look; he then confessed to Sam that his first assessment had been a little too optimistic. Sam was almost as proficient as the doctor when it came to treating the wound, stopping the bleeding, and suturing. It was amazing, and surreal to see the two of them performing like Bethseda Hospital surgeons, solely under a single light bulb hanging from a wire strung over a small log beam, under a plank and thatch roof. Jungle doctor was an understatement. It was soothingly hypnotic to watch their gloved hands move, the flashing of the yellow incandescent light on the forceps, scissors and needle; but, the red color of blood, the dark ale color of the iodine—and the smell of it—almost made me puke. All in all, it was impressive how fast their hands danced in and around the wound. And I was even more amazed and horrified that it was only one bullet that had done so much damage by unzipping him from right to left, all the way across.

I would have remembered it as a stupendous moment, an instance in which Man had been truly challenged by Death, and then won. But, Lor's breathing stopped and all pandemonium let loose. "What do I do?" I pleaded. "What do I do?"

"CPR!" Sam yelled as he and the doctor tried working faster. Xiong grabbed the plasma bag from me.

With only the dim memory of pretending to blow air into a classmate's hand-covered mouth, and massaging his heart with my weight on intertwined hands during a safety drill at the Singapore American School, I began CPR. "Faster!" Sam said. "Faster!"

"He's not coming around, Sam!" I blurted. "Sam?!"

Sam finished a suture, tossed the forceps and scissors into a metal tray with a loud clatter, and moved quickly over to my side. He put his ear to Lor's nose and parted mouth. Discoloration was already beginning to appear around Lor's lips.

"Blast! We're losing him, Sam," the doctor said.

Stunned, I just stood to Sam's side, my hands dangling like leaves on a tree in a still night. "Get over here, help me!" Sam barked.

Shocked out of my trance by Sam's first emotionally charged words to me, ever, I went into action, following his orders to breath into Lor's mouth, while he pounded and pressed on Lor's rib cage. At one point someone suggested cutting him open and massaging his heart directly. But, by then it was too late. All the action and emotion that had collected around Lor's barely alive body had dissipated into the far edges of the home, moving out of the light and into the shadows. Xiong and his aunt collected in the kitchen corner to share tears. Others squatted and sat down against the walls.

Sam patted me on the shoulder and said, "he just lost too much blood." We rolled him over to get more of the sheet he was laying on around his body to wrap him in it. There was a large multi-colored stain on it, right where the blood and iodine had soaked through, along with other stuff never described in the war propaganda movies: urine and feces. When we were done bundling him up in the sheet and securing him with twine, I put my head in my hands and didn't know whether to cry from emotion, or groan against a very real physical pain that emanated from my very core.

I had not thought about my young friend, Chester, in a long time; such a long time that it was shocking. Recalling his sudden death gave me chills, and as I sat there on the dirt floor, I realized that I still didn't know how to handle death.

Chapter 6

"Many people when they fall in love look for a little haven of refuge from the world, where they can be sure of being admired when they are not admirable, and praised when they are not praiseworthy."— Bertrand Russell

Light of Respite

Carlisle had a friend who often visited Hong Kong on business. If I had the money, it would be no problem for me to quickly replace that equipment tumbling along the bottom of the Maekong. Definitely much cheaper than trying to buy new cameras in Bangkok, what with the heavy import taxes levied on products like Japanese technology and American motorcycles. I accepted his offer with a click of our Singha-filled tumblers. Suddenly relieved from a stress that had hounded me for the last week, I looked out on Soi 22 and breathed a sigh. Once again, I felt that there was a reason I was supposed to be here and not back in the US. Carlisle chuckled, and said, "You were worried?" I raised my eyebrows a couple times in acknowledgement. I was about ready to throw in the towel and go back home.

Anne was over by the kitchen chatting away with the food stall owner. "He say will be ready in just a moment," she said after giving Carlisle a hug and kiss upon her return. "You tell about my mother?"

Refugees of war, famine, political and religious persecution, and hurried mass exodus, orphans from all over Indochina and Burma filtered into the back alleys of Bangkok. Anne was one of those who had lost touch with her mother in the escape from Laos. And, like many Asians from the countryside she was very superstitious, seeking solace in the advice of soothsayers.

The one they visited at one of the large markets by the bus stop had told her that she would find her mother in a refugee camp up by the border of Laos.

"That's like finding a needle in a haystack!" I told Carlisle. "And I could have told you that was one of the places to go."

"I know; but, Anne wants to go back to the fortuneteller and get some more information. What you might find interesting is that she wants to talk to you. She even described you to us."

My posture stiffened as I became instantly alert.

"There's something she wants to tell you. Said she wouldn't charge the normal price. Said it'd be cheaper."

"You didn't tell her about me did you?"

Anne grinned at me. "Want talk to you. Very special!"

"Interesting, don't you think?"

Leaning back in my seat, I asked, "What does she want with me?"

"Wouldn't say," Carlisle said and took a swig from his beer. "Do you believe there's no such thing as coincidence?"

I shrugged my shoulders.

"There's a saying that there is no such thing in life as coincidence; that we're meant to go and meet every individual and every moment. You know, I've read about cultures where they don't even have the word for coincidence in their vocabulary. Many of them are your own American Indians."

"What's the purpose then? Where is it all supposed to lead?"

"Peace."

"Peace? I don't think that's it." My thoughts flashed on the last time I saw my father, and I suddenly became aware of a tightness in my stomach.

"Peace," Carlisle said. "Divine peace. Peace with every soul we meet over and over again."

I laughed. "I think you've been here too long with all this Buddhism and reincarnation. Am I going to come back as a dog owned by some asshole because I didn't make my peace?" A feeling of uneasiness hit me.

"Haven't you wondered why you and I met?"

"Yeah, we're just kindred. . . souls," I quipped. "So when are we going to see this woman who'll read to me from my book of destiny?" I had always been curious about palm readers and fortunetellers. I attributed it to reading fairy tales and myths as a child, where the protagonist always had to meet a gatekeeper before venturing on.

"So you'll go?"

I nodded as a waiter brought us our meals. After the dishes were passed around, I dipped a spoon into my bowl of *gang gari gai* and shoveled it onto my side plate of steamed white rice. The delicious scent of yellow curry, basil, and chicken perked my senses up, making me salivate in anticipation of that sweet chicken curry. Carlisle yanked me back from my food-induced trance by asking, "Did I ever tell you about a friend of mine who went to a clairvoyant who told him he should get his life in order?"

I shook my head as I chewed and reached for my glass of Singha.

"Three weeks later he was on his motorcycle and a plate of glass slid off the truck in front of him. Cut his head right off."

* * *

Markets are the center of a wheel that spins wildly across the large cities of commerce in Asia. My childhood memories stand within that wheel, memories of trips with my mother and our *amah* on Saturday mornings from home to the local Singaporean or Saigon markets. We'd get Singapore-style noodles and *pho*, the Vietnamese noodle soup passionately enjoyed nowadays as faraway from Asia as the Silicon Valley, the main excuse for broth spots on a shirt or tie during lunch; the candy-apple red *char-siu* Chinese pork, and all the fresh vegetables and fruits that would impress any connoisseur of Asian cooking. It's the bananas that enchant most of those on their first visit to Southeast Asia. In the States, there is only one type, the yellow ones, picked green in Ecuador, and then, if not ripe by their arrival at the local supermarket, are hit with sulfur dioxide to improve their color. But, the process does nothing for their taste. In Asia, you find little red ones that taste like honey, and green ones that are actually ripe. And papayas. Real papayas! The diameter of footballs, and sometimes almost twice as long! Just from a small papaya tree that is maybe six feet tall. We're not even talking about the lychee and rambutans whose sweetness taught me as a child that the Divine meant that people taste not just of the salt, but of the ambrosia of life! By the time these two fruits get to North America and Europe they're canned and taste, unfortunately, like canned pears.

As I reminisced and took in the sights and smells of the market, I felt lonely. Maybe it was seeing Carlisle and Anne, relationship smoothed, or maybe it was all the senses brought to delight, but I felt that there was someone special who should be walking with me, too. I'd been told that when the time was right it would happen. The lack of female companionship never really affected me much when I was working fast and hard to get an assignment, or when I had family around me, but being alone in a foreign country somehow made my solitude that much more acute. I tried to picture someone, and a woman with blonde hair and blue eyes came to mind, which made me laugh. An understandable fantasy in Scandinavia or California, a fantasy which had started with my first kiss from a blonde little girl at my fifth birthday party. I chuckled, took a deep breath, and pulled myself away from the chasm in my heart.

The market was one giant mass of vendors and hawkers haggling over prices for their produce and wares. A belief prevails among

Asians that only fresh ingredients must be used for cooking; not doing so results in a meal that doesn't taste as good and only has a fraction of the nutritional properties. Meat vendors waved us over to show what they had. They kept their *meats* in bamboo baskets and cages. There were pigs and piglets, giant lizards, turtles, chickens. . . pythons.

"Look at that." Carlisle pointed to a vendor over by a mound of cages.

The hawker pulled a python out of its cage. It fought for its life by wrapping its seven-foot length around the snake seller's five-foot frame. His deft blade started at the neck and sliced its way down to the tail, spilling an amber fluid out on to the street and down an open drain. Just as quickly, he gutted and skinned it, and wrapped it up for a little old Chinese lady.

The skinning left me sad. The snake reminded me of Kaa, the large python, in Kipling's *The Jungle Books*. As a child in Singapore, I was a young Mowgli who revelled in the hunt for ghosts of tigers, leopards and panthers through the jungle lots behind our home.

We left the dead snake and continued browsing. "Look at that! . . look at all those rabbits! There must be at least a hundred. . . hey, look at that one. He's just like the one I had in Saigon."

A lone white rabbit curled up in a corner, pink eyes wide with terror as he held himself against the suffocating mass of gray and brown rabbit fur around him. The rabbit reminded me of when these markets were my pet shops. Most of my menagerie in Saigon was filled with animals from just such a market.

"There she is," Carlisle said and pointed to a woman sitting on a corner sidewalk above the market. Like an old Buddha she seemed to have a better view from her high seat. We climbed a short set of stairs to the woman, who wore a sarong and sweater, and watched pedestrians walk past giving her looks as if she were begging. Lady Buddha sat cross-legged on a mat with ordinary playing cards on top, her rubber thongs to the side. She smiled when she looked at me. A chill ran up my spine as she waved us over to sit next to her, if for no other reason than Carlisle's previously having told me she wanted to meet me.

Anne and Carlisle crossed their legs and sat down. Not limber enough, I knelt. Anne and Lady Buddha talked for awhile, then the woman pulled out a cigarette and lit it. She then touched the stack of cards.

Anne pointed at the cards, too, and said, "Touch cards."

Lady Buddha dealt them out from the stack after my touch. She was quiet for about five minutes as she just gazed at the cards and me, taking long drags on her cigarette as she squinted. My chills became more pronounced. Lady Buddha got into a long conversation with Anne. I looked at Carlisle, but he could only shrug his shoulders and remain quiet and watchful with me.

Anne's voice took on a sullen tone. "She say you go dangerous place, very dangerous, but learn much, get many answers."

"Where exactly?!" Mystery suddenly muffled the distracting crowd sounds.

"To east she say. . . Very important you stay away from border. . . If you come back, much money. Much good luck!" Anne stopped for a moment as Lady Buddha took a drag on her cigarette, the glowing embers contrastingly bright against her dark face. I thought about asking whether she was talking about the future or the past, but then Anne grinned, and even giggled as she kept her ear to Lady Buddha. When Lady Buddha stopped, Anne translated, "She say you meet woman with long gold hair, good teacher about yourself, then marry Thai woman with long black hair who teach more."

I just sat there and smirked at Carlisle. He gave me the shrugged shoulders again.

Anne said, "She say, very important you stay away from border. Border no good."

"Where? Laos?"

"She no sure. You stay away from border. Very dangerous."

I laughed it off. I was intrigued. But I was more intrigued with the women to come than with Laos anytime soon.

* * *

The bus was late. The sun was beating down on me. And Carlisle had gotten me into a Singha drinking match last night that left me with a raging headache. Most of all, I was feeling anxious. The previous week's debacle on the Maekong was really beginning to get on my already frayed nerves, leading me to the unthinkable. I had begun to weigh other options: whether to go back to the States and become an electrical engineer, or enlist in the Marine Corps. Either choice would make my parents happy, and now I was beginning to see no escape. I had already given my money for the equipment to Carlisle, so I had to at least wait until his friend came back from Hong Kong in a couple days.

I was uncomfortable not only from last night's alcohol that made me smell like a brewery, but also that my jeans and polo shirt stuck to me like plastic sheeting because of the intense heat. I wanted out. I wanted out of my skin. I wanted out of all hot, sticky places where people got killed for just a few dollars. I glanced down at my untied shoelaces and lost it. The scream came from a place I had never been to. It was a place so dark and repressed that I could only hold myself against the raw emotion by clenching my fists as I let loose.

Relieved by the outburst and inaccurately thinking it was only because of the stress of not having made a name for myself yet, this was actually just the beginning of the effects of post-traumatic stress from the Hmong episode. I composed myself enough to bend over and tie my laces. A moment of embarrassment caused me to quickly look around as I stood back up. A khaki and white uniformed policeman was directing traffic and I worried that he had witnessed my outburst. It was lucky for me that he paid me no attention, because he probably would have thrown me in jail for suspected drug use, or for some type of psychological disorder. Such an outburst is definitely not accepted in Southeast Asia.

"Excuse me. Would you have the time?" The voice was pleasant, soft, and made me want to hear more. Not wanting to appear rude, I removed my black Ray Bans as I turned to answer the face that spoke the words. I stared at the woman who looked as though she'd fallen off the Marrakesh Express, and fought the urge to hum a Crosby, Stills and Nash tune. Her breathtaking beauty put me into a kind of brain-numbing trance as such women do.

She repeated her question. With my face turning warm with embarrassment, I looked down at my watch. "Two p.m.," I said and found myself staring into her eyes that seemed to lock onto mine. Surprisingly, I felt a sense of calm and it didn't seem as weird and intrusive as I imagined it would have had I gazed for that long into someone else's eyes. She had the deepest blue eyes I had ever seen. A bus that seemed driven by a tornado blew by, causing us to recoil against the blast of air. As she recovered from keeping her dress from flying up, she took on a coy expression, a flirtatious tilt to her head as she now looked at me. "Where are you going?" I asked, suddenly short of breath and mesmerized by her features that were as striking as those of Anita Ekberg.

"Do you know what time is the river market?" she asked. *German? Norwegian? Dutch?* I thought to myself. *Where is the floating market?* I had to get to know this woman better: the Oriental Hotel always had tours!

"I'm pretty sure it's right now. Matter of fact that's the direction I'm going. Would you like to take the taxi with me?!" I hoped she didn't notice how much my heart was pounding.

She faced me, seemingly taken aback by my forwardness. Her eyes carefully read my innocent smile as she said, "Yes. Thank you."

I hailed a taxi and we got in, she being careful not to close the door on her waist-length blond hair. I got the driver from sixty baht down to twenty, and off we went. On the drive I learned that her name was Erika, and that she had just arrived from Ceylon. Morning intentions of visiting the AP office completely disappeared. Catching myself humming *Norwegian Wood*, I berated myself in thoughts. Erika looked over at me with a smile that made me wonder what it would take for her to share her lips with mine in a kiss.

She started telling me about herself and I learned why my ferang friends on Soi 22 call these northern European travelers "pilgrims." In the United States, she would have been called a hippie chick. She had traveled all the way from Stockholm by land, had bought the leather money pouch around her neck in Turkey, the earth-and-cream cotton blouse from India, and the rock-washed, gypsy-style skirt from, of course, Marrakesh. A sneaked glance at her feet revealed leather sandals. She told me she was a college student from Stockholm. When I told her about my career goal of becoming a well-known combat photojournalist, she gave me her full attention. I felt rejuvenated! And as she found me interesting, I couldn't help but find my own interest in her building. I forgot not only about the day's plans, but also about how poorly everything had gone up at the Lao border.

When we arrived at the Oriental, the driver tried to get more money out of us, but she refused and it showed me that she hadn't let anyone push her around during her trip by land to Southeast Asia. The driver left in a huff with the initial bargain of thirty baht. The Oriental is a hotel where the rich and famous stay, and they don't like journalists taking pictures of their guests. I was neither rich nor famous, so I never felt the hotel an inviting place either as a Bangkok resident or a journalist. It did have an interesting history though. The old wing is Victorian, a remnant of the Joseph Conrad days. Inside they have books, some signed by famous authors who have stayed at the Oriental. And if you can afford it, they serve a great high tea.

When we finished our short walk to the river market ferry station we were first greeted by the stench, and then the sight of the debris floating in the brown river: human feces, fruit skins, plastic bags, and who knows what else. The Chao Praya is a river that flushes much of the debris of Thailand before it gets to Bangkok, from rice fields to village outhouses. I directed her attention toward the river, and the dock conspicuously devoid of the market ferry.

"I guess we're late. . ."

She nodded sadly.

"What are you doing for dinner? There's a great place just around the corner from where we met."

"Dinner? Isn't it a bit early?" She sure seemed depressed about missing the river market ferry.

My watch read 3:10 p.m. "We can see the town, and then have dinner at six or so. I don't know this area too well, but there are lots of places to visit back near Soi 22."

Her face relaxed and was overtaken by another smile. "Okay!"

We caught a taxi and I learned that even without her beauty, she would still be very attractive. Not once did our conversation die, as she easily kept it running.

Dropped off by our taxi, we passed through boutiques along Sukhumvit from Soi 22 to Soi Cowboy, and back. They were full of wonderfully intricate Thai art and curiosities. Brass trays, carved wooden pictures of Thai country life, wooden elephants, multitudes of stuffed mongooses and cobras, and BUFEs—pronounced like the girl's name, Buffy—filled the shops. I enjoyed telling her the story of how the green, two-and-a-half-foot, ceramic elephant received the name of "BUFE."

"You see, during the Vietnam War lots of GI's on R&R in Bangkok spent their pay on these guys. BUFE was the pet name given it by US Postal Service, who hated having to process them through the mail. Stands for Big Ugly Fuckin' Elephant."

She laughed.

"Try and pick one up."

Walking over to one standing by the shop entrance, she put both hands on it and lifted it. Her eyes widened as she exclaimed in Swedish. Erika strained to lift the elephant a couple of inches off the ground. We laughed together as she lowered it.

At another shop, they sold brass tables with wooden legs. Engravings of elephants and tigers in the jungle adorned the tables. My focus rested not on the tables behind the window, but on Erika's reflection. She caught me and smirked, but said nothing.

"Are you hungry?" she asked in a playfully seductive way that made me uncomfortable.

Her eyes and hair color stopped me. I stared at her, shocked after just remembering the fortuneteller's prophecy from two nights ago. But even though I was shocked, a light feeling of happiness filled my center being.

* * *

Erika stood in the lobby of her hotel, as we had planned at dinner the night before. Her western clothes revealed a curvy, model's body that had been so well hidden by the dress from the day before. Instead of the dress, she wore faded blue jeans, and a tucked in light-blue blouse with rolled up long sleeves. The hiking shoes were a finishing touch that could have easily put her in an Eddie Bauer catalog. Erika's hair was free-hanging again, but blow-dried full. She wore make-up as though trying to please and sensed that I considered none better than too much. Erika trusted her natural beauty.

"I don't dress like this when traveling alone; men always ask me ask to go out on a date with them."

"You look very nice." Amazingly my words had come out softly and smoothly, without even a stutter. Such was not the rule considering the feelings I hadn't experienced since my first crush.

Bangkok always moved fast during the day, only stopping for a moment between one and four in the afternoon, when the heat caused most of the populace to go home and take a nap. Only crazy ferangs like us would spend the day running all over town to see the sights in such heat and humidity.

Erika declined my offer to take her to a Muai Thai fight that evening, for she preferred to only remember the calm ambiance of the morning market. She bought a bag of rambutans, which are like the sweet lychee except they are covered by red skins with soft spikes, looking like golf-ball-sized sea-urchins. While walking up the street, we tore open the thick skin of the fruit, revealing the white meat. The fatty-looking layer of fruit tasted like wine and honey.

With Erika, boutiques, custom tailors, places I hardly visited on my own, were immediately interesting. Tuk-tuks and taxis were used sparingly. Erika loved to walk; by the way she walked it was evident that she had an intense love of life. Her steps were light but deliberate. My body weight must have dropped by four pounds during our walk that day.

My infatuation was overpowering, blowing away any shyness that would have kept me from sneaking glances at her beauty. She was at once exciting and terrifying. Romantic love had always been to me like the little treasures we now gazed at behind the walls of glass display cases—most times I never asked how much they cost; they attracted me so much, but I didn't want to deal with the added pain of not being able to afford them.

* * *

Patience never suffocated Erika's gusto. She even wanted to go with me up to the Laos border and sneak in alongside Hmong guerrillas. My confidence in my career choice grew in answer to her words of praise. The hint as to what a perfect mate could be sometimes became too much, and knowing that she was not mine always brought me back down to Earth. Still, the decision to come here, without so much as a true contact, didn't feel insane anymore.

"I respect fully what you have done. To say good-bye to home, completely unprepared for what awaited you," she said over a lunch of curry and rice, "But also, I do see your father and mother's viewpoint."

I set my finished Singha down on the table and frowned at her last statement.

"It's my life, right?!"

"Yes, as long as you pay for everything." There was no intimidating this woman.

Our conversations were spiked like that for the rest of our time together. Her agreeing with me all the time would have taught me nothing. There were enough street vendors who agreed with me all the time, to complete a sale. Carlisle's Thai girlfriend always agreed with him and look how she treated him.

"Why are you smirking and shaking your head?" she asked.

"Oh, nothing. Nothing at all."

We entered Wat Po, a temple complex built by Rama I. Because of its size and age, most tourists tried to visit it.

In the northwest corner of the temple, a large golden Buddha lay resting on his side, an enlightened smile on his face. He was an easy hundred-and-fifty-feet long and plated in gold. Incense scented the breeze.

"We're going to have a storm pretty soon. Feel that electricity in the air?"

She looked around and the breeze picked up the ends of her hair, making them seem to catch afire in the smoky light.

"Lots of thunder and lightning will be here in a little while."

She squeezed my hand and let go. Kneeling in front of the Buddha, she brought her hands together the way Thais did when they went into deep prayer, and closed her eyes.

"Are you Buddhist?" I asked after she rose.

"No."

"Where do you want to go now?"

"Home," she said.

* * *

"Now be prepared," I warned, as we took the first plank into my neighborhood. "We have rats as big as cats."

"Have you forgotten my visits to India and Pakistan on the way here?" Erika stopped. "Where is your house?"

"Over there." My extended index finger pointed to a two-story wooden bungalow, surrounded by a fence.

"Why is there so much water here?" she asked.

"Bangkok is built on a swamp."

Erika gave a questioning look. "Why isn't the rest of the city sinking like your house?"

"The newer buildings, like the high-rises, have foundations that are sunk deeply into the muck." We stopped at my gate and I slid open the wooden latch. "My place is like those houses on stilts the Thais live in at the coast. I like it; the shape, and the redwood color of the place makes it look like a houseboat moored in Sausalito."

She stepped in three inches of water as we entered the yard. "A leaky houseboat." Erika kicked her foot to rid her shoe of water.

"My room is upstairs." Closing the gate, we made our way across the water by stepping gingerly along the concrete slabs that had been set down for that purpose.

"This is my room." I led her upstairs, and unlocked the door. Moving aside, I motioned for Erika to enter, and then pointed to the switch just on the inside of the doorway. "Would you turn that light on?"

The room looked as though it belonged to a stressed-out college freshman. "Sorry about the way the place looks."

"You need a woman."

While I opened the four shutters, she perused my collection of tapes. Most of them were of bands from the 1960s and 1970s. She stopped at The Association.

"Where'd you get these tapes?"

"At the bootleg store down on the corner."

"Bootleg?"

"Yeah, they're homemade copies, black market. Drives the recording artists nuts. The copies even have the same packaging as the authentic tapes. But even the packagings are bad, too."

"Where is your cassette player?"

"Here."

Erika accepted it and inserted the tape. After turning it on she looked up at me. "The bathroom?"

"It's in the room back down the hall."

Left with idle time, I read, for what seemed the millionth time, the issue of *Surfing* magazine purchased back at San Francisco International Airport.

Erika's mischievous grin disappeared as she locked the door behind her and turned out the light. In a moment she was removing my clothes and with them, the insecurities about my body, making me feel that I had finally found someone I could really love.

Later, *The Association* song, *Never My Love*, came on over the cassette player. Opened up by having just made love for the first time, and listening to such a caressing melody; suddenly, my throat tightened. No teenaged sexual fantasy could have ever prepared me for the intimacy.

"Why are you crying?" Erika asked, cautiously.

"Memories of loneliness back in California."

She propped up her head with a pillow.

"Boy, how I fed into ignorant stereotypes of Vietnam. I acted like the crazy Vietnam Vet just because of a need to fit in at high school."

"Why do you have such an obsession with Vietnam?"

"Maybe it's because I remember more about the war than I should. So damn surreal! One moment the Vietcong are trying to take Saigon, the next I'm water-skiing with my father up and down the Saigon River. Seemed pleasant and safe. And then I learned that a French ex-pat had been shot off his waterskis by a Vietcong sniper, in broad daylight, on that same route up the river! Too damn surreal!"

She gave me a quizzical look, and I lay back and stared up at the ceiling.

"I remember the war in Vietnam in colors; colors of red and yellow, the colors of the South Vietnamese flag and also the color of the smoke jets that used to leave long stripes across the sky during political events."

Erika reflected my smile as she wiped away the tear that had left a trail on my face all the way down to my earlobe.

"There were other colors, though. There was the red, white and olive-drab of the military hospitals. Those are the colors that come to mind when someone talks to me about the war."

I glanced back at Erika. "I've never told anybody this. Not even my parents know."

She looked flattered and empathetic. "Tell me more."

I gazed back up into the emotional safety of the blank ceiling. "When I was seven we lived in Saigon and my father took me to the hospital, because my tonsils had to be removed. I actually used to go there a lot. Almost died of typhoid once; the Army doctors thought I had cholera, something more prevalent there. I remember my dad telling me that I would be safe and that he and my mom would see me after the tonsillectomy."

Erika laid her hand lightly on my forearm. "They left you alone at that age?!"

"He said I would get as much ice cream as I wanted when I came out. He and my mother left me with a bunch of comic books."

"Then what?" she asked, fidgeting slightly.

"A medic kept me company the first night. He read my comic books while I watched one of my favorite shows on Armed Forces TV called *The Glen Campbell Goodtime Hour*. The next morning a blonde nurse came in and gave me my shot. Funny how I remember being surprised that someone as beautiful as she could lie to me and say it wouldn't hurt as she gave me the shot."

Erika's smile faltered, making me feel as though I had killed her puppy.

"Is there anything wrong?"

She said, "No." Still, her smile did not return with the strength it had before.

"They took me to the operating room soon after, and wheeled me down a corridor, past an African American soldier. For a while I barely remembered that soldier," I said and took a deep breath. "Man. . . to this day the look in his eyes. . . It was the kind of look you see in movies of people trapped in silent limbo. His expression will always give me the creeps."

"What was the expression on his face?"

"Something like, 'what the hell are you doing here in Vietnam, kid?' Poignant, don't you think?"

Erika said nothing.

"Anyway, as I was wheeled past him, I saw that his legs had been amputated and that blood was soaking through the bandages on his stumps."

Erika winced.

"Do you want me to continue?"

She nodded, and held her hand over her heart and drew a labored breath.

"When I woke up, I was in the recovery room where they had put all the wounded Vietnamese. I was the only American there surrounded by Vietnamese and their babies, who were wrapped in blood-soaked bandages. Oh, and the moaning. God, the moaning."

"And you were only seven years old?!"

"Yep. What I remember most was me yelling, 'no!' and the taste of blood, and pain from the sutures in my throat. You should have seen the excitement as the Army nurses yelled for someone to wheel me out." I chuckled, a safety measure I employed to distance myself emotionally from the experience and the resulting sarcasm.

Erika reached over and kissed me softly. As I pulled back, I said, "You know, sometimes it seems as though these dark memories are all locked safely away in a fantasy or a dream. And then other times it's as though I'm going mad, 'cause no matter what I do, I can't get them out of my mind. And whenever I tell anyone about these experiences, I can't get anyone to understand."

Considering how intimate our lovemaking had been, I had never felt so lonely.

* * *

Erika and I were shielded from the humid atmosphere outside Winchel's by the glass wall and the donut shop's air-conditioner. We had come to Pattaya to say good-bye to each other after almost two weeks of sightseeing in Bangkok and northern Thailand.

But, something was wrong. She had been uncharacteristically silent for an ungodly length of time. Every time I spoke of wanting to visit her in Sweden, she averted her eyes.

Like a surprise ending in a mystery novel, a myriad of images filled my mind's eye, creating a wall between us: "Erika, is there someone waiting for you?"

She nodded and I realized there wasn't anything I could do or say.

"The man in the photo album, who I told you was my brother, is my fiance."

"What?!"

In the long, painful silence that followed, she reached over and held my hand. It felt good, but it was all I could do not to jump and run out of that place as fast as my feet could fly.

"Fred, are you feeling okay? You look a bit pale," she asked after we took our seats in the air-conditioned bus back to Bangkok. I had met my own truck full of plate glass, but unlike the hapless motorcyclist beheaded in Carlisle's tale, the plate of glass sliced my heart in half instead.

With a forced smile, I lied to put her at ease.

Erika slept with her head against my chest. I looked out of the tinted window, reminded of how as a child I had been blinded by silent, shimmering tears, and felt removed from those around me as though the remoteness were a defense against rejection.

Chapter 7

"Defeat doesn't finish a man—quitting does. A man is not finished when he's defeated. He's finished when he quits."— President Richard M. Nixon

Virgin Soldier

Aussies turned out to be the cure for the pangs of puppy love. We met at the Crown Hotel, a hotel known for its drugs, prostitutes, and guests after a wild vacation. I went there because the hotel security never asked ferangs if they were actually guests at the hotel—sadly, just like dark-skinned peoples around the world who shy away from the sun and tanning because they want to be as light as white, a preference for the lightest of color twisted into the culture of many Third World countries through a history of European imperialism. The small pool next to a large tree sat in the middle of a circle formed by the hotel. Attired in swim trunks, a T-shirt, rubber thongs, carrying only a towel, and looking very much the tourist, I knew any hotel official would be hard-pressed to consider me anything other than a hotel occupant. After about an hour, the desk clerk came out once to chat with a security guard, and performed the motions of a person wanting to know of my right to being there.

But it was too late. An hour had been spent with me floating on my back in the pool. A couple beers had been ordered, and I had been invited to join a group of Australians at a table next to the pool. I adjusted my Ray Bans and smiled at the desk clerk, and then turned back to the Aussies, deep in conversation about sailing the Thai Gulf.

"Mate!" George Gaebler blurted. I've always liked that about Aussies: everyone's considered a mate, a friend. "You've got to watch yourself in these waters. Those Thai pirates are nasty!"

"What kind of boat did you say you have?" I asked, and took a swig of beer.

"It's a sixty-two foot sailboat. My wife and I sailed up from Sydney in it. It's moored down in the harbor."

"Beautiful boat!" Len added from across the table.

Quite a mixed party at our table. Len was the tattoo-covered, sunburned Aussie from West Hedlands, who drove bulldozers for an oil company in the Great Australian Desert. His red mustache, facial expression, and build made him look like a short, stocky, wild-eyed Yosemite Sam. On his flank, a very quiet and watchful Marty, a former burger joint manager from Melbourne, he was now making much more money as a model in Bangkok for the modern Europeanlook-hungry magazine readers. Trim and tanned, with hair slicked back, he looked perfect for the job. Dressed in only a Speedo, he kept himself marketable by tanning for at least an hour a day at the pool. We joked about our both being non-hotel guests, infiltrating for some free pool time. Both men in their early thirties, each had their arms draped around a bargirl, bargirls who just moments before had dropped like coins from heaven into their laps.

In contrast to them were George and his wife Mary, an older couple. George was old Australian Navy, with a body and tattoos like Len, except George seemed to hide from the sun with his white skin and thinning hair. Mary, a mousy woman with spectacles and curly hair, sat meekly and quietly at his side, more like an overbearing CEO's downtrodden secretary than a wife. The way George acted towards her was the stereotypical interaction between Australian men and women, a stereotype that depicted women as second-class citizens. They were making their annual visit to Thailand so George's young son from a previous marriage could visit with his Thai mother. The sixty-two footer we were talking about seemed to be only a hint of his wealth. George made his money in the loan business. By his demeanor, he seemed to be a loan shark.

"Go get me some panther piss, Mary!" he said. I winced slightly at his loud, grating voice, and sat amazed and irked as Mary meekly scooted away to get him a beer.

A silence hung over the table until Mary was out of earshot. Len spoke up, "Why don't you give her a break there, George. She's doing the best she can for you."

"Listen Len, I married her only so the boy would have someone to take care of him. Other than that she's nothing. She's still a secretary in my eyes. I only married her for the boy. . . You remember that."

From the expressions traded around the table, I'm sure I wasn't the only one who thought George was being an ass.

George turned to me. "So what kind of a photographer are you?"
"I'm a photojournalist."
"I know the story for you—Thai pirates! . . Now that would be an adventurous story. That is if you made it back alive."
"Tell me about the pirates."
"They're a mean lot. They patrol the Gulf just outside of Vietnamese waters, searching for Vietnamese refugees."

"Why Vietnamese refugees?"

Because they were slow, unarmed, and had with them all the gold and cash saved and hidden from the conquering tax man of Hanoi. When people think of the escape from Vietnam, the image that first comes to mind is that of the American choppers on the top of the American embassy in 1975. The mass flight was much longer and lasted from 1975 to 1989. It was typified by wooden fishing boats in dire need of repair, crammed not with anchovies, but people, similar to how the slavers of the 19th century packed their ships. The difference was that these Viets were not being sent into slavery, but escaping it.

The odds were horrible, dangers numerous: hulls cracked by wave swells, or simply disintegrating due to poor materials and workmanship (much of the skilled and educated population of Vietnam had escaped the Communists by the end of 1975, in the initial wave), passengers being washed overboard in a storm, and piracy, to say nothing of the little and big creatures in the water. Let's not forget that they often had to escape at night with poor navigation, and with captains whose furthest voyages were the fishing limits of Vietnam. Maybe the worst part of the escape was that it meant that relatives and elders would have to be left behind. Not much could be worse for a population whose culture is based on ties to ancestors and the burial plots of those ancestors. This was one of the numerous reasons so many South Vietnamese military personnel decided to stay in Vietnam. They actually thought that they would be greeted openly as cousins from the south. Boy, were they surprised as they were handed their marching orders to Communist re-education camps based on the designs Stalin implemented in his own Soviet Union. (The press corps and history teachers used the label "concentration camps" when referring to the Nazi labor/death camps, but Ho's "reeducation camps"—sounding like summer school camps—were the same bloody thing!) Hanoi told them that they would be away from their families for only a couple weeks. Two weeks turned into at least five years for most, some ten. These were years plagued by malaria and starvation as the cousins from the south were turned into a free slave labor force for the Hanoi regime. Many souls didn't make it and gave up, freeing them at least in spirit if not body.

For those who did make it to the boats and into the Gulf, they might find themselves sitting dead in the water, a failed motor being the culprit.

"And this might happen even before they meet any pirates?" I asked.

"Better sitting dead in the water," said George, "with at least the hope of being picked up by a ship, than the pirates! Pirates shoot the men, steal the cash and rape the women. After they rape the women, they kidnap them and the children for sale into slavery and prostitution. Sometimes they simply rape the women first, shoot everyone next, sink the boat, and then get away with the refugees' life savings. They try to leave absolutely no sign of who they are since many of them would be easily recognized in any of the fishing villages around the Thai Gulf."

George accepted his beer from Mary, who then skittered over to the pool to be with George's son. "See, most of the pirates are fisherman who've realized there's more money in pirating than fishing. All they have to do is buy a few machine guns on the black market. And you know how easy it is to buy anything in Bangkok!" Actually it was more than that. Though piracy had been conducted in Southeast Asia since time immemorial, it reached a zenith in the 20th century. Not only were there pirates plying the Thai Gulf in Thai fishing boats, there were also pirates to the south. Because of the large amount of money brought in by the oil off Sumatra and Borneo, Muslim pirates marauding out of those areas were equipped with heavily-armed speedboats equal to a US Navy SEAL team's.

Len broke in. "Did you read in the paper about the oil tanker hijacked in the Gulf by pirates only a little while ago?!"

"Geez! No I didn't!" I made a mental note to pick up a copy of the *Bangkok Post* every day, and berated myself for not having done so all along.

"Yeah, they held it for about four hours or so, and took everything they could!"

"I'm amazed you even brought your boat here, George. You don't seem so intimidated by them. Why's that?" I asked.

"Don't you worry. I'm protected."

"What do you have?"

George turned a smile and a knowing glance towards Len, who chuckled, and then looked back at me. "Let's say it's big enough for you to fit your fist in the barrel." I asked him again to tell me what exactly he had on board for protection. My persistence got me a cold shoulder from George for at least an hour.

Finally, he once more warmed up to me and our conversation went on to cover George's sailing in the Bali race, Marty's surfing experiences around Melbourne, and Len's drilling in the Australian desert for oil and blowing all his hard-earned money to drill bargirls in Thailand. George and Mary left when the sun set, leaving us young men to feebly fend off the evil spirits living in our Singhas. Then night came, the Singha beers stopped, and the Maekong flowed, drowning me.

"You know, I visited the... Maekong whiskey distillery up... by the Maekong River... up near Laos," I said trying to keep my wavering body from falling, and unable to distinguish the dark shimmering shadows that were my new-found friends, Marty and Len, and their girls.

"You vely dlunk, buttahfly boy," Marty's girl blurted at me and grinned a smile that stood out like a light.

"I–I–I'm... not... druuuunk... I'm O–O–kay." I caught my head from slamming down on the table. "What's a butterfly boy?"

"You buttahfly boy. Buttahfly. Fly from flower to flower putting in stem."

" Ha-ha. No, I'm—not a butterfly boy."

"No, no. You buttahfly boy."

Suddenly, I was extremely ill, like the time in Saigon when I almost died from typhoid. The vomit flew between my legs barely missing my shoes, or so I would think until the next morning. With a loud thump, my forehead hit the concrete table.

"Mate! Is he okay? Is he okay?!"

I felt myself rising from the table, my arms suspended in a Christ-like position, Len and Marty flanking me.

"You got 'im?" Marty asked to my left. "... You know, he's a good mate."

Len answered on my right, "He is a good mate, but he's got to learn how to drink. Let's take him up to my room. We can leave him in the extra bed."

"I'm okay, you guys... really I'm, uh, O... kay..." My feet slipped out from under me, shifting all my weight on to Len and Martys' shoulders, as my feet dragged behind me. We went up a flight of stairs that took us to a hall. Walking through the dark hall, we arrived at Len's room. They dropped me off in the extra bed and left me with a waste basket.

"We'll stop in to see how you're doing, mate. Get some sleep, and don't forget where the basket is. Cheers!"

"Cheers!" I waved to them as I rolled to edge of the bed and vomited up some more of my hamburger lunch. "Please someone shoot me!"

* * *

A giggly, young attractive Thai woman looked down at me as she sat on the edge of my bed. "You virgin?!" she said, her head haloed by the morning sun peeking through the half-closed curtains. Because of the light and my previous night's drinking, I had to squint at her and her friend who had me pinned between them on my loaned bed.

"What?!" I asked, sluggishly trying to pull myself out of bed in order to push away unknown, pawing hands. Unsuccessful because of my hangover, I fell back, and felt hands touching my painfully throbbing temples.

"He virgin all right." Len yelled from his own bed. He had been lucky during his bar-hopping; a naked Thai girl lay beside him. These two girls were her friends.

"Oooh! I never have virgin ferang before!" the girls said as they lifted off their dresses with one quick movement, turning my drowsy eyes into large round saucers. In one more quick movement they were in bed with me and taking my clothes off faster than I'd ever been able to do on my own.

"What the hell are you doing?!"

"Oooh," they chimed, "we going to make you feel soo goot, virgin boy!"

* * *

Virgin, virgin, virgin, virgin. Five times I was a virgin, tagging along down Soi Cowboy with me mates Len and Marty. Five times I ran to one of a multitude of neighborhood VD clinics, only to be told everything was okay and stop worrying. Back then we all thought the worst worry was herpes.

The world of prostitution has thrived in Thailand for thousands of years, mainly because of a traditional ease with sex, a Southeast Asian culture of *free love*. So much at ease was the culture of Thailand that it offered the Chinese traveler, Ma Huan, the opportunity to record in 1433: "If a married [Thai] woman is very intimate with one of our men from China, wine and food are provided, and they drink and sit and sleep together. The husband is quite calm and takes no exception to it; indeed, he says, 'My wife is beautiful, and the man from China is delighted with her'."

And as for my having been approached by cab drivers at Bangkok's airport, that was a history going back at least to 1603, when Dutch adventurer Van Neck noted, "when foreigners come there from other lands to do their business. . . men come and ask them whether they do not desire a woman."

Prostitution was even more an institution back then. In 1655, according to Gisbert Heeck of the United Netherlands East India Company (VOC), "Most of them had concubines or mistresses, in order to avoid the common whores, and they maintained them with all necessities, buying or building houses for them. . . . they rarely refer to them other than as whores, sluts, trollops and the like, up to and including the director [of the VOC Bangkok office], for hardly anybody was free of this failing. Anybody who earned enough to keep such [a] trollop had to have one, even if it meant they had not a penny to their name afterwards—indeed, some were deep in debts, as I saw for myself."

But, prostitution didn't become such a big commercial institution in Thailand until the 1960s, with the wave of American soldiers to R&R destinations like Patpong, Soi Cowboy, and Pattaya, bringing with them their foreign ideas, modern goods and the money with which to buy them. And, if a bargirl was from up country, which most of them were, and naive to Western culture, she would quickly become addicted to it, finding it impossible to return to the small rice farm from which her father had probably sold her to bring in a little much needed cash.

She would quickly become jaded, thinking of true love as a luxury only afforded by the unworldly girls back in her village. She would instead go after a ferang as a prime source of income, commanding more money than her father, back home behind a water buffalo and plow, could even imagine. As with everything, there were exceptions, and these were the ones who actually fell in love with a ferang because he was so nice and treated her like more than just a partner on a sex vacation. But, these moments away from their reality faded quickly, and the soldiers went back to their war, and the bar-girls went on to their next customer.

By the early 1980s, the soldiers were gone, replaced by the curious travellers from Europe and the US, and the notorious Singaporean, Japanese, and Taiwanese sex tours, bringing with them bus loads of new diseases to add to the already unsavory stew of gonorrheas, syphilis, herpes, and various sexually transmitted diseases called "non-specifics". The worst was the mythic, super-powerful, black gonorrhea[16], the V.D. that quickly made you persona non grata in the US, because it was incurable and would actually make your penis fall off. One frequenter of Soi Cowboy had told me that he knew of a guy in the US Navy whose penis, because of this monster clap, had simply fallen off into the urinal while he was relieving himself. AIDS was still way off on the distant Western horizon, and hardly anyone really understood it, or the effect it would later have on the Thai population. Nobody knew that it would become like the communicable diseases that almost wiped out the free-loving indigenous peoples of the Americas and Caribbean when Europeans first arrived there.

So, my only worries back in 1983 were contracting herpes and the monster clap, but even that didn't keep me from joining Len and

Marty on nightly patrols of Soi Cowboy. I carried on so because I was searching for an emotional patch, a Band-Aid if you will, one to cover up the pain of my feelings towards Erika and my steadily fading dream of fame as the result of getting the "breaking story," the fame that was supposed to make me happy.

Not attracted to drugs or alcohol, I turned to the Bangkok sex life. Being young and single, unique among the majority of middle-aged customers, I found myself not only getting buckets of sex, but free sex at that. The bargirls wouldn't even think of charging someone whom they considered a prospective mate, one who would whisk them away from Thailand and poverty. Now mind you, I didn't feed these fantasies, but as I would soon learn, it's easy to be taken in by fantasies that can make the whole world a much more pleasurable place in which to survive.

Soon though, even indiscriminate sex offered only the drained feelings of post-masturbation, lacking the exaltation of profound emotional connection I had felt with Erika. I was inefficiently trying to fill my emotional and spiritual body with every outside experience I could. While clutching at everything to keep me from sinking, I tried something I'd sworn I would never do. It was Len who suggested I try recreational drugs after a night of Soi Cowboy debauchery. One of his many bargirl friends had bought the opium-laced Thai stick for him on Soi 22. I was surprised to hear that as I was still a bit naive about my neighborhood. My neighborhood, though a slum, was a place in which I felt quite safe.

I watched intently as he sat down in a lounge chair against the bedroom wall and took a Marlboro from its pack, returning the pack to the table next to him. Spotlighted by the bright fluorescent light emanating from the open bathroom door, his fingers moved deftly as he used a small pair of manicure scissors to cut up a Thai stick. While my new-found Thai girlfriend, Moi, sat idly waiting, Len's Thai girlfriend urged him on with the words, "Hurry, hurry, give me big smoke. I give you big bang-bang."

At first it was terrifying when Len suggested a joint. I never touched drugs in high school; I mean, what would John Wayne have said? And in Singapore, that was absolutely out of the question! There were too many stories throughout Southeast Asia of people getting thrown in jail because of drugs and never seen again. And you get hanged in Malaysia for illegal drug use! I'll never forget the shock and sadness of my classmate when he learned that his older brother was being kicked out of the Singapore American High School and deported back to the States because of drug abuse. My friend's brother was lucky. If he hadn't been an American teenager, the amount of heroin (more than one half-ounce) he was arrested for would have put him on the gallows.

In high school and college, I wasn't stupid enough to believe the elitists who reasoned that recreational drug use was the only way to become enlightened. "Open your mind, man," they'd say, and make reference to famous artists who had supposedly talked with God via the chemical telephone. "Indian shamans use it to see the other side," they'd throw in, completely ignorant of the fact that *shaman* is a word that comes from Siberia, and *real* native healers don't need a drug in order to reach the Spirit World: drugs are just training wheels for those who are afraid to see beyond what little is offered by our physical eyes. In their drug-induced feelings of superiority, these "enlightened" children also ignored another fact, that when indigenous people's holy leaders, such as in the Native American Church, use peyote, only one person is supposed to make the voyage to the other side. The rest are in the circle to provide the necessary support and guidance for the spirit world traveler, through song and prayer. Imagine what a peyote circle would be if everyone was taking the peyote: you'd get the same gibberish at a Friday night stoners party.

Too many horror stories. So, it was with great surprise that I found myself sitting next to Len, waiting for him to roll my first doobie. I nervously jumped in my seat at every passerby in the hallway outside, and every knock at a door. I thought I was going to pass out from paranoia. To evade my fears, I concentrated on his meticulous attention to detail as he cut up the Thai stick with a pair of small beautician's scissors. Then, he emptied one of his Marlboros, cautiously making sure that he didn't flatten the paper tube as he twirled it between his fingers. His actions seemed even more spectacular and mesmerizing because as he worked, he listed back and forth from over-intoxication, chanting like a fakir. Len had had just a few bottles too many of the panther piss.

"Here, hold this, Fred." He handed over the filter-tipped tube, and then took some marijuana from the tray and filled the tube. I wished that he would hurry up as my nerves were shot. When he was done, he put it to his mouth and lit it. The embers crackled as he took a drag. His eyes bulged as he drew in more air and held his breath. Then he choked as he couldn't hold it any longer, letting it out with the heavy sigh of a dying man. From the pained look on his face, I didn't find it very inviting. Still, I accepted the joint when it passed my way. I would at least try it and then make up my own mind. The smoke burned as the sage-scented cloud filled my lungs for a moment. I coughed violently, spittle and phlegm flying over my hand. I was not impressed.

"That's not the way to do it, mate... What you do is smoke it in slow so it doesn't go straight back hot. Then you hold, and maybe even add another two or three tokes to the one in your lungs so that you have the full effect."

I followed his directions to the letter, fighting the urge to cough everything up immediately. He took some tokes from the joint and passed it on to the girls. "You know, I really don't know what's so great about this Thai stick. Nothing's happening." I was now impatient, not only because of how anxious I was about being thrown in the slammer, but how stupid it would be to be thrown in jail for something as unimpressive as a stinky cigarette.

Len seemed hurt by my statement, but that quickly disappeared. "Just wait a while, maybe you just need another hit."

Disappointed in having wasted my time with the marijuana, and being much more interested in the girl, Moi, who had come back from Soi Cowboy with me, I stood up from the bed and took a step toward her lithe nude figure, reclining on the bed near the air-conditioner. "No, I don't think so..."

A gasp and a look of surprise overtook Moi's provocative smile.

"What... the... fu...ck is happening?!" I grabbed for the end of the bed to make the world stop spinning and keep my legs straight. Moi grabbed my arm and helped me into our bed. Once she had me laying on my back, she removed my clothes and covered our naked bodies with a thin sheet. My head spun as she cradled the back of my head with her right hand and offered the dark nipple of her large breast, and the words, "It okay, baby. No worry, no problem. I make you feel good." Everything went black, and I would never again risk my freedom on something so pointless as a recreational drug.

* * *

When I pried my eyes open the next morning, Len was still in his chair, like a fat troll sleeping on a king's throne. He grumbled for a moment, and then continued snoring. His girl, in the dim light, was sprawled out on their bed, naked, and sucking slowly on her thumb.

Moi brushed her lips up to mine and said, in her drowsiness, "I love you."

She was very beautiful, surprising tall, almost as tall as Erika had been, and I fought the urge to jump out of bed and run out into the hall, naked or not. Just as suddenly, my previous intention of having sex with her again subsided. I returned to staring at the ceiling. I wanted absolutely nothing to do with true intimacy.

She slipped my arm around her as she rested her head, and her healthy black hair draped across my shoulder and chest. She stroked her foot up and down my calf and relaxed into a deep sleep, leaving me to smile at how attractive she was because of her height.

Erika's smile flashed across the back of my closed eyelids. Perplexed, I wondered whether my attraction to Moi lay only in the past memory of Erika, and how Moi had the same height and jubilant attitude. Only depression resulted from those thoughts, as equally depressing as the experience with the marijuana.

In the same manner that marijuana was so unappealing to me because it was an illusion, and a buffer against reality, I looked at Moi. No matter how attractive she was, and that she wanted to be my Thai wife and take care of me, I couldn't help but think that if I stayed with her I'd become like Carlisle, a self-abusing savior, or Len, who always wanted to be something else other than a person working a nine-to-five job, killing the pain of staying in a job he hated with any drug he could get his hands on.

Suddenly fidgety, I whispered to Moi that we would go and watch a video at a club on Soi Cowboy. She nodded. I shook my head, because I knew of a multitude of men who would have loved a woman like her: never saying no. But every time she nodded and agreed with me, I shuddered, as though I'd just been dropped into the slave business and that her complying with my every request was a double-edged sword that would soon have me on the other end. I was a no-strings-attached kind of guy, and I meant to keep it that way. It was safer.

At the bar lit only by a television screen showing Oliver Stone's *Midnight Express*, I sat with Moi, who drank Coke and stroked my arm and said nice things, reminding me of how much she wanted to "make much love" and please me more. During my beer-filtered thoughts of how to move out of this relationship that had so quickly entrapped me in barely a week, and find a better way of getting stories than hitting bars, I looked up at the TV to see the protagonist being hauled away to a Turkish prison. "You'll never see me get into something like that!" I said.

Moi only smiled in her sly, secretive way.

* * *

Three Thai MPs trained their M-16s on the teenaged boy's wide-eyed face. With his hands clasped on his shaven head, the terrified Thai did everything he could to keep straddling his dirt bike right there in the middle of Soi 22. The large wet spot on the crotch of his pants where he had urinated on himself stunned me. White powder lay fanned out from a burst bag by the boy's left foot. Plainclothes officers screamed at the boy, their hand-held radios, and my gawking neighbors.

Standing across the street from the ruckus, I watched the drug bust, not knowing why I had such an empathy for the boy, along with an intense interest in his expression of fear, as he stood with his hands behind his head.

* * *

An hour after the neighborhood drug bust, I was at Everingham's house still trying to get the teenager's expression of terror out of my mind. Everingham, dressed in sandals, slacks and a dress shirt, with a camera bag slung across his chest, was mounting his motorcycle when I walked up the driveway.

"Fred! Where have you been?" he said as he slipped his helmet on. "Have I got the story for you! Definitely along your lines." Everingham had heard all about my planning to do a story on the mercenaries sneaking into Laos, so he knew I was up for just about anything.

"Oh yeah?!"

"Yes, I had a talk with this guy in Pattaya, named Knight. He's going after treasure."

"Where?"

"I can't tell you exactly, because the treasure hunter swore me to secrecy."

I could only think it was Vietnam, but Everingham kept true to his promise of silence.

"Seemed to be along your lines. . . I told him there was no way I was going." Everingham would later tell my father that he didn't think that I would actually go and see this guy. I guess Everingham didn't really know me that well after all.

Chapter 8

"If we do not find anything very pleasant, at least we shall find something new."—Voltaire

Just the Ticket!

O 290834Z JUL 83

FM AMEMBASSY BANGKOK

TO SECSTATE WASHDC

"Meanwhile, a consular officer in Singapore spoke with Mr. Grimley on July 28 about this treasure hunt in which he was to take part. Grimley, in a detailed story that can shiver timbers, identified the treasure island as the largest and northernmost in an archipelago appropriately named Iles des Pirates, 18 miles east of the large island of Phu-Quoc, just off the Kampuchean/Vietnamese border. Luckily, Grimley did not know or chose not to reveal the exact locations of treasure on the island, else the vice consul in Singapore may have set her jib by now."

    What a mess! I thought my room in Bangkok was bad, but Richard Knight was a hardened veteran of disorder. Medium-rate and dimly-lit, Knight's room at the Sun and Sand Motel was strewn with luggage and clothes. As though trying to hide something, Knight rushed over to his bed and hurriedly tried to even out the rumpled sheets and blanket, and stash some of his equipment to one side. Maps and cheap cameras lay under and on top of the guest table. A spade in the near corner drew a chuckle; it was such a Hollywood cliché.
    My hopes were way over the top, I knew; I had expected someone with the robustness of Errol Flynn or Mel Gibson. There was a robustness in Knight, who seemed to be in his early fifties, but it was more in the physical form, especially his sunburned-red, hairy belly, nurtured by a lot of beer drinking. His appearance made him look like a chunky miner; he was a foot shorter than me. But, by his odor, he could have easily been a well-fed street urchin. He did seem to have a genuine smile, one that was calming. I was still a little too inexperienced to recognize the difference between the smile of a friend, and that of a cobra.

Knight blinked away sleep from his bloodshot eyes as he invited me in. He said he had gone to sleep just before my knock. As he closed the door behind me, an overpowering odor of stale beer engulfed me, causing me to fight back a cough.

"I've been out celebrating, you know," he said with a sheepish grin that turned into a wide grin. "Tomorrow's the big day!"

I didn't think my hopes could have fallen any lower, but they had. The whole idea of going on a dangerous mission and sneaking into Vietnam with this drunk, simply because of my dire need of an assignment explosive enough to blast open the tightly locked doors to the press corps, hit me hard during that moment of silence in which he looked at me with that crocodile grin.

Knight pointed to a seat at the table against the wall, and then made a detour to the bathroom to splash water on his face and style his greasy, white-speckled red hair. I sat with my back against the wall at the round table.

"Cigarette?" he asked, scratching his facial stubble, and quickly brushing away a bead of water hanging on the tip his large beaked nose. I shook my head as he sat down and said, "No, thanks."

Knight seemed very nervous as he held his match to his cigarette and took short, shaky drags, the end seeming almost never to light. Sucking on the cigarette overemphasized the sadness, and nervousness that dragged the corners of his eyes down: Knight had been weathered by life experience.

He finally got his full drag and relaxed into the smoke expanding out of his flared nostrils. "What has Everingham told you?"

You'd better tell me something more awe-inspiring than what Everingham did, I thought. "Well, he told me you were planning to look for treasure in Vietnam, and needed a photographer. He said he wasn't going; but that's understandable, considering he has a family."

"I'm going after treasure on an island off the coast of Vietnam."

"Whose treasure?" I sat up from my slumped posture.

"Captain Kidd's."

"Huh?! I thought Captain Kidd was in the Caribbean." Thinking of ways to excuse myself from this nut, I wondered if Everingham was playing a cruel joke on me, and whether he was truly my friend.

"Here! Look." Knight handed over photocopies of pages from a small paperback. It told of an English Navy Captain William Kidd, accused of piracy in 1699. According to the story, he surrendered in that same year to Lord Bellemont, Governor of New England, in the hopes that the governor would offer him a pardon since he was married to an upper-crust New York widow, named Sara Oart. Instead, Bellemont put him in irons and kept him in a New York prison until he was transported by the HMS Rochester back to London in 1700. In England he was held in Newgate Prison—not one of the better prisons to be held in at the time—and then put on trial for pirating British ships. He was also accused of an equally notorious crime, that of killing one of his crew by knocking him on the head with a bucket.

"He was hanged by chain, until his body fell into the River Thames." The words held in my mind like foreboding dialogue in a horror flick. Actually, he was first tarred and then hanged, which made it even more gripping as I read the rest of the story. But no more gripping than that the rope had broken during the first attempt. You'd think the court would have accepted it as Divine intervention, but no! The second try did the job.

I continued reading.

"Kidd bargained for his freedom," Knight said, "by promising substantial wealth to King William of England, who ruled as cosovereign with Queen Mary until her death in 1694. There was an issue between William III (of Orange) and the many secrets associated with signing on privateers to basically pirate in the King's name. I'm sure that Kidd would have been freed, but Kidd had run aground with the East India Company, when he took to robbing the Quedah Merchant. The King had to cover his reputation with regards to licenses for Kidd to raid French ships, which has never really been cleared up, so the question is, did Kidd have papers to do so, or not?"

Not an Errol Flynn, much less a Sean Flynn, nor even a John Wayne; but I was finding it hard to remain objective in the ever-rising onslaught of Knight's charismatic, damn-the-torpedoes enthusiasm for the adventure of pirates and the potential of finding pirate booty!

"You see. . . there is no record of Kidd until his early thirties, when he married an American from NewYork, and became a captain in the British Navy. The theory, or I should say my theory, is that he had been a pirate long before he started using his British warships for piracy. He probably started as a deckhand on a pirate ship. Most of all, I believe by the time he was in his twenties, he had his own ship and was doing quite a bit of piracy in the China Sea."

That Kidd was a Scotsman made the story especially appealing since my father had raised me to respect my Scottish ancestry, that of the Clan Graham of Montrose. The physical description of Kidd's execution was similar to the betrayal and hanging and quartering of our romanticized clan chief, James Graham, Duke of Montrose, by the English in 1650.

I stared at Knight, my interest rising.

"See this map here? It's a map that was found in his strong box, a map I first saw described in a book called *The Money Pit Mystery*."

"Do you have the original map?"

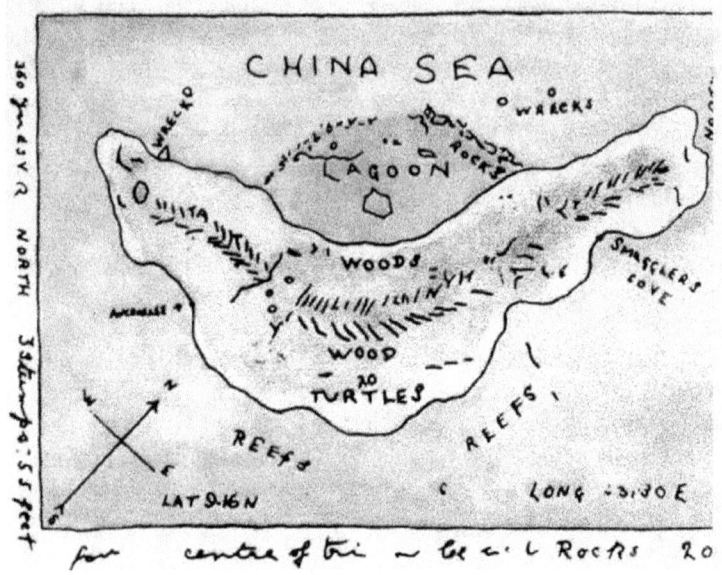

Captain Kidd's Map

"Yes," he said, his eyes jumping away. There are times to know absolutely when a person is lying, and this was one of them. "It's been authenticated. Here's a copy. The map was found in a 17th century strong box bearing the name 'Captain William Kidd' and 'Adventure Galley, 1669' on it. Adventure Galley was one of his ships. The map had on it the date 1669, and the initials W.K. A relative of mine had bought it from a London collector in 1929.

"He had found the map by using the bureau as a table, and accidentally broke one of the runners which exposed a secret compartment, revealing a brass tube that had been sealed inside with wax and an anchor insignia. Inside the tube was the map, from which this copy was prepared."

Knight handed me an 8x10 photocopy and continued, "It's absurd that the author of *The Money Pit Mystery* would even infer that the island on the map is actually an island off New Brunswick. Have you heard the story?"

"Saw it on some show narrated by Leonard Nimoy," I said. "I think it was *In Search Of.* It's a pit into which they've been digging deeper and deeper, and still haven't found the treasure. Even after almost continuous digging since the 1600's?"

"Yes." He looked at me as though cheated out of telling a grander tale. "But all you have to do is see 'China Sea', plainly written at the top of the map, to realize that the book's assumption is ridiculous."

"Don't you think someone else has taken the treasure by now?"

"I don't think so. If you look for this island using present-day coordinates, it's supposed to be off the Philippines. . . but there's nothing there but open ocean. If you use old French navigation maps, it puts the coordinates just off the Vietnamese-Cambodian border." He handed me another map. I'd seen its type before, while studying navigation at Pensecola Naval Air Station.

"I bought those through the mail from the CIA," he volunteered. "When I was living in California."

The topographical similarities were astounding! There was the sand spit jutting out on the northwest; the crescent shape of the island. The treasure map had a submerged rock circle at the north end of the island. The CIA map was really a Defense Intelligence Agency (DIA) map. Like other maps of Indochina, these were easily ordered from the DIA until Colonel Gritz's notorious raids into Laos after MIAs brought an onslaught of interest from other Vietnam Vets who wanted to win the war in their minds by bringing back their own.

"How can you be sure this is the island? There's no rock reef here."

Knight shifted in his seat, then said, "While I was in Australia, I met a Vietnamese doctor who vacationed there. He said he had snorkeled the area many times, and there *is* a submerged circle of rocks on the north side."

I looked at the treasure island and the islands around it, my mind spinning, going round and round about this vagrant-looking madman; and, as my mind did circles, my eyes danced across the map, repeatedly resting on the name of the island group—*Iles des Pirates*.

"What is the name of the specific island?"

Knight looked me straight in the eyes and said, "Grand Pirate Island." The over-dramatization caught me off-guard and I laughed.

Knight had invited me, with such enthusiasm, to a land so close, yet so remote; a place I had for some reason felt such a need to return to. Non-Communists were still very restricted in their options when visiting

Vietnam, especially the area Knight had outlined. The adventure appealed to me because it made me feel as though I could unearth a truth that journalists who went to Vietnam legally would never be able to do. I would get to see the true Vietnam behind the political charades of the dictatorship.

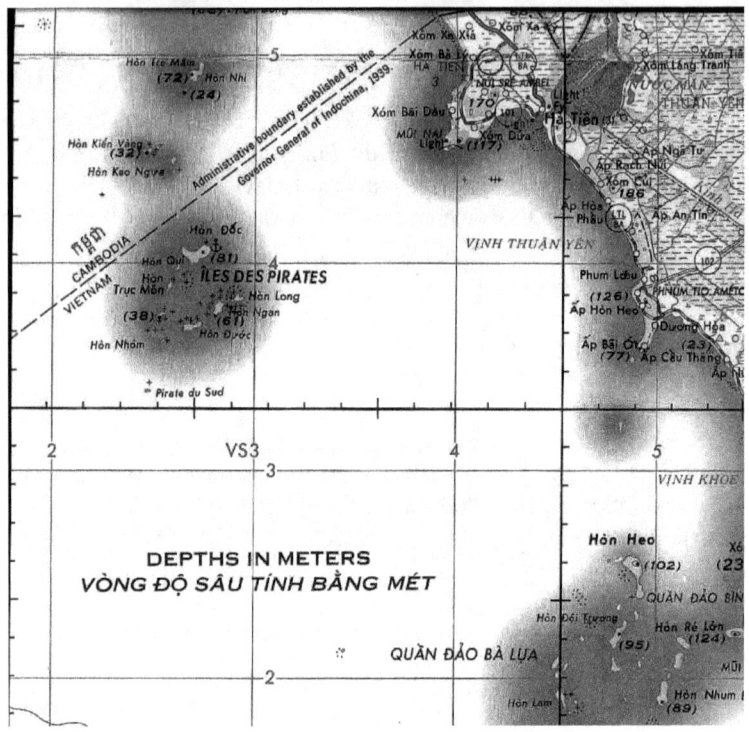

DIA Map of Iles Des Pirates off Ha Tien

Though the packaging seemed a little disheveled, this adventurer's gift seemed to be unwrapping itself into one helluva first story and a chance to see once again the land that imprisoned my mind and soul. To have Vietnam offered to me like this was too much to turn down. So enthralled by this offer of adventure was I, that I barely noticed Knight nervously sucking on his lower lip as he watched me.

Suddenly, he asked me, "How old are you, if you don't mind me asking?"

Reminded of those who, because of my baby-face and youthful questioning, had underestimated me throughout my life, I smiled wryly and answered, "Eighteen."

He eyed me, more seriously than before, gauging me in his mind, deciding whether I would do. My grin faltered as I tensed: now I was more eager than ever. He reeled me in even closer by reaching for an eight-by-ten blue book. "Look at this," he said.

"This is a market survey I had done for me in London." He opened it to a page, and passed it over.

Price estimates pulled my excited interest from page to page: "book rights, one million"; "movie rights, 300,000"; "story rights, 60,000." Knight's grinning, almost gloating face, made him look like a cook who had just put the icing on an already rich cake.

"Those figures are in English pounds."

My chin dropped. Knight snapped the book shut, making me wonder what else the book held.

"And if you go with me all the way to the island, instead of staying on the mother boat, you'll get six percent of the treasure."

"How much is that?".

"One million dollars."

I gasped, "One million dollars?"

"The rest of the treasure, of course," he stated in a now disinterested manner, as though he realized that he didn't have to work hard on me anymore, "will be divided among the Thai crew, my investor, who has already put $30,000 into the expedition, and myself.".

Thirty-thousand dollars! I thought. *Must be something to his claim or else he wouldn't have gotten so many people to put that much money into his operation.*

"What kind of equipment are you bringing?"

"I've got some filming equipment, a camera, a compass, food, a specialized metal detector that can go down 15 feet, shovels, and the rest of the equipment to dig it up." He turned jovial. "And, I'll be bringing a bottle of whiskey to toast our success."

I grimaced. "I don't feel comfortable about having booze along on something like this," I said.

"I assure you, Fred. There is nothing to worry about. And you must realize that if you come on this adventure, I will be the captain. Our only worry will be the Thai pirates and the Vietnamese government."

Remembering the conversation at the Crown Hotel's pool with the Aussies, especially George Gaebler, the old yacht racer who had a gun with a muzzle "big enough to put my fist in," I asked Knight, "What do you have planned in case we run across the pirates?"

He smiled cockily, and said, "I have a special plan, but I prefer to keep it a secret. It's foolproof." I guessed he had his own big secret weapon, like George Gaebler: I should have paid more atten tion to the plastic toy guns laying on the bed.

"Okay. Is the treasure going to be brought here?"

"Yes, but it will then be hidden on one of the Thai islands. The investor, who owns a thirty-five foot yacht, will sail up from Singapore. We will then sail to the Philippines, where there are no diplomatic ties with the Vietnamese, and put it in a bank."

"How long will the trip to Vietnam and back take?"

"No more than seven days," he said confidently. I made a mental note to write a letter to my parents and give it to a trustworthy friend, with instructions for him to mail it if I hadn't returned in thirty days.

"Well, Fred, I have to have your answer tonight, as I am leaving tomorrow." He yawned.

Ignoring the sudden tightness in my stomach, I nodded twice.

* * *

"Appear more amorous Fred, won't you? We're trying to create an impression!" Knight yelled, his hair whipping like flames in the wind, his head bobbing as our yellow and white thirteen-foot motorboat leaped from wave to wave. Waves so tall I could easily have surfed them! I looked at the bargirl whom I was cuddling. I bowed to Knight's request by putting my arm more snugly around her and wondered how in the hell I had let myself get into this charade.

Earlier in the morning, I had arrived back at Knight's room just in time to wait for another couple hours while he set up the rental of the boat, and hired the bargirls. Our façade was that of being a couple of tourists with our dates, motoring out for a picnic on one of the islands off of Pattaya. Our equipment had already been carried ahead to Bangsare, where the main fishing boat that would take us to Vietnam was docked. "Back in a few days," he had told the boat rental owner, as we jumped in and the owner yanked the outboard to life.

From the looks the girls gave each other, they were very eager to land. What had looked like two very made-up prostitutes, now looked like two wet rats on a sinking ship. A mile out we turned east. The brown cliffs seemed only another mile away. Waves crashed over the side. The girl next to me pulled a handkerchief out of her purse and daubed the cheap makeup that was streaking down her face. Even in their mess both girls tried to smile.

At first tight and stiff against my arm, the redhead soon relaxed, sitting softly back into her seat. I envied her ensuing freedom that would come when we beached below the hotel on the cliff.

As we closed in on the hotel's private beach, the waves turned even more menacing. Knight was unsure as we attempted to land. I swung my legs over the side and into the water that at first had seemed shallow. Knight looked down at me with an idiotic grin as I came up for air.

"Sorry Fred, didn't realize how deep it was here!"

A group of waiters hurried out from the palm frond-roofed bar. I felt like a shipwrecked sailor beset by 18th century scavengers. Clustered around the tossing boat, they assisted Knight and the two girls out. I breast-stroked for shore and walked up onto the beach, my steps leadened by my soaked jeans and polo shirt. Knight tried to help the Thais pull the boat up the forty-five degree incline. With an accommodating smile, one of the waiters gestured us towards the bar, and away from the boat. Probably so the others could complete their task of securing it without Knight's redundant commands.

Dry loose sand made the steep walk to the hotel bar slow and taxing. Knight's false flirting with his girl made the short walk seem that much longer.

We both ordered Singhas at the bar. Knight's smile dimmed as he hunkered slightly and whispered, "Fred, I'm going to give the girls their money, and get rid of them. What did she tell me to pay them?"

"Oh, yes," he answered himself, and looked at the girls sitting side by side between us. "Here's 30 baht, each of you. Here's 40 baht for taxi."

They stared at him for a moment, a look of bewilderment on their faces, and then hesitantly took the money.

"It's okay," Knight said. "Too dangerous for you. You go taxi. We take boat. We meet you at bar."

Up the stairs that zigzagged up the cliff face went the bewildered girls, probably trading stories about crazy foreigners. Knight said, "We'll leave in a little while, after the girls are well on their way and out of sight. There should be a lull in the waves. We'll make a try then."

Knight finished his beer, and I would have left my half-finished beer on the bar, but he looked sourly at me. I finished it in a couple gulps. We waved our thanks to the bartender and walked out to the boat, waves crashing over its stern.

"How far down do we have to go?"

"Only a couple miles, we'll probably be there within a half-hour," Knight said over the beach break.

Knight engaged the drive and scrambled up to the pilot's seat as I pulled myself out of the water. A push on the throttle lifted the bow and we plodded over the waves. He inched further on the throttle and we began bouncing from wave to wave, coming round the curve that made the eastern point of the hotel's crescent bay. Taking the calmer water as an invitation, Knight gunned the throttle all the way and we flew from wave to wave like a flying fish.

Villages on stilts lined the coast, and we sped for the partner's house, where the large boat that was to carry us to Vietnam was docked. I wondered out loud how Knight would recognize the house, as they all looked the same.Talk about looking for a grain of sand on a beach.

"Our boat's docked in front, it's easily recognized," Knight yelled over the engine.

"What does it look like?"

Knight grinned and pointed. "It's that green and blue Thai fishing boat with red trim!" He pulled back on the throttle, and the boat slowed. Planks held up by pole stilts made the dock that we floated to. Running out to meet us was a stout Thai and his four slim and trim assistants.

"Hallo, Mistah Knight. Good to see!" cried the stout one as he directed us along the planks to his bungalow on stilts.

"Beer?" the stout one asked as he ushered us into his home which had a picture of the King of Thailand above the doorway, the way some devout Catholics have a picture of the Pope.

"Thank you, Mr. Muk." Knight said as we all collected on crossed legs on the mat that barely covered the bamboo floor below us. The spaces between the bamboo were wide enough to make me feel as though I was sitting on a high unicycle, balancing to keep from plunging to the water far below.

"And you're the journalist." Mr. Muk asked. "Good to meet you," he said as he handed a beer to me, and then Knight.

"Is everything ready to go?" Knight asked as he sat back on a pillow.

"My men need a little more money to get gasoline."

"I've already given you a lot of money, Mr. Muk."

"Just a little more, please, for gasoline."

Knight pulled his wallet out and went through the baht, and handed Muk a few.

"Thank you. I'll have my people get everything done, and we can wait here." Muk spoke in Thai to one of his men, who took the money and quickly left for shore.

"Would you like to see what we fish for here, Mr. Journalist?"

"Sure."

He pulled out an album filled with photos. He must have recognized me as a kindred fisherman, because he quickly pulled out another two albums. There were pictures of grouper, sailfish, and one that seemed to be a yellow fin tuna. Halfway through, I stopped at an 8X10 photo of a large shark hanging on a meat hook.

"Tiger shark?"

"Yes, many. Very dangerous."

* * *

"Sure you don't want to come along, Mr. Muk?" Knight yelled as Pi pushed us off, and Ti edged us out into a bright green sea.

"No! No! You go. Bring back much treasure!" Mr. Muk and his four men waved.

It felt good to have Mr. Muk's two other hands, Ti and Pi, along. They were fit, looking the part of experienced Thai fisherman. Ti was in his mid-thirties, and Pi in his mid-twenties. The two of them, wearing only black pajama bottoms, were darkly-tanned from many days at sea. Tattoos of Thai prayers, a leopard and a Buddha adorned their chests, identifying the village from which they had come, and the village from which we had all departed, Bangsare.

I left the Thais to their work and went up to the bow to sit on the starboard bench. After saying a little prayer for our voyage, I got a full view of our fishing boat. It was a typical Thai fishing boat hired out to ferangs wanting to do some deep-sea fishing. Constructed of wood, the craft was propelled by a giant diesel engine that took up most of the hull. The cabin above it had a three-foot ceiling, and served not only as the wheelhouse, but also as our storage compartment and sleeping quarters. It would prove to be cramped, since there was barely enough room for three men to sleep side-by-side, along with the equipment. The putt-putt sound from the engine, and the musty smell, reminded me of the junks in Hong Kong's harbor. It was definitely going to be difficult to sleep in that space with the engine noise. I hoped that at least none of the others snored.

From my view on the bench seats from which many a tourist had caught fish, I watched as we motored along the coast toward Cambodia, and Bangsare gradually turned into little match-boxes on match-sticks. Knight stepped out for a brief chat during which time we came around the short point southeast of Bangsare. The point protected Bangsare against stormy seas, for just outside the point, the calm sea rose into four-foot swells. Knight became uneasy, saying he'd take the wheel. Every once in a while, the small yellow-andwhite dinghy would come into view as it trailed behind our boat on a tow line.

Left alone, I held my seat and turned anxious. The incoming swells grew, reminding me of the seven-footers I had surfed in California on the back of my longboard. The dark clouds to the south did even more to turn my knuckles white. A tap at my shoulder turned me.

"You want Maekong?" Ti yelled over the pounding and hissing of the waves that smashed against the starboard hull. There was a glaze in his eyes. By the adept skill with which he balanced the large glass of whiskey in his hand, it was evident that he had done this before.

"Maekong?! Are you out of your fuckin' mind?! No."

Ti finished it off himself as he raced from balance point to balance point, not spilling a drop. I followed him to the wheelhouse. Knight sat at the wheel, trying unsuccessfully to feign calm as his eyes turned into those of a goldfish and darted excitedly.

In an I-told-you-so tone, I asked, "I thought the bottle was for the trip back?"

A wave slammed into the gunwale.

"They're very stressed, Fred, you can understand that, can't you? They just need a drink to relax."

He stared at me as though he were waiting for me to agree with him. Behind him were the seated and teetering silhouettes of Ti and Pi, and the half-finished pint of Maekong whiskey.

"Ha!" Thinking the worst, I went back to the bow and prepared for my final walk with the Creator.

"You don't know where we're going?!" Knight's screaming jolted me out of my meditation at the bow.

I dashed back to the wheelhouse. "What now?!"

"Well, they've had a little too much to drink, Fred." I didn't know a man's eyes could bug out so far without them falling out, but there Knight was. His sun-burned knuckles were white as he clenched the wheel. Ti and Pi were out cold and flat on their backs. The empty bottle rolled back and forth between them.

Disgusted, I shook my head and went back to my mental refuge of solitude at the head of the bow. My plan was that if the boat capsized, I would swim hard for shore and be free of this enterprise. A nervous giggle overtook me and turned into an out-and-out laugh. *So much for toasts to success and gold doubloons.*

* * *

Knight roused me with a couple taps on my shoulder, and pointed out the window. As I became more awake, I thanked God for not having let me drown in my sleep. Though the grimy window blurred the island, the grime couldn't detract from its beauty. I scrambled out of the cabin and stood in awe of this mythical-looking isle that is one of Thailand's national parks.

Named after one of the many species of trees on the evergreen-and-deciduous-blanketed island, Ko Samet is a naturalist's paradise. Covering about eighty-five square miles, and shaped like a 'T' with the wide part being three miles and the length of it seven, it attracted many tourists. Surrounded by beautiful white sandy beaches, it also served as a warning of the encroachment of man on a pristine environment. Legally, nobody was allowed to build on the island, but it was quickly being invaded by resorts, even in 1983. It was still small then, with only bungalows on the major part of the island. If I were ever to become a castaway, I hoped that I could be lost on such an island. There were coconuts everywhere. In the island's forest hid mouse deer, squirrels, long-tailed macaques, and fruit bats. Only monitor lizards and some snakes represented the more varied and much more threatening reptile population of Southeast Asia. The cobras weren't that big, wanting more to get out of your way than do anything harmful. The waters were still full of fish, and the reef so beautiful. It was paradise!

As we chugged into one of its many little turquoise-blue coves, the clandestine nature of our visit played with our emotions. Knight stood at the bow, searching the shore with his binoculars, looking apprehensive. Knight was worried that the police were probably already looking for him, after having rented the small dinghy under false pretenses. At least the bargirls must have said something to the owner by now.

At the far end of the cove a peninsula of gnarled, black rocks jutted out, protecting the small cove from the crashing waves that rolled in, creating a wonderful sense of tranquillity and safety. Bamboo bungalows lay nestled among the grove of palms that stood along the edge of the long sweeping beach. Their thatched roofs danced like anemone fingers in the wind. Behind the small village rose the forested mountain. The view made me want to sing a tune from *South Pacific*. A quick glance at Knight told me that no matter how relaxing and inviting the island appeared, he would be a very stressed man until we returned from Vietnam.

Chest out and chin up, elbows sticking out, he peered through the binoculars and let out a sigh of frustration

"I see some people on the beach. They're Caucasian. This must be one of those resort villages advertised in Bangkok," Knight said.

He lowered the binoculars, and said, "We'll stay here tonight and let the storm pass us by. We should also pick up some supplies here." Knight looked at me. "Do you have any money on you?"

"Only about ten baht," I answered, irked that he had suddenly shifted me from the position of observer to investor.

Knight sighed again and moved away from the window. Ti eased off the throttle, and we anchored. Leaving the cabin, I held myself against the boat's rocking by grabbing hold of the leg-thick bamboo pole running from the top of the cabin to the top of the bow. "Will this put a damper on our schedule?"

Knight's face darkened slightly, then cleared, "Shouldn't. . . maybe a day or so."

The gray clouds that had been at bay to the south rolled in quickly to belay Knight's last thoughts.

* * *

Knight flew over my head, from the top of the wheelhouse, splashing water back onto the port side as he hit the water. This was his release from the cooped up conditions on board as we waited out the storm that had hit the island for the two days since we arrived.

"Come on in Fred, the water's nice!" he said while treading water.

"That's okay! I'll wait till the sun comes out." It did look inviting as I looked over the side. The emerald green was intense, but I couldn't see the bottom. I was reminded of why I surfed only in the safety of kelp beds, and why Mr. Muk's photos disturbed me so. When the movie *Jaws* came out I read too many books about shark attacks, and about the U.S.S. Indianapolis tiger shark feeding frenzy, and I apparently hadn't gotten over it all.

Inside the cabin lay Ti and Pi. The Thai talent of catching a few Zs is truly amazing—they can sleep anywhere. They often travel by bus, and sleep with their heads leaning against a hard glass window. Eyelashes never flicker, even when the window rattles loudly and their heads hit the pane with a loud rat-tat.

According to Carlisle, anemia was the reason for this ability. He always had a lot of theories about life. I thought about Carlisle and my excited good-bye to him as I had gathered my equipment to join Knight. What would Carlisle's theories be on my reasons for attempting this adventure? Success as a photographer at all cost? Maybe. I remembered Carlisle's profanities shouted to me about my slim chances of surviving this adventure and smiled.

Knight pulled himself out of the water and went to confer with the Thais. I entered the cabin to retrieve my cassette player. Ti had been listening to it and had left it near the windshield. I took it, along with my Crosby, Stills, and Nash tape, and returned to the bow.

"You bloody fucking thieving cunts!" Knight stomped over to me with blood in his eyes. "Can you believe those fucking assholes?! They pocketed the bloody money I gave them to pay for all the diesel fuel we would need for the trip!"

"What?! What're we going to do?"

"We'll have to go to the beach and scrounge up some diesel." He went back to the stern for another volley at the Thais.

"What—ever," I said and put my headphones back on. *Southern Cross* took me away from the dark emotions and drizzle that dampened me.

That evening Knight paced the deck. He knew the weather would persist and we needed fuel. "Enough! Ti! We go island, buy food and diesel," he commanded, after the constant drizzle broke. "Do you want to come along, Fred?"

"Sure."

"Great. Pi will stay here and take care of the boat."

Ti jumped out of the wheelhouse and drew the dinghy in at the stern. He yanked on the starter cord and it started immediately.

"Come on Fred!" Knight yelled to me.

I thought about changing my camouflage cut-offs for jeans since a breeze had picked up.

"Well, are you coming along?"

I should have told Knight to shove it and give me the time to put something warmer on, but I jumped in, and he pushed forward on the throttle. The ride was slow and smooth as we idled around the rocky outcropping to the southeast of the boat. Knight confessed that he had been to the island before while doing research. And it hit me: if he had been to Ko Samet, why did he have such a question on his face as to the first village we'd seen? In the coming adventure, Knight would have more question marks on him than the Riddler!

The rocks seemed so much more jagged and sharp as we closed in on them. I speculated on how much more hazardous they would be to navigate around at night, and hoped Knight's search for diesel would be quick, lest we be stuck or worse.

"There's a resort around the other side that will be a good place for us to get some last minute provisions," Knight said as he scanned the water.

Barely missing a submerged boulder, Knight yanked hard on the wheel and steered us farther out to sea. He grinned abashedly. Drizzle started hitting the back of my neck, sticking my T-shirt to my body and the air turned colder as we went round the point, pushing me to ask, "How much longer?"

A twin of the village resort off which we had anchored came into view. Knight made a wide opposite turn as though preparing to make a U-turn on a city street, and brought the bow straight onto the beach. Cool, white sand greeted our feet as I jumped out with Ti to moor the boat.

"Now make sure everything's secure. . . Fred, are you sure about anchoring it there. . . Ti, it's better if you tie it 'round the tree. . ." Ti looked at me, vexed. I bit my lower lip to keep from laughing at our own version of Captain Bligh. Ti looked up again and rolled his eyes.

Knight yelled out another command "Now pull boat!"

"Why don't you get out of the boat and help us?" I said. *Dumb-ass!*

Ti grinned as though having read my mind.

"That's better," Knight said after he jumped out of the boat, and helped us pull on the anchor rope. A Thai with wavy hair to the middle of his back came running out and tried to help, but to no avail. That boat was much too heavy for anything other than being floated by thousands of gallons of seawater.

"Let's see about provisions," Knight called over his shoulder as he dropped the line and headed for the huts.

Looking up at the sky as we walked up the beach, there was less than a half-hour of light left.

The long-haired Thai, who we learned was the owner of the bungalows, invited us into the resort's restaurant, a thatched-roof hall. No walls. Only poles supported the palm frond roof. He motioned for us to sit on a wooden bench at one of five long dining tables, laying parallel to each other.

Knight, Ti and I sat down as the owner disappeared behind a woven palm frond wall that divided the kitchen from the dining area. He returned with menus, taking a seat with us.

A young Caucasian woman in her mid-twenties came in, just as three bare light bulbs above us went on. She ignored us as she sat down next to the owner, touching and holding him. The owner acknowledged her by putting his right arm around her. He then turned back to Knight, and they talked business.

The lights inside became brighter as the sky outside turned black. They caught the woman's strawberry blonde hair and made it glow. Her shoulder-length hair was attractive, distracting Ti and me from our reading of the menu. She was a "pilgrim" and had the same hippie style of dress Erika had worn when we first met. I looked at this pilgrim across the table and had pangs of longing for Erika, wishing I was with her on a plane to Australia.

Knight made menu suggestions. They were the cheapest. I picked my favorite, squid sautéed in garlic sauce. Knight didn't like the rubbery texture, so he ordered chicken curry. Ti joined me in ordering squid in garlic sauce. Knight asked him if he wanted a beer. Ti glanced at me, told Knight no, and then shook his head while making a remark about our first night at sea.

While we gave Knight our orders, the blonde carried on a conversation of whispers with the owner. She fidgeted in her seat the way women do in great anticipation of doing the *boom-boom*. Frustrated by the owner's lack of interest, she got up and gave all of us a harsh look and left. Having our orders the owner got up and took them to the kitchen.

"It should be quite good, don't you think?" Knight said.
"What did the owner say?" I asked.
"About what?"
"Supplies. That's what we came here for, right?"
"There'll be no problem with the supplies, but he says there's no diesel on the island. I think we have enough food to last us the trip. We can try and get some fuel from a boat in the Gulf. It'll be okay. . . But, this is the last chance to return to Bangkok, if you're having second thoughts."

Many who couldn't understand the grip of Vietnam and effects of PTSD have asked me why I didn't just grab my stuff and jump on a ferry back to the mainland at that moment. Looking back on that time I see now what a grip they both had on me, and how memories of having been deemed a quitter by my parents were too strong a motivation for me in those days. I said, "I gave you my word in Pattaya."

Knight pulled a pack of cigarettes from his shirt.
"Would you like one?" he asked.
"I don't smoke." It was the twentieth time he'd asked, and the question had already turned grating long ago. He smiled apologetically, then began talking about California. He wanted no mention of our trip. People filtered in for dinner as a waiter arrived with our meals, and there was the hedging of our words.

"After dinner we'll go to the dinghy," Knight said
"What about getting the dinghy *back* to the boat in the dark?"
"We shouldn't have a problem. Pi'll have the light on," Knight said. I sat with the uncomfortable feeling left over from the previous nightmare when the crew were supposedly going to have only a small drink, but ended up flat on their backs.

* * *

"Shall we?" Knight asked, as he finished wiping his mouth with a paper napkin. Ti and I slid off our bench and we headed towards the boat, just ahead of the waitress as she came running up with our bill. Knight gave her thirty baht. I gave Knight a dirty look. He evaded my eyes. "Let's get to the boat so we can sleep," he said, as he began walking faster.

The tide had come up drastically during the setting of the sun, so much so that I could barely see any beach, and the dinghy was bobbing and bouncing like a toy against grass just under the coconut palm! Ti and Knight jumped in while I pulled the anchor out of the sand and wrapped large coils of anchor line around my open hand and elbow. Ti started the engine, making me coil and walk faster. I ran towards the bow, throwing the line and anchor to Ti.

"Jump in!" Knight yelled as I ran through the waist-deep water and then jumped in, assisted by Ti. The dinghy accelerated as Knight pointed us back towards the rocky point.

The rocky point was black against black—invisible! "We'll go wide of the point so we don't run aground!" Knight yelled over the engine.

"Rock!"

"Christ!" Knight yelped, yanking on the wheel. The starboard-side planed out of the water. We barely missed the white froth-circled rock by a foot. Our course turned into an even wider circle as we finally came round the point.

"Where in the bloody hell is the boat?" Knight yelled, calling our attention to the dark void off the bow. To our starboard side were lights from the resort.

"Where in the bloody hell is it?" Knight mumbled. "That idiot! That bloody fucking idiot!"

Ti took the brunt of Knight's ranting for the rest of the fifteen minutes we spent circling around like a crippled duck.

I sighed. "Why don't we just beach it and search in the morning?"

"Yes. . . We'll go back to the resort." Knight turned the wheel one last time, heading us in. As we motored, Knight blurted, "These people can be so stupid sometimes. They're all the same!"

I ignored his racist remark by keeping my attention on the darkness and the threatening rocks.

We were all quiet the rest of the trip in. The tide had come up even farther. Knight steered us straight in, landing us within ten yards of the restaurant. Surf reached up the last two feet of sand, spraying the restaurant's lawn.

The owner grinned as he came out to meet us. "You come back?"

"Do you have a place we can stay?" Knight asked, as we moored the boat.

"Uh. . . yes.You can stay in the bungalow there," he said. Our evening abode would be a bamboo shack fifty feet away, in the shadows, beyond a coconut palm.

Knight finished tying the anchor line to a coconut trunk, opened his wallet, and thumbed through his bills.

"You don't by any chance have any cash on you?" Knight asked me.

"I told you, I don't. My wallet's on the fishing boat anyway."

Knight continued to look through his bills as if he'd lost imaginary money. "Here you are," he said. The owner handed Knight a lit kerosene lantern.

Inside the hut was a dirt floor, with three grass mats strewn about. The walls stopped two inches short of the floor, barely a buffer against the increasingly chilly draft coming in off the Gulf. Knight scowled, unknowingly creating a humorous monster face in the bottom light from the hand-held lamp. His bushy eyebrows relaxed, as he said, "Well, get some sleep and we'll leave early in the morning. They say the weather's supposed to end tomorrow."

"Which mat do you want?" I asked.

He didn't care, so I took the one next to the wall nearest the water. Wrong decision. I woke up countless times during the night, shivering from the cold sea breeze that shot under the bottom of the wall and into my face. I didn't know which was worse, the cold, or the ground that seemed to rock like the boat every time I closed my eyes.

We awoke to another gray morning. My seasickness had subsided, but made me hesitant to get back on the fishing boat.

"Shit." I whispered to myself, as we came up on the dinghy.

"Damn!" Knight bellowed.

On the beach, a mere five yards from our bungalow, but more than a hundred yards away from the water, lay our dinghy. Off in the distance, tiny breakers curled softly along the shore. After a long pause to stare at the result of a very low tide, he sighed, "Well, let's get to it."

Ti pushed at the stern, while Knight and I took both gunnels. We could only move it a foot at a time. A German tourist offered us a hand, enabling us to move it ten to twenty yards at a time. I chuckled inside as *Yo!Ho!Ho!And a bottle of rum*, played in my mind. Leaving a trail in the sand like a giant sea turtle, the dinghy finally hit the waterline with the help provided by the German. We thanked him, and were off.

This time the ride was quite enjoyable: a glassy light green sea and blue sky peeking out through the high clouds. There was a pleasant feeling all around from us having had a good meal and respite from the cooped up environment of the fishing boat.

We rounded the point again and there was our red and turquoise boat bobbing softly, not beached or lost at sea as our vivid imaginations had led us to believe.

Pi smiled and waved to us from the front deck. His smile faded rapidly, as we boarded and Knight reminded us who was in charge. "You bloody fucking idiot! Why in the hell didn't you leave a light on for us last night?!"

"Sorry, sorry, sorry. Is okay, sorry, sorry!" Pi pleaded, his hands going wildly between pointing at nothing in particular, and clasping together in the form of prayer.

"It's not okay! You're just a bloody idiot!"

Ti empathized by uttering a few Thai words. Knight seemed possessed by the ghost of Captain Kidd; I half-expected him to pick up a bucket and pummel Pi.

Chapter 9

"What one hides is worth neither more nor less than what one finds. And what one hides from oneself is worth neither more nor less than what one allows others to find." — André Breton

Evasions

Anchor up and bow aimed out to sea, the world was full of new and grand opportunities. Pi put more pressure on the throttle, bringing the diesel to full-bore and those possibilities shined even more vivid and exciting! Far to the southeast, the sun offered an added hoorah by breaking through the clouds and throwing javelins of light into the bright emerald horizon. Off our stern, a couple of tourists strolled hand in hand along the beach. Were I just a tourist, I would have been despondent about leaving Shangri-la. Instead, I paced back and forth on the deck, as if my movement would somehow add a few knots.

Knight intercepted me at the wheelhouse.

"Yes?" I answered, beginning to feel a queasiness returning as the rocking of the boat became more pronounced.

"Would you like to know how far I expect us to get today?" he said and led me into the cabin.

While emptying one of his flight bags of its papers, maps and photos on to the area behind the pilot's seats, he motioned for me to give him some room on the sleeping area, and then spread out a nautical map of the Thai Gulf.

"You see this island right here?" he said, pointing at the large, elongated island of Ko Chang.

"Yeah?"

"That is where we should be by this evening. It'll be our last bearing, before heading south to stay out of Cambodian waters. By early tomorrow morning we should see the lights of the oil fields in the middle of the gulf."

"Who's that?" I asked, pointing to a photo of a man who was in too good of a shape to have been Knight. With a confused look on his face, Knight reached for the snapshot, half-hidden in the mound of papers. The photo held an image of a muscular, thirtyish-looking man seated on a lawn chair. A trim, brown beard covered the man's expression as did his dark Vaurnets. Still, he seemed to have a very serious aura about him.

"Oh, he's the Frenchman who's place you have taken. He quit because he had become fed up with all the delays we had in getting a boat. Likable fellow. He was with me for a few months." Knight quickly hid the photo under the others. "You've been quite lucky. You've only had to wait a few days for this adventure to begin."

"Great, Richard. I'll take a nap now," I said, as he collected his maps. Laying back and propping my head up with some of my rolled up clothes offered a view of the disappearing white line of Ko Samet's beach. Soon, only the dragon's back of green Cambodian mountains and island tops of eastern Thailand would stand above the horizon. I closed my eyes and had an unsettling thought: *what had the Frenchman learned in two months that I didn't have the chance to learn in two days?*

* * *

Stifling a yawn, I rubbed my eyes and squinted out over the stern at the phantom gray horizon that barely marked the split between Heaven and Earth. *What a headache!* I clutched my head as I had done as a child when I slept too late into a tropical morning. I motioned for Ti to move out of the pilot's seat for me to take my turn at the wheel. He mocked me by holding his forehead and crawled out of the seat and took my place on the foam sleeping mat. Knight scooted up to me, a large rolled up map in his hand. He caught himself, as a large wave rocked the boat.

"You know how to read this, don't you?" he asked.

"Good," he said when I nodded. "You shouldn't have to mess with the throttle. Keep it all the way forward. Our course right now is east, southeast. Just keep that compass reading."

The compass was still in its packaging, vacuum sealed in plastic against a cardboard backing. Knight had nailed it to the console. I laughed at the cartoon on the cardboard backing of a blonde woman driving with her children in the country, a copy of the compass stuck to the dashboard. God! I'm so glad I've brought my own compass, I thought.

Vacillating between a smile and a look of concern, Knight said, "It should do fine, don't you think?"

"I've got an army lensatic compass in my pack. Would you like to use it?"

"That would be very nice."

Knight took the wheel and I shuffled back on my hands and knees to my equipment. Pi moved his head slightly in his sleepiness in order to let me pass. Rummaging through the three small outer pockets of my ALICE pack, I found it and offered it to Knight. He grabbed hold of it by its olive-drab cord, and then inspected it with great interest after we traded places behind the wheel.

"How do you use it?" he asked.

Dividing my attention between the wheel, the horizon, and the compass, I gave Knight a quick lesson in using a lensatic compass. "See this here?" I said. "That's the lens used to view the readings. It also acts as a latch. Turn it up, then open up the cover. See that black wire in the slot down the middle of the cover? You line it up with the notch on top of the lens. After you line it up with your target, you look down through the lens to read your bearing."

"Great, and these are luminous?" he asked.

"They're painted on. I don't feel they're that effective. . . then again I haven't had much use for them at night."

"I'll put it right here," he said, as he put it on the window sill next to his.

"I'm going to take a nap. If you see any other ships, or any kind of emergency, give us a shout," Knight said, turning around and shuffling back to a foam mattress.

I enjoyed piloting the boat; it distracted my attention from motion sickness, like when my parents permitted me to drive the car on family trips along curvy mountain roads. Our course paralleled a lowland string of mountains that stood sheltered from the sun by a thin strand of rain clouds. Knight said the mountains were Cambodia, Thailand long having disappeared below our aft horizon. Such a beautiful country in memories and issues of *National Geographic*, but Cambodia was scary with all its rampant xenophobia and self-destructive history that forced it to mix with its neighbors like oil and water.

By 1983, the border of Cambodia and Thailand was more like the wild, wild west than just a front dividing Thailand from further expansion by Hanoi. Communist Vietnam had not only conquered South Vietnam, but also Cambodia, giving it the reviled and internationally unrecognized name of *Kampuchea*. That was the name Hanoi used when they invaded, "to help the Cambodian people who are being oppressed" and started throwing banner slogans around to aid their puppet regime, like *Kampuchean United Front for National Salvation*. All I could think about was what I had read in a history book the week before, while enjoying a Thai iced tea on Sukhumvit, and cogitating on possible story ideas. I did that often in Bangkok, read history books, especially after Jacqueline had expressed her disgust at how journalists trained in the

United States were so lacking in their understanding of the countries they covered. She blamed it on American journalism schools stressing only the writing without forcing students to look outside, something that comes so naturally to natives of countries like Switzerland, where everyone speaks at least two foreign languages. Basically, her opinion was that because of poor training in global matters, American journalists weren't much good for anything other than chasing American ambulances and fire trucks.

So, I read. I read everything I could get my hands on, not only about Southeast Asia, but also about every other country that took my fancy. I learned that to understand Cambodia, and the rest of what became Indochina, I had to look to a time so far back that my ancestors were still getting used to the idea of being called *Scotti*, or Scots, instead of Picts. With the ninth century arrived the dawn of the more advanced Khmer in Cambodia; their king, Jayavarman, was already orchestrating the building of the majestic reliefs at the base of Angkor Thom, depicting his naval victory over the Chams, and amassing a total acreage that topped at the middle of what is now Laos, and bottomed out as far south as the Malay peninsula. By the time his descendant, Jayavarman VII, was in power, Siam to the west had gained strength and interest in Cambodia's land holdings, an interest matched by its enemy to the east—Vietnam. Fighting the Siamese elephants to the west and the Vietnamese tigers to the east, the Khmer lost the area that would be called Saigon, along with the rice-rich Mekong Delta (the darker-skinned Vietnamese who reside in South Vietnam, especially in areas near Rach Gia, and Saigon, are descendants of this ancient ruling people, a fact that Pol Pot used when trying to excuse murderous raids into Southwest Vietnam, in order to *reclaim* lands). But then the French landed. By the third year of the American Civil War, Cambodia was a strand of Thai silk away from losing its complete political leadership to the throne of France. On April 17, 1864, Napoleon III of France included under his *protection* Laos, Vietnam, and Cambodia. An appropriate example of French occupation was soldiers sending postcards with black-andwhite photos of lines of decapitated Vietnamese, Khmer and Lao heads to their girlfriends and wives back in Paris. Just a continued spin into horror and despair for countries so ironically known for their qualities of Buddhist gentleness and kindness.

For a moment, during the reign of Prince Norodom Sihanouk, there was hope that Cambodia would finally come out of its thousand-year tailspin. By 1954, France had pulled out of Indochina. Then the United States made its idealistic attempt to defend Vietnam from the Communist invasion, but left. And then Pol Pot reared his ugly head. Some reports put the total number of Khmer murdered by the Khmer

Rouge at around 2 million, one out of every six. That's an earthquake killing every man, woman and child on the San Francisco Peninsula, or a nuclear bomb annihilating almost half of Finland's population. Such was re-education as taught by Pol Pot and the Khmer Rouge: shooting, torturing, and starving, while brainwashing children to commit many of these atrocities, from 1975 to 1979. America is always so proud of having rescued all those prisoners held in Nazi concentration camps during World War II. I have never stopped wondering why this pride never carried over into rescuing the people in Southeast Asia, especially when reports of these atrocities were released into Thailand by refugees from Cambodia, Laos, and Vietnam. In Bangkok, I'd heard these tales of atrocity from vagrants who had escaped not only Cambodia, but the appalling conditions in refugee camps along the Thai border.

Sporadic clouds continued throughout the day. My enthusiasm for piloting waned as the seat cushion gradually turned to rock. I shifted my weight to relieve the numbness in my legs to no avail. It was so painful, I ended up standing behind the wheel during the last hour of my watch.

By the time my shift had ended, the evening sun was painting the mountains of Cambodia in shades of rust and orange, and the salt air was so fresh it revived. Sitting on the starboard bench at the bow, I closed my eyes and breathed in deeply. The fresh salt air brought back memories of sunny weekend mornings spent surfing at Santa Cruz. I was now a far cry from the innocent pleasures of surfing at Pleasure Point.

Being that I was the only other real English speaker on board, and the close quarters, made Knight open up a bit more about the history of his treasure hunt. He told me about an American sailboat owner he had tried to interest in Kidd's treasure. And then he tossed the grenade: our present voyage was not Knight's first attempt. We were hundreds of miles from Thailand and I guess that was the only way he thought anyone could be trusted was by that barrier.

Knight said he had initially tried to get a boat in Singapore, but couldn't interest the owner. The sailboat was the *So Fong*, owned by an American, Bill Mathers, who had been a US Navy officer and diver in Vietnam, and a well-known treasure hunter in his own right. (Imagine my surprise about reading in the news that Mathers was imprisoned by the Vietnamese in 1984). Knight met him in Singapore, but he didn't show any interest because he said he was soon flying back to the States. From the look on Knight's face and his description of the *So Fong*'s state-of-the-art navigation equipment, I could tell he had really wanted that boat.

Since Knight's search for a boat in Singapore was unsuccessful, he went north. In that adventure he made an initial attempt to sail to *Iles des Pirates* in a Malaysian fishing boat from Chennering, a village on Malaysia's northeast coast. There was a heavy mystery surrounding that trip, especially since the owner wasn't told of Knight's intent. He said the crew he had hired was to drop him off the Vietnamese coast, and return later to pick him up. A few days before the voyage, the Malay crew went AWOL. An expression of scorn covered Knight's face as he told the rest of the story. He gave it a try on his own, he said, but was turned back by a monsoon.

This was quite a different story from the one relayed to the London writer who later wrote Knight's adventure narrative, and a lot more believable. Knight lied to her and Viking Publications by saying he had succeeded and found part of the treasure, that the trip with me was just to secure the rest, and that he was able to drag the dinghy ten yards up the beach on his own. This was the same type of dinghy for which we needed the aid of the German tourist on Ko Samet to move it two feet at a time!

Suddenly, Knight changed the subject by rambling on about his failed acting career. He almost became joyful as he reminisced about days studying in Paris with Marcel Marceau, and landing a part as a drunk in the Jacques Tati comedy called *Playtime*. He then went to Los Angeles. The city of entertainment didn't have the production deals that he'd visualized, but that gave him free time to research. Knight spent months in the UCLA basement map library, until he found the irresistible map of Grand Pirate Island.

He stopped talking, just as abruptly as he had begun, and returned to the wheelhouse. My mind went in circles trying to decipher what Knight had told me—he said he had found the map in a library book while out of work in Los Angeles, yet back at the motel room, he had said that the map had belonged to a relative of his.

Since there was nothing I could do now about his tale that was quickly unraveling into a disquietingly incongruent story, I relinquished myself to the scenery. The intense color of the mountains increased, along with the darkening red sky. *National Geographic* colors, I thought, and smiled as I remembered that Asians view red and orange as fortuitous colors, and that I had finally gotten my big break.

* * *

"Tell them we're just fishing!"

I jumped out of bed and searched blindly for a weapon of any kind. Squinting hard, I saw Pi and Knight silhouetted by a spotlight. He was wrapped in an eerily illuminated fog, almost as thick as one you would find in San Francisco. Beyond him loomed an imposing, large, dark monster with a big, bright red eye, the monster spotlighting Pi.

"What the fuck is that?" I yelled as I brought my hand up to shade my eyes.

"Gunboat. They're patrolling for pirates," Knight answered. Nothing worse than being surprised by a patrol boat with twin MaDeuces[17], and at this hour the gunner was most assuredly tired.

"It's okay," Knight said. "Don't worry. Ti told them we're just out on a fishing trip. You can go back to sleep." I couldn't go back to sleep after that red cyclops eye, so I took the wheel, more willing to do two watches back to back than be shaken out of another sound sleep.

The window was covered in condensation, and I was surprised that we'd been navigating like this. I wiped a hole in the fogged window. What looked like an aurora borealis glowed straight off the bow, marking oil rig lights at the center of the Gulf. Our course was now one-eight-zero, straight south; we were doing everything we could to ensure that we didn't cross into Cambodian waters. Withdrawn into himself, Knight stood alone in the mist, eerily reminding me of scenes from *Moby Dick*, as *our* Captain Ahab prepared to challenge the White Whale and the spirits of dead adventurers.

Knight walked along the bow, reaching up every once in a while to the pole that went from the top of the wheelhouse to the bowhead. The pole was intended for hanging nets, but Knight used it for doing pull-ups. Knight did a lot of pull-ups during my shift to relieve stress. What a bizarre scene in this fog! I wished Knight would go to sleep, and leave me to my own inner thoughts, instead of giving me the unsettling view of a worried ghost captain walking the deck of a ghost ship. He was giving me the creeps, the way some people do when you don't know if they're really joking about killing themselves, or not.

* * *

Next to scaling mountains in Mendocino County in search of the family table's holy sacrament of fresh venison, I loved nothing more than flycasting a silver hilton, or a glo-bug for steelhead on the Trinity River of Northern California. I just loved to fish. My step-grandfather, Ed Thompson, instilled in me the love of fishing, and seemed more like my blood grandfather because of it. Every time we'd visit from Southeast Asia, Grandpa Thompson took us to Newman or Loon Lake to fish for bluegills. My passion for fishing was so great that I had not missed a fishing outing since. So, when I heard the hooting and hollering going on outside the Thai fishing boat, and the sing of a fishing reel, I thought I was dreaming.

Rushing outside, I saw Pi holding the rod and cranking on the reel. "Big fish!" he yelled and a three-foot long dorado shattered the glass-calm water, shooting six feet into the air. After flashing its brilliant green and gold colors in a wild and unrestrained shake, it plunged back in with a slap. The fish was a hundred feet off the port side, and slowly getting closer. My stomach grumbled in anticipation of fresh fish, and there's nothing better than fresh mahi-mahi!

Knight, who had been coaching the reeling, said, "Don't lose him now."

Line peeled off Pi's reel. And then he gained it back. A voice in the back of my head told me the fish would be lost. Pi yanked on the rod. The fish, barely twenty feet away, jumped more than ten feet up, and then the rubber squid fishing lure dislodged, becoming a missile headed straight for us.

"Look out!" Knight yelled, too late for anybody to do anything as the lure and line slammed on to the deck.

Like spurned lovers, the men returned to their chores. I went over to Pi to help him reel in the line that lay at our feet. Reaching the end of the line, I checked the rubber squid lure and straightened hook, not realizing yet how soon our boat would be like the lure, zigging and zagging in the water, bringing out big, hungry fish.

Pi took the fishing equipment back to the stern and started to prepare lunch. Squatting by the clay stove in black pajama pants, a white T-shirt tied around his head as a headband, Pi could have easily passed for a Khmer Rouge if the headband had been checkered white and red. He smiled a wide, pearl-white grin as he looked up at me through the smoke from his little clay stove. Pi fanned the flames briskly, until all the charcoal turned white. He put a wok half-filled with oil on the stove, then cut sand-dollar-sized slices from a football-shaped loin.

"Buffaloo!" He shouted, grinning and pointing at the meat. We shared a thumbs up and a smile, and then he tossed the slices into the wok. The fragrance of meat frying amplified my hunger pangs. I went out on the front deck, with a tough water buffalo steak on rice, dreaming about how tender that mahi-mahi would have been. I could almost see myself back in California seated at the Fish Market in Palo Alto, a lightly grilled and buttered mahi-mahi steak nestled next to a bed of spiced rice. I looked at my plate of water buffalo and plain white rice again and sighed.

Pi suddenly yelled, "Look! Mistah Knight look!" and pointed to the small gray form of a fishing boat on the horizon behind us. Knight grabbed his 8x30 binoculars from his bag and ran out to Pi, who stood on the stern deck.

"What do you think it is?" I yelled out the window.

"I don't know; could be pirates."

"Pirates?"

Knight walked up the port side and spoke, "I'm not sure, but we'll see if he follows us. Keep our present heading."

"Okay. What are we going to do if they chase us?" The conversation with the Aussies back at the Crown Hotel's pool came to mind, making me sick with visions of brutality.

Knight took a deep breath, sucked on his lower lip, and then divulged his foolproof plan which he'd kept secret at the Sun and Sand, "We'll have Ti and Pi negotiate with them. Most Thai pirates are just fishermen adding to their income by pillaging Vietnamese boat people. And, if Ti and Pi aren't able to persuade them, we'll use those plastic toy guns I brought to bluff them."

"Plastic toy guns?!" I could only stare in disbelief. Knight's statement reminded me of a robber back in the Bay Area, who'd used a toy gun to rob a number of Fotomats. One day he pulled the toy gun on some cops, and they blew him away.

The common arsenal for pirates in the Thai Gulf consisted of weapons freely available from the region's revolving wars: AK-47s, M-16s, M-14s, RPGs, M203s, high explosive grenades, old trusty .303 Enfields, M-1 Garands, M-1 carbines, and Thompson sub-machine guns. The shortest ranging of them all were the carbine and the Thompson, and those were effective to at least a hundred yards in the hands of a novice. All they had to do was pick us off from that range and then pick up the scraps. We had no place to hide. Those full metal jackets would punch through our wooden boat like a cheese cutter. And we didn't even have the luxury of a visible shore to swim to. With no cover of darkness, they'd assuredly finish us off in the water with a few bursts of automatic fire. Listening to Knight, I wished we had George Gaebler's secret weapon, "in whose muzzle you could put your fist."

Knight said, "I really don't think there'll be a problem. Ti and Pi are Thais. They'll be able to convince them. We'll hide our precious gear when we're sure they're following."

Knight watched the suspected pirates for five minutes then came into the wheelhouse and assessed his equipment, like a squirrel going through nuts. When he was finished, it was a cluttered mess.

"I'll take this shift Fred," Knight said, motioning for me to scoot away and take a break.

"Sure, Richard, it's all yours. Any orders?" I said as I crawled out.

"Keep an eye on the boat." His eyes bulged as he spoke. The severity of his terror and the insanity of everything made me laugh. It wasn't a funny scenario at all, but it was that realization that made me laugh.

Out on the portside, Pi and Ti each had a pistol in one hand, and a cleaning rod in the other. They smiled at me and then continued cleaning their weapons.

Amazed and curious, I asked Ti, "Can I see that?"

He nodded and handed me his revolver. Rust pitted much of the chrome plating. The barrel had ".38 Special, S&W" stamped along it. Smith & Wesson. I pulled the locked rod, and unloaded it by popping the six cylinder to the side. The barrel's rifling had been almost all shot out; it looked more like the inside of a container used for motor oil. Overpowering, the odor of gun solvent suddenly filled my nostrils.

"Nothing like counting on a well-maintained weapon," I joked, and handed it back to Ti.

Handling Pi's semi-automatic Army Colt .45, I realized there was no clip. It wasn't a .45! Pi laughed as I tried to eject the magazine. He motioned for it back. With deft action he pushed a lever, causing the barrel to break away from the pistol grip, like a break-action shotgun. A shotgun was exactly what it was! Pi took a 12-gauge buckshot cartridge from his pocket, chambered it, and closed the action. An amazing weapon. More amazing was that he was prepared to use it. Because of the amount of recoil a 12-gauge delivers, I couldn't see how he'd be able shoot it without breaking his wrist.

With a sly grin, Pi said, "I kill two in bar fight, Pattaya. Goot gun!"

He stowed it in his bag. Before closing it, he extracted the *pièce de résistance*: a fragmentary grenade! It was the WWII pineapple type. He dropped it in my hand. Heavy for something that compact.

Carrying the grenade hidden from view, I made my way to the window of the wheelhouse and grinned as I ducked my head in. "Richard, we're going to die."

"You're so bloody melodramatic!"

"Oh, *really*?" I answered, mocking him in my most outrageous Noel Coward accent. I was getting really peeved not only at him, because he was such an imbecile, but also at myself for having been so easily taken in by that pleasant charm and daring do. Like a trophy exonerating me of anything wrong I may have done in my life, I revealed the grenade for him to stare at it wide-eyed. *Well*, I thought, *I guess you didn't know about this either!*

"Where did you get that?!" he asked, clenching the wheel to steel himself.

"It's Pi's, and they've both got handguns. Quite powerful persuasion, don't you think?"

"Uh, yes, yes."

"You do realize that our chances of surviving a contact with pirates is ninety to one, don't you?" I said coldly, as the back of my neck turned hot. I wanted to have it out with him right there. Since I was the only one on board with any real naval training, and he had shown himself to be so incompetent, I was sure that no naval court would bring charges against me if I took control of the ship. I wasn't sure about the Thais, and there's a rule I was quickly learning, and that is you've got to listen to the ones with the guns. Since I had no guns, I was powerless; but, had I a better grasp of the Thai language, I would have learned that Ti and Pi would have backed me up one hundred percent. They would have turned that boat right back to Thailand without a second thought.

"I assure you, Fred; I had absolutely no idea. . . I'll have a talk with them." He did have a talk with them later; they should have paid more attention to his suggestions because of what would later happen to them in Vietnam.

With a shake of my head, I returned Pi's grenade and climbed the step ladder to the deck of the wheelhouse.

The sun had heated it, burning the soles of my feet, but I got used to it. Solitude was more a necessity than protecting myself from the intense heat. Taking my T-shirt off, I laid it down and stretched out so I could tan while I watched the boat that was definitely following us. Visions of the pirates garbed in head bandanas and cut-off pants, heavily armed and storming the boat, Ti and Pi desperately trying to keep them at bay. We were going to die!

"No," I said to myself, shaking my head. *Too good of a day. Bright sun, beautiful sea; people don't die on days like this. Do they? Quiet the mind and peace will follow.*

Stress gripped the next two hours as I lay on the sun-baked top deck, turning into a well-done ferang. The alarm was set on my wristwatch for fifteen-minute intervals. Like a chicken on a rotisserie, I rotated from laying on my back to my front at each beep from the alarm and then back again.

"Richard!"

"What?!" he yelled back up.

"That ship seems to finally be veering off."

"Are you sure?"

"Yep, absolutely sure."

"Give us a minute. I'll come up," he said. "Pi!" He yelled, "Come drive!"

Knight pulled himself up the ladder. "Are you sure?" he asked in a lower tone of voice, as though to say it out loud would jinx it. I handed him the binoculars. He smiled as he focused on the boat.

"You know, you're absolutely right."

"Yes, Richard." I'd had enough of his treating me, and everyone else on board, like an untrustworthy child. "I'm going inside, Richard."

"Oh yes, yes, don't let me keep you. You can take a nap if you'd like. We've got it quite under control now."

"Yeah, Richard, I can see that. If you'll excuse me."

Nothing much happened that day or the next, except the continued beauty of the glass ocean. At one point the next afternoon, while I sat on the bow with my legs over the side, a dark oblong shape sped up from behind. It was so fast it startled me to jump almost into a standing position. Another similar form sped up to the first one. A dorsal fin broke the surface, signaling the arrival of a mystical friend. The dolphins played in the wake of our boat, rekindling a childhood fascination and afternoons of watching TV's *Flipper*.

"Richard!" I yelled back to the wheelhouse. "Do you see the dolphins? Aren't they great!"

"Yes they are," he said.

"You know what?"

"What?"

"It's good luck to be visited by dolphins. It's a sign!"

Knight grinned.

"Thanks," I whispered to the dolphins, and waved. Suddenly, the fortuneteller's words came back to me—*STAY AWAY FROM THE BORDER. Which border was she talking about? Laos and Thailand or Cambodia and Vietnam?* Lady Buddha gave her prophecy during my preparation for the MIA story, but what now as we headed for an area split by Vietnam and Cambodia? Had she been talking about this voyage all along?

* * *

A conical-shaped island rose above the horizon. We had been away from Ko Samet for three days.

"That's Paulo Panjang!" Richard said gleefully. "We'll be on the island this evening." He climbed down from the roof of the wheelhouse.

We kept our bow pointed straight at the island.

"Fred, would you come down here for a minute?" he yelled up to me after about a half-hour.

Gathering up my shirt and towel, I climbed down off the top deck.

"What's up, Richard?" My eyes adjusted to the light in the cabin; black silhouettes turned into Knight, the crew and our equipment.

White spots still danced before my eyes as Knight spoke, "Come look at this." He slid a nautical map to me. "See this here." He pointed to an island at the southern tip of Vietnam. "I'm thinking that this island could be Hon Khoai. Paulo Panjang and Hon Khoai have the same tops. On the map they both have conical tops."

I grunted in agreement, an uneasiness coming on.

"What do you think?'

I pointed at the southern tip of Vietnam. "All this land below *Quan Long* is flat, right?"

"Yes."

Sliding my finger across the map, up to the largest Vietnamese island in the Thai Gulf, I asked, "Phu Quoc is higher than *Hon Nam Du*?"

Knight nodded.

"So the only thing to do is see whether there's a peak that comes up on the horizon, or a bar of land, right?" I jabbed back and forth between the two islands.

"Yes, thanks Fred, that's what I thought also."

"Yeah, Richard, no problem." *Nothing like a confident captain.*

We went up together to watch for the next confirmation of our position. Since we had been navigating through pilotage and dead reckoning—without any compensation for drift, basically a wing and a prayer—Knight was worried that we had traveled too far south before heading east. If we saw a conical-shaped island appear on the horizon we were in luck. If we instead saw a piece of land that was flat and continued to spread out as we neared, we were lost off the southern tip of Vietnam. Within an hour, Phu Quoc revealed its identity with its unmistakable razor-back ridge rising above the horizon.

"We're here!" Knight said. That he had a look of surprise immediately put me on guard. Because of a solid understanding of how appearance effects the confidence of a team, good leaders are never confused in their bearing. Knight was always confused!

Five hours passed as we skirted to the south of Paulo Panjang and I was blown away by how easy the trip had been. All our navigation had been done using only landmarks: the Thai mountains before we headed south and lights from oil rigs in the center of the Gulf, a clock, the cheap compasses, and the inaccuracy of reckoning our speed between 8 and 12 knots.

We continued our course towards our drop-off point at Hon Nam Du. Once, a small boat appeared on the horizon, over towards Vietnam. It turned tail. Knight suggested it was probably a refugee boat thinking we were Thai pirates. An hour later Hon Nam Du betrayed its identity by forming into a fat cone on the horizon.

"Run down and tell Ti and Pi that we'll be separating in about an hour or so."

I slid down the ladder, making it to the bottom in almost one complete jump.

"We go Vietnam! One hour!" I told Ti as I took the wheel from him so that he could bring the dinghy alongside.

"Vietnam, Vietnam!" I said to Pi, who seemed to be dazed. As if trying to get him to believe me, I kept pointing at Hon Nam Du and Phu Quoc, the dark green tops of the islands looking like conical Vietcong hats slowly edging above the northern horizon.

"Vietnam!" Pi said, recovering and breaking into a jig on deck. "Vietnam, Vietnam!"

Chapter 10

"If you hear that I'm coming back soon, forget it. I like this place. It's really great over here for the newspaperman." — Oliver E. Noonan/ AP photojournalist, killed in a chopper shot down en route to Danang, 1969.

Departure

People react to fear in a multitude of fashions. Over the years, I've had the luck, good and bad, of experiencing and observing quite a few of these reactions. I've boiled them down to three: an urge to fight, an urge to flee, and an urge to wait for it all to blow over. The latter reaction can be seen as someone laying back and accepting what comes, like a dying man. Or like a person curling in like a pill bug, doing what you're supposed to do when a grizzly bear is playing soccer with your body, and you're praying he doesn't get you by your soft underbelly and lap you up.

Driven by fear, Ti fought the motor with a wrench and screwdriver, trying to get it to do what it was supposed to do. Every once in a while it would tease us with a pop and a short growl. A few times, small waves that had been patting the dinghy's sides would become large swells; and Ti would jump back from almost being dropped into the drink, and respond with a spicy Thai tongue-lashing, cursing our bad luck. The only distraction he had from his rage was sucking on his fresh wounds scraped open by the sharp edges of the outboard engine. Pi would laugh, but I didn't find much humor in our predicament because the tip of the island of Phu Quoc was looming closer, with precious minutes flying by while we grappled with the outboard. Our only option in our continuing enterprise to Grand Pirate Island was that motor.

"Are we going to make it?" I asked, my arms crossed in the unenviable position of being the pill bug because of my lack of experience in tinkering with engines.

"No problem," Pi said. Rule number one in placating the distressed: never use a negative because the subconscious has to process a positive in order to process the negative. That's why telling a toddler "*don't* touch the stove," and telling an adult "*don't* think of pink polka-dotted elephants" has the opposite effect.

Knight startled me out of my tense concentration on Ti's efforts. "Why haven't they been able to start the engine?"

"No idea."

Ti and Pi spent the next fifteen minutes jerry-rigging a throttle system by tying twine to the fuel valve. Instead of pushing forward on the throttle handle as we had done during the trip from Pattaya to Bangsare, we would now have the twine taking the place of the throttle handle and the cable. The sun was quickly making its way to bed. Night comes fast in the tropics, and not just in the jungle. We had barely an hour before dark. Ti yanked on the starter cord, charging the air with a roar. While he kept the engine running, the rest of us loaded on the plastic jugs of gasoline.

At thirty and fifty gallons each, the jugs were beasts. I didn't relish the idea of trying to balance them while filling the dinghy's gas tank from them during a high-speed crossing, which is what Knight had planned. The jugs made a second deck, amidships, causing the dinghy to sink even deeper in the water. If we came up against any rough weather we'd be sunk!

"What was wrong?" I asked when Ti and Pi were done.

"No problem!" Pi said.

"Shouldn't be any problem. What do you think?" Knight asked.

"No problem" I said. Ti and Pi laughed. Knight raised an eyebrow, and I hoped that the Vietnamese would not be too brutal with us when they nabbed us.

The dinghy ready to go, Knight ran over to the wheelhouse, and returned with two walkie-talkies. Knight gave Pi and Ti a crash course in radio communications and then signaled me that it was time to go. He climbed in the dinghy with me and took the wheel.

Ti handed me the throttle cord, and after shaking my hand he re-boarded the mother boat. Eerily, the scene seemed to me like that of a NASA technician shaking the hand of an astronaut, just before they shut the hatch on a Apollo capsule readying for countdown.

"Ready?" Knight asked.

I nodded.

"Start the engine."

I yanked on the cord, the engine roared to life, and Pi exploded into crazy laughter. He danced up and down on the deck of the fishing boat, and then gave a thumbs up sign. "You clazy! Clazy muddha-fucka! Clazy!"

Holding back my own laugh, I returned an excited thumbs up and a wave. Pi joined Ti in a somber wave, yelling, "Good luck! Get much treasure!"

It didn't take more than a couple minutes to speed out of earshot. In five minutes they were gone in the twilight. I closed my eyes and clenched my fist as though my life depended on it. *This is it; three days and we'll be outa here*, I told myself, arrogantly thinking like Knight—that it would be as easy as the voyage from Thailand. No sooner had we lost Ti and Pi in the dark than the engine stuttered. Then it died!

"Oh Christ!" Our wide eyes mirrored each others'.

"Get it going again!" Knight bleated. I was already out of my seat and rushing for it. My ears were pounding—it was the blood from my wildly thumping heart trying to escape through my eardrums. After a couple deep breaths, and crossing myself for luck, I yanked the starter cord. So much for begged luck; the engine only farted.

"Please God, please God, please God!" One yank. One more yank. And again, and again. Twenty yanks later, I was exhausted. A painful feeling swirled in the bottom of my gut. "Jesus Christ! How 'bout lending a hand, Richard!"

"Oh, okay." We traded places, and Knight had a go at the engine, silhouetted against a starry sky. Ten tries later he lay back and cursed God.

"We'll try and call Ti and Pi," Knight said as he grabbed the stowed walkie-talkie, and extended the antennae. "Hello, One. . . Hello, One...This is Two."

There was no answer except the doubts and despair screaming in my mind.

He pushed the speak button again, paused, then, "Hello, One...Hello, One...This is Two." He let the button go, the two of us hanging on the radio static. He pushed the button and shouted, "Answer!"

I jumped in my seat.

"What do you think we should do?"

He took in a loud and trembling breath, then answered, "We'll give the engine another try and then see what we can do in the morning."

"Where's the flashlight? I'll see what I can do."

"Over here," he said as we traded places. He got it from somewhere up in the bow and reached it back to me.

Back at the stern, I popped the engine cover and turned on the flashlight, hiding the glow with my body, so hopefully no one on Hon Nam Du could see it. Revealed to me was a puzzle that with my meager knowledge of engines I could only fiddle with. I wished that I had learned more about motors from those dropouts in the Carlmont High School parking lot, so I could magically breath life into this dead engine. Pulling and pushing all the moveable pieces in the same way a chimpanzee might, I yanked on the cord so many times that the apparent futility finally got to me. Out of energy, I finally flicked off the flashlight and plopped down on my back.

"Give it a rest, Fred. Let's trade," he repeated my efforts, and then he too plopped down, exhausted. He lay there, his belly silhouetted against the clear night sky, like the fabled mounds in ancient Irish and Scottish mythology. Wishing for a moment that Knight's belly was just such a magical mound, and that if I were to sit on it like the Celtic hero Cuchulainn, I might be visited by a wise wizard from the Otherworld, one who might lead us to safety.

But this was no myth, and there was no getting out of our predicament this night. I curled up in the bow against a chill that had come on suddenly. Never in my life had I felt so alone. Now I really understood how Columbus and other adventurers must have felt when they were so far away from home. Knight said, "We'll get some sleep now, and give another try in the morning."

"Okay, Richard." I closed my eyes and wondered which was to be our end: Thai pirates in the Gulf, armed Vietnamese waiting on the beach, or a hammerhead shark circling the boat, waiting for us to roll off the dinghy in our sleep.

* * *

I squinted at my wristwatch. It was 9 a.m. Yet another tropical late sleep headache throbbed at my temples. What with the sun and the featureless sea—except for the tops of Phu Quoc and Hon Nam Du—it was as though we were in a desert.

Knight was already awake. A sullen gaze on his face, his mind was in some far distant place, farther away than the furthest horizon. The bright, cheery white and yellow of the cocktail ornament upon which were we floating was really getting on my nerves, like someone trying to cheer me up when I would prefer to sulk. I glared at Phu Quoc as Pi's last words echoed in my head: "You clazy! Clazy muddah fucka! Clazy!" Shaking myself out of it, I stretched, only to recoil from a sudden sharp pain in my back, the result of sleeping like a contortionist amongst the equipment.

"So what's the plan, Richard?"

"I've been thinking about a few possibilities," he answered. Knight's lack of optimism and enthusiasm surprised me, I'd never seen him so accepting of a sentence of death.

"We could row, or wait until the water takes us in."
Neither sounded inviting.

"I've been watching the island." He motioned over his shoulder at Phu Quoc with his chin. "It hasn't changed position. I think we're moving out to sea. If we could just land, then we could dump all our equipment, and present ourselves as castaways to the authorities. But, we could be on a current headed for Australia." Actually, we'd be hitting Borneo, or Indonesia long before Australia; but, that was geography according to Knight.

Weeks or months at sea in this floating coffin definitely had no appeal. "What about rowing?"

"We've got one oar, and the shovel for digging up the treasure."

"Let's give it a try." At least the hypnotic rhythm of rowing would take our minds off our predicament.

"Okay, . . here," He handed me the shovel. Keeping the oar for himself, he took the starboard side. His cushioned seat must have been comfortable. My seat was a plastic gasoline container which cut the circulation in my legs, making them numb. Rowing with the wide-bladed spade, I quickly tired. Knight paddled as lightly as though he were floating down the Thames. Finally, after twenty minutes, Knight offered to use the spade. Five minutes later, Knight clanked the spade against the side one last time.

"Let's give it a rest," he said.

He crawled into the bow which afforded some shade. The heat from the sun had changed from hot to unbearable. We floated along helplessly on what I still considered more a cocktail ornament than anything else. Fear that had set in the night before prostrated me with fatigue. There was no large amount of drinking water, no escape. Our only hope was that useless outboard.

"Mind if I give it another try?"

Knight looked over at me and grinned half-heartedly. Removing the top cover of the engine, I fidgeted with it like I had the night before, but now there was a cognitive curiosity to my method, a method of deduction. Within minutes I had deduced that all the other thingamajigs had nothing to do with the throttle. I reached for one last piece that I had noticed Ti fiddling with the night before. It was the fuel control, and it went over easily into the full open position. With one yank of the cord, the engine started. "Yahoo! Richard!"

Knight was already getting up as I spun around to face him at the end of my quick jig. A look of bewilderment and a smile of joy covered his face. Catching up with the action, he stumbled about by the steering console. He was too impatient to take my suggestion that we wait until the cover of darkness to approach the island. "Kee–keep it going, Fred!"

"A-okay," I answered over the putter of the engine. "Are you ready to go?"

Knight nodded excitedly from his seat behind the wheel, and I slammed the shift lever forward. The boat leapt, almost sending me over the side. Regaining my balance, I took out all the slack on the twine, and made my way over the gasoline jugs to my seat next to Knight.

"What did you do?!" he asked, as we quickly went to full power.

"I just fiddled around with a lever on the engine. It must control the fuel intake somehow," I yelled over the engine's roar.

"What?"

I waved him off, not wanting to repeat myself, preferring rather to feel the full exhilaration of speed. It was a rush flying along on an open throttle, especially after having been restricted to such strained immobility. My smile lingered at least a couple of miles. Color shades became more defined on the islands as we sped closer to them. Burnt olive turned to a mosaic of light and dark, browns and greens.

"There's a naval base on Phu Quoc. They've got a radar station there. It used to be American during the war," Knight shouted, to be heard over the wind. "But we should be safe from the radar," he added, obviously aware of the apprehension that hit me.

"What about the patrol boats?"

The engine died, and I was once again doing the investigation dance over the fuel jugs. Thankfully, it wasn't anything that I hadn't already dealt with. The fuel control had slid over. Drawing my USMC Ka-Bar knife from its scabbard on my belt, I used it to move the control over again and jam it in place. Another yank on the cord and we were once more speeding along.

"Should be there in only a few hours, don't you think?" I asked, while slipping on my tiger-stripe field jacket. Pulling out my cassette player, and balancing against the jolting waves, I inserted *The Eagles' Greatest Hits 1971-1975*. The dinghy bounced to the beat of *One of These Nights* as we came to a point directly between Phu Quoc and Paulo Domo. It was an exciting beat, both the song and the rush of my heart. Knight looked at me, grinned and nodded his approval at our speed. His grin faltered as a sail came into view, then another, and then a third! Knight veered wide and to the right towards Paulo Panjang. Our course brought us around wide enough to evade them, just in time to spy another boat coming up on our right.

"Crikey!" Knight yelped as the engine died again.

I ripped off my earphones, and scrambled back to learn that the fuel control was still in the same position. Knocking on the fuel can, I heard the sound of emptiness. "Gas, gas!" I said as I picked up one of the jugs.

Surfing with a tapir in my lap would have been easier than pouring fuel out of that thirty gallon container into the small opening of the five gallon steel tank. But I took three deep breaths and felt another surge of adrenaline that filled me with strength. Still, the rocking of the small waves made me spill the gasoline all over my legs, soaking my socks and sneakers. Much of it ended up on the bottom of the dinghy, turning into pink waxy globs floating on the saltwater we'd taken in. Some even happened to go into the gas can. Carefully, I set the half-full plastic container back down. After screwing the top back on the engine's tank, and squeezing the gas line pump, I looked up to see Knight nervously dragging on a cigarette.

"Put that fuckin' thing out!" I yelled, yanking the butt out of his mouth and tossing it over the side. "I'm soaked to the skin in gasoline and you're gonna smoke a fuckin' cigarette?!"

He stared at me, apparently unsure as to what to say, and rightly ashamed. We shared no words for the rest of the boat ride in.

"There are the islands!" Knight said, pointing ahead. In the distance, just off the bow, lay a group of small islands. Beyond them was what seemed to be a larger island. Cambodia.

"Man, nobody's going to believe me back home! . . And what did you do for your summer vacation, Freddy? Why, I sneaked into Vietnam!" I said, imitating memories of my elementary school essays about summer.

Knight gave me a queer look, but flashed a grin and an emphatic thumbs up. We arrived at the islands, circling wide, and in those ten minutes I felt the true intense excitement that I was searching for: the sun and wind on my face; the sea; the warmth and beauty of it all concentrated into small, intensely iridescent moments of time.

There was a village on the south side of Grand Pirate Island. A more immediate danger floated just off the starboard bow. What did that old fisherman, hand-lining for fish from his dugout canoe, think? A conical Vietnamese hat covered his head, hiding his expression. *Tourists!* He probably would have hissed ten years ago.

"Wave!" Knight said. I didn't know what to do, so I did. If I had been more assertive and confident, I would have demanded that Knight turn the boat around and get us the hell out of Dodge!

The fisherman waved back.

Knight didn't seem to realize what had just happened: we had been seen arriving in broad daylight. He was just high on his own excitement. Knowing that we had been seen, my thoughts turned heavy, making me want to crawl out of my skin, making me wish I had some kind of magic wand and that all I had to do was wave it over us, and we would magically turn into inconspicuous Vietnamese fishermen. We might as well have been a Bob Hope road show, scantily-clad girls hanging off the gunwales, waving and giggling at the locals, with two blondes trailing on skis behind us. We couldn't have stood out more. I just knew we were about to be screwed horribly, so I checked my watch to remember the exact time. It was 3:30 p.m., June 16th. Hard to tell the expression on the fisherman's face as it was hidden by his conical hat, but he just kept jigging his hand line as we left him behind.

The western tip of Grand Pirates Island lay barely a mile ahead. A white sand spit, thirty yards long, jutted out from the jungle-covered island, with a few mangrove trees growing on the tip of the point. Knight steered around, a hundred yards off. Continuing past, we saw some houses on the north side. These were built of brick and stucco, not bamboo shacks standing on stilts like on the other side. The stucco houses were a beautiful postal blue, Chinese pagoda style.

"Look!" Knight pointed down into the water. We decreased our speed to a crawl. Just below the surface of the water was a boulder the size of a baby elephant. Just like on Kidd's map—but not on the satellite photos because they only offered a surface view. My eyes turned wide in my stare at Knight—*this is Treasure Island! This is Kidd's island!*

"This is part of the submerged rock reef that goes around the north cove in Kidd's map." Knight joined me in the same amazement.

It was incredible. Up to this point, whether Knight's version was true or not, I had a story. With this new evidence, I was completely convinced that the madman was right. I envisioned articles in *National Geographic*, articles with Richard and me as great explorers, the treasure spread out before us on a table in Manila. Dad would read of my accomplishment; he'd had a subscription since the 1940's.

Knight steered in a circle, bringing us back inside the white sand spit. One last thrust of the engine brought the bow up on the beach. Running a line to a coconut palm, we tried dragging the dinghy further up the sand. Both of us barely moved it a couple inches.

After three tries, we finally fell on our butts in the wet sand to rest. Knight stood up and searched inside the boat for a green tarp. He planned to use it to camouflage the boat! I couldn't help scoffing and asking him how serious he was about his intentions.

He threw me the other corner and said, "Take the other side!"

Not only was it fluorescent green, but it didn't even cover half the dinghy! I was beyond worrying: it was though I were already out of my body, looking down and thinking to myself, "WOW— unbelievable! *C'est la vie.*"

Knight compromised and draped it over the stern. The hope was to hide it from boats traveling by. For added cover, Knight draped a small homemade Vietnamese flag over it. He had me sew the yellow star on a small red rectangle of cloth during the voyage over. For those who don't have a close personal connection or history with Vietnam, or seem to think that a flag is just a bunch of colors on a piece of cloth, it might be hard to understand why I detested the duty if for no other reason than I had to touch that symbol of repression.

To shed some light on why South Vietnamese refugees, and those who haven't forgotten that Ho Chi Minh had envisioned Communist domination from the very start, hate that flag (all the way back to 1930 when that banner was the official flag of the Indo-Chinese Communist Party), let's clarify what the five points of the star represent: the three historical areas of Vietnam (Tonkin, Annam, and Cochin); plus Cambodia and Laos. Even in 1930, Uncle Ho had his own plans to replace the French Imperialists with himself. Contrast that meaning with the original flag of the Republic of Vietnam that was three red horizontal stripes on a yellow background, recognized by the United Nations from 1950 until 1975, the flag that soon came to represent the Republic of South Vietnam from 1954 until the fall of Saigon. That flag represented *only* the three regions of a unified Vietnam: North, South and Central. No intention of annexing two other nations. Had I known that I would soon share a re-education prison with those who fell under the control of the gold-starred flag and the Resolution 49-NQTVQH it represented (The resolution enacted on June 20, 1961 basically stated that everyone not toeing the party line be "concentrated for re-education." Originally it was designed to throw all personnel under Bao Dai, plus those discontented with the new Marxist-Leninist regime, namely Buddhist monks, Catholic priests, lay Catholics, *bourgeois* capitalists, and intellectuals left in North Vietnam after the 1954 Geneva Accord, into labor camps), I *absolutely* would have refused Knight's request.

With the camouflaging and flag laying done, we began exploring the near terrain, and found a deserted, run-down shack just a few yards from the beach. It must have been a vacation house at one time. There was a concrete foundation, but the other sections had turned into a heap of rotted beams with the corroded remnants of a tin roof.

My stomach grumbled as I noticed the fresh green coconuts above us. Deciding to go after them, I prepared a rope to aid the climb, a technique island natives use to retrieve coconuts. It involves using the rope as a brace to help one walk up the trunk, like a logger, except without spiked boots. What a lesson in futility for someone as out of shape and stiff as me. It sure looked easy when I was an eleven-year-old, watching a villager accomplish the feat during a summer vacation in Indonesia.

Knight got a laugh out of my attempts. All of them ended in falls. The third try put me within a yard of the coconuts. After another drop into the sand, a fifteen-foot fall, my ankle throbbed painfully from a sprain.

Knight suggested we see if there was a path to the north cove.

* * *

Knight was no help. I'd been digging all by myself from the moment we finished clearing brush and breaking ground. That was an hour ago and almost six feet into the ground.

"Hurry, Fred. It's getting dark."

"Who am I, your pit bitch? I'm a goddamn photojournalist for Christsake!"

"What's that?" Knight said, as I picked up another shovel-full of dirt and not so accidentally tossed it his way. "Watch it will you?" he said, as he kicked the dirt off his sandal.

I grinned as I raised the shovel again, and drove the tip deep. The answering thud was deafening.

"Did you hit something?"

"No way!" I said, as I quickly set about for another shovel-full. This time there was the snapping of wood and chink of metal against metal. With a quick scrape, I saw what I thought was the dim gleam of gold.

"Oh my God! It's the chest!" Knight whispered, as if anyone were within earshot and not at least as far as the other side of the island.

I knelt down and got hold of a small piece of dark wood. It almost fell to pieces when I tugged. "It's…true!" I said, as I gazed at the revealed small mound of gold coins and jade pieces.

Knight said."Cover it up! Cover it up!"

"—What?"

He said, "We'll come back tomorrow."

"Bullshit, Richard let's grab what we can carry, take it down to the boat, and get the hell out of here!"

"We've got two more caches to dig up."

"Your greed's going to get us killed, Knight! We're asking for it by staying one minute longer. Let's get outta here!" I said, and reached for my camera, taking a couple quick photos of the treasure.

"Cover it up," he said. Before climbing out of the hole, I did so, but not after having grabbed a coin and hidden it away in the pocket of my cut-offs.

Most everyone I can think of would be completely elated were it they who had just found that treasure. Personally, I was totally depressed. During no other time in my life had I ever had something so wanted be shown to me, and know it would soon to be yanked from my ever seeing it again. No more present in my mind was that fisherman hand-lining off his boat and returning our wave. It was all too easy to imagine him on the other side of the island telling the militia commander that two American spies had just landed.

Elephant grass slicing my bare legs aside, the return descent wasn't much easier than the climb. From my north-facing position, I photographed the sunset that looked, appropriately enough, like a phoenix, fire wings stretched out along the horizon. Finished with the last of the roll of black and white, I quickly loaded another by feel, pleased that practice had enabled me do so without shifting my sight from what I planned to shoot. Photo opportunities followed of the different steep landscapes of Grand Pirate Island, Cambodia, and Vietnam. They were average pictures, but pictures that easily could have been construed as military reconnaissance photos. If I had known how incriminating they would be to me in the future, I would probably have taken more shots of Knight, but Knight was an uninteresting subject and was doing nothing to merit a photo as he strolled, shovel in hand. I continued on with my shots of the coast. To the northwest rolled the mountains of Cambodia. Vietnam lay twelve miles to the north, a dark, gray-green. Silhouetted against the silver, burnt-orange light reflected off the water, sailed a small, fifteen-foot dugout trimaran. I enjoyed how photography could take mind off my most depressing thoughts about impending capture.

"Man, I'm going to start a resort here, when the country opens up again...If I get out of here alive." Postcard-perfect, the island was for romance, not danger. What a waste it was that no one was able to visit this beautiful island because it had the bad luck of being controlled by a Stalinist-style government. Ironically, it was the forbidden notice set in place by the government that had protected the pristine quality of Grand Pirate Island while other islands around the Gulf were taking on the look of roadside trash left by inconsiderate tourists and resort owners.

"Get down!" Knight hissed, as he noticed the dugout sailing around the point. I crouched down in the grass, though I didn't see the point. They were coming from Ha Tien, surely Knight must have realized they had already seen us. With my face down to keep the sunset from illuminating my face against the green grass, like I had done for years to keep mallards from noticing me in a duck blind, I listened as he whispered, "We've got to keep hidden."

I wanted to yell, *well, no shit!* But, I distracted my attention by studying the cracks in the dry dirt between the grass roots. Knight was beyond reason. If he weren't, I would have pressed him to just get back in the boat and salvage all that we had left: our lives. Twirling a blade of grass I had snapped off close to its root, I thought of what to tell the Vietnamese when they captured us.

"You've really got to be more careful, Fred," he said, as the boat sailed around the sandy point, barely fifty yards from our dinghy.

"Richard, if he saw anything, it was our boat."

He ignored me and walked past, leading the way back to the beach.

Moon and stars appeared in the dark purple light of evening. Richard opened a can of Spam and offered me half. Not being Polynesian or Hawaiian-born, I had never really nurtured a craving for the cold, fatty meat that sluggishly slid down my throat, helped along by a couple swigs of water. But it was all we had. We didn't even have any spices to do some food doctoring—I would have given anything for a sliver of chili pepper from our mother boat. Knight finished the other half and offered me some Vegemite, an Australian concoction made from the yeast residue of the beer-making process. He loved his Vegemite. My dislike of its bitter taste hadn't improved since my first experience with it in Singapore. He helped himself to a heaping spoonful. With the sudden thought that this might actually be my last meal on this planet, I became very sullen.

We ate quietly as we sat facing each other on the cool sand. Above, palms loomed, slender monsters with long fangs silhouetted against the moonlight. The beach, though, looked very peaceful, the dark shape of our dinghy resting on the silver sand. Knight and I whispered good night to each other, and separated. He lay down where we had eaten under the coconut palms. A search for a place to sleep led me up from the beach to a patch of waist-high grass, barely thirty yards from Knight and the dinghy. My field jacket spread out over the grass, created a comfortable sleeping mat.

Suddenly, I had the urge to run, run until I was out of breath, run until I arrived home safely—a good little college boy. I fought the urge by telling myself I was in the jungle once again, in a safe place. Jungles, after all, used to be my playgrounds in Singapore. If anyone was out of place it was Knight, and considering what I now thought of him, I took comfort in that. Sitting down on the jacket I tore a blade of grass from the ground, and frayed the ends with my worries.

For some reason I can't explain, other than perhaps it was reassurance that all we had done, and all I was sure would happen, would make sense, I pulled the coin from my pocket and held it up to the moonlight. Gold is amazing! And I mean real gold, not that plated, or low content, offering in most jewelry shops. I mean the kind of gold so pure that its softness easily takes a handstamp. It felt good as I twirled it between my fingers. Then, I put it back in my pocket. Having calmed what I hoped were the last urges of fear, I closed my eyes.

I never have been able to sleep on my back—subconscious protection, some say—but I did that night, completely open and relinquished to the future, or lack of it. Everything was so peaceful. Soft light illuminated the area. Small waves, washing the sand behind me. A breeze from the south lightly caressed my face, and filled my nostrils with its cool saltiness. My fears made my heart jump with one last apprehension, the memory of the old Vietnamese fisherman handlining from his canoe. I thought about all the possibilities and prayed that if this was the end, that the ambush would be quick and painless. I worked hard to concentrate on the waves; there would be rest in them taking me away.

Part Two

Vietnam

Chapter 11

"The test of an adventure is that when you're in the middle of it, you say to yourself, 'Oh, now I've got myself into an awful mess; I wish I were sitting quietly at home.' And the sign that something's wrong with you is when you sit quietly at home wishing you were out having lots of adventure."— Thornton Wilder

Capture

It was still night when I stirred. The full moon shone high above. And I was restlessly dreaming of my childhood in Singapore, about days and evenings adventuring after school. We set many traps then, in the elephant grass near our neighborhood. My friends and I would flip a coin to see who would be the Japanese or the American GI's, the heroes of our fathers who thought America's last good war was WWII. I'd always flip the coin in the hope of being my comic-book hero, *Sergeant Rock*. It was a carefree time. Dad's warnings of no Air Force commission or flight school if I didn't develop good study habits in middle school, went unheeded. Concentration was not one of my natural abilities at that time, except maybe when we hunted the imaginary enemy and shot them with our plastic toy guns. It was only a game back then; people didn't really die.

In the blackness, the enemy moved out from behind a tree. *That must be Jimmy Ellis*, I thought. *He was always a short kid.* Jimmy brought up his toy gun and fired a burst over my head, shattering my dream!

"You've got us! You've got us!" I heard Richard Knight scream.

I was wide awake now, but it would be a few years before I would receive the proper training that would teach me that the first five seconds can decide the outcome of an ambush, or an escape. After all, the Vietnamese didn't know where I was. Their tracers were not only flying into the sky in shockingly beautiful red and green streaks, but also into the brush just beyond me. Had I been trained, I would have quickly rolled onto my belly, slithered my way over to the water and swam over to one of the nearby islands. I would then have waited for an opportune time to steal one of the small fishing boats that surely would be moored at the village on the other side of the island. But as yet, I didn't have the solid training in escape and evasion. As though testing hot water, I raised my hands and stood up.

Three dark figures encircled me, jabbing the muzzles of their assault weapons at my face. One of them came round behind me and bound my elbows. The twine cut into my elbows as he yanked on it. Another one rifled through my pockets. And another said some heated words in Vietnamese and pointed toward the water. And yet another nudged me with the butt of his gun. I tripped and fell, driving my face into the sand and hard grass roots. If that wasn't painful enough, the sand that lodged in my left eye would be a maddening source of irritation for days. Two of the men yanked me back to my feet and directed me forward again, a little more compassionately this time, with a not-so-friendly young militiaman behind me who repeatedly nudged me with the muzzle of his AK-47. I tripped a couple times, and suddenly became acutely aware that the militiaman's index finger was resting on the trigger, and his weapon's safety was off. All it would take would be one trip on his part and I'd be zipped up the middle by a burst of copper and lead. Finally, he stopped me at the water's edge and then he yelled out into the darkness, as though calling someone.

"Where are you taking us?"

He ignored me.

A dark mass offshore caught my eye, a mass blocking the light of the moon and stars reflecting off the slowly rolling ripples of the Thai Gulf. The dark mass grew larger and larger until it took the shape of a Vietnamese fishing boat, similar in size and shape to our thirty-foot Thai fishing boat, except it was piloted with an open tiller instead of a housed steering wheel.

Tied to the Vietnamese fishing boat was a small canoe, shallow like a Cajun's pirogue, but wider and with oarlocks amidships. Someone on board disembarked from the fishing boat and started rowing towards us in the canoe. Dark and mysterious, it was as though Charon were rowing across the river Styx to come and take me to hell. Suddenly, a commotion erupted behind me. Knight was spotlighted in the middle of the coconut grove by flashlight beams. Around him circled the silhouetted forms of armed looters tossing our equipment in the air, searching for something that wasn't there. The angered look in the face of the young militiaman who guarded me was a perfect reflection of his cohorts' actions.

"Where are you going to take us?" I asked.

He yelled and kicked my left leg out from under me. I fell, the twine cutting deeply enough into my elbows to draw the sting of blood.

He motioned for me to stay down by sticking his AK-47 in my face. I didn't move, I didn't twitch. I just lay patiently for the vomit of fear to subside. A few minutes passed and the canoe beached right in front of us. Stepping out of the boat, the oarsman came over and helped the guardsman get me to my feet. It was tricky at first for they were so short and I was so heavy, and we kept sinking into the sand.

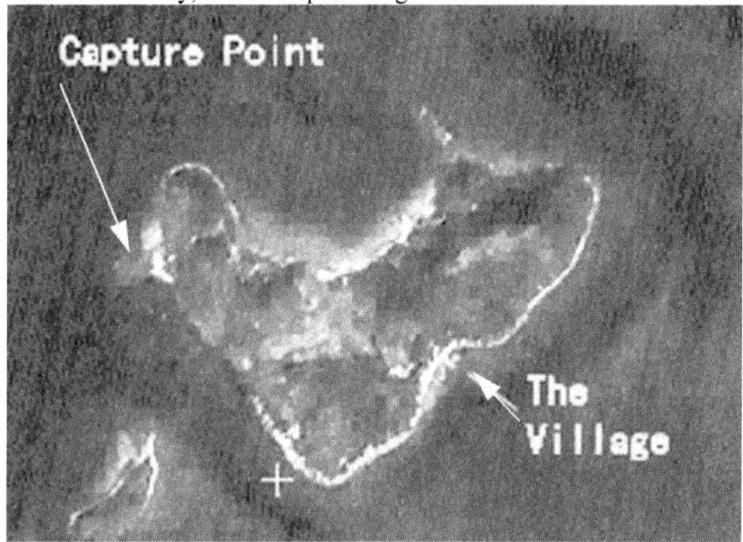

DIA satellite photo of Grand Pirate Island

When we got to the water it was refreshingly cool, and for a split second took my mind off the danger at hand. The militiamen rushed into the canoe and motioned for me to quickly sit down. What was cool and refreshing for my feet, was very uncomfortable for my crotch as the two inches of water in the bottom of the Vietnamese pirogue soaked my shorts. The young militiaman took his place at the bow and his kept his weapon trained on me, along with a hard look of contempt. We started backing our way out to the fishing boat, while two guards led Knight down the beach. I wanted to wave to him and tell him I was okay, and make sure that he was, too.

When we got to the larger boat, three militiamen on the large fishing boat reached down and pulled me in by dragging me on my belly over the splintered gunwale and onto the rough deck.

"Hey, what's the big idea, you assholes!" I screamed, feeling as though I'd been dragged by an automobile over asphalt.

Without warning, the belligerent militiaman who had watched me on the ride in the canoe, came up from behind and gun-butted me with his AK-47. Trying to reach for the sudden dull pain at the right side of my head, I fell to the ground. A warm wetness ran down my temple. The unmistakable iron smell of blood made me woozy. I was lucky that I had caught his movement out of the corner of my eye, and that I was beginning my evasion right before he hit me. The strike was only glancing. A direct blow would have killed me, or atleast slowed my cognitive ability. I yelled more insults, as I tried to wriggle my arms free from their bindings to protect my head from the blows I was sure would come. When he lifted his AK-47 for another blow, making me flinch, my thoughts were in such disarray that all I could manage this time was a primal yelp.

One of the other two men who were on the boat jumped at the assaulting militiaman and blocked his AK. "Stay away from me, you motherfucker!" Tears filled my eyes as I flipped on my back and tried scooting away like an inchworm. "God. . . I WANT TO KILL YOU!"

The militiaman who had defended me grabbed a rag and came to my side. Before he touched it to the side of my head he dipped it in a can of something. I smelled the gasoline before I myself felt it, and it burned like a red-hot poker. "What are you doing?!" I asked as I recoiled from the sting.

The man raised his hand and smiled, trying to pacify me by speaking softly to me in Vietnamese. At first, I wanted to punch him, but the tone of his foreign words soothed me. It soon became clear that he was simply disinfecting my wound.

Angry words were shouted by the guard who had clubbed me. The man assisting me yelled his own angry words back. In a huff, the man who had hit me stomped off to the bow.

The militiaman next to me put his hand on my shoulder and said more comforting words in Vietnamese. I wished for my past fluency in Vietnamese, attained as a child in Saigon, but I could only smile weakly, my eyebrows heavy and quivering from the pain—one beat puppy!

After a bit of silence that seemed long because of the glares leveled on me by some of the militia, especially the angry one, I heard the splashing of oars come closer to the boat. The men rushed to the side and shortly thereafter pulled Knight up onto the deck. They plopped him next to me on the center deck, and for a moment he looked just like a freshly caught fish on the deck of that fishing vessel. I savored the only light moment I had on the boat that night by turning my head away for a stolen smile.

Knight worked his way into a sitting position and asked me if I was alright. I nodded, and then the angry one rushed at us, yelling at us with gestures that demanded that Knight and I keep to ourselves.

* * *

Smiles, proddings, and questions greeted us after we motored the route around to the village on the south side of Grand Pirate Island. Small, and consisting almost completely of bamboo huts, the village seemed to have been there a long time. I was happy when the one who hit me disappeared along with the boat that had carried us over. When someone who seemed to be the island commander made gestures for us to follow him, the crowd parted as he led us to a small shack. It seemed to be one of only five huts with electricity. In the room was a bench and a strip of fluorescent lights. I chuckled because the light caused Knight's speckled red hair to glow.

No one spoke English, but Knight was fluent in French and a couple of the villagers also spoke French. Even those who knew only a few words of the language tried to get in on the act.

"Why are you here?" asked one of the men who had introduced himself as a college student on leave from a university on the mainland.

"Treasure," Knight said. "There's a large treasure." The college student translated this to everyone in the room, which was now full of villagers. The villagers went between gasping and chatting elatedly amongst themselves.

Knight then drew a map of Grand Pirate Island on the dirt floor and marked the first cache with an "X". With a hard look on his face, the officer glanced at the map and then back at us as the student translated rapidly with him. I expected the militiaman who went through my pockets to chime in, but he remained silent, even trying to back into the shadows. I motioned to him with my chin, and said, "He took a coin from my pocket!"

Knight's eyes went wide. And they may not have been able to speak English, but they sure must have understood it. The officer yelled at the thief, who then quickly left the room, followed by two of his comrades. The officer then gestured for Knight to continue his explanation—I never saw the one who took the coin again.

While they talked I slowly slipped my bindings off my arms. Knight noticed my actions and scowled. I wanted to tell him to fuck off, but instead said, "They hurt."

One of the guards standing by the officer noticed, too, and helped me get the rope off. He then helped Knight with his. The officer left the room and disappeared for what seemed an hour. I assumed he went to call someone on the mainland.

During our time there, I developed a better understanding of the villagers and their views of us. One of the women had seen me combing my hair with my fingers. She pointed at my hair, spoke some Vietnamese and then disappeared. She quickly reappeared with a comb and hand mirror. I took them and combed my hair. The villagers smiled. Women pointed at our eyes and giggled.

"Your eyes are blue and green like the sea," the student said. We laughed. Suddenly one of the boys who had been hiding behind his mother's leg ran up and touched me on the arm. As the boy ran back to his mother, the rest of the villagers broke into laughter again. I felt like the first white man to arrive in Vietnam.

"Have you a wife?" asked one of the middle-aged men, through the translator.

I shook my head, and, in the French of my childhood, said, "I have a girlfriend." Erika's deep blue eyes flashed in my mind, making me wish I was with her in Australia. As though matchmakers, the Vietnamese pointed at their younger women and me, and making the hand gestures of two people joining.

"I had a wife," Knight said. "She lives in Paris."

"Ah, Paris," said one a man with crew-cut white hair. "Have you lived there?"

"I was an actor in Paris," Knight said. "I studied under Marcel Marceau."

The old man's eyebrows rose, and he smiled.

Suddenly the officer returned and along with him a gray cloud. He talked with the translator, who then came over to us, and smiled, "You go Saigon."

* * *

Knee-deep in the water, I watched as the militia loaded most of our equipment on board—one of the militia had already pocketed my Canon AE-1. Knight stood at the gunwales and watched, also. The old man in shorts and undershirt who had recognized Marcel Marceau stared at me. He made me nervous. He was no longer the jovial and talkative French speaker back in the village. He didn't say a word: he just stared! Initially, I thought it was because I didn't have enough command of French to keep a conversation going with him. But, now I wasn't so sure. Every once in a while I would look around at the villagers and my eyes would run across him. He just kept silent and continued staring. I was happy when the last of our equipment was stowed, and we were ordered aboard.

Finally, he spoke, in French, "Are you American?"

It was the same question he had asked Knight and me when we were back in the hut. Knight had lied then—"English!"

I smiled as I nodded to the old man and said, "Oui, je suis américain."

"Oh. . . Au revoir, monsieur. . ." he said, which seemed such an oxymoron considering the literal translation is "see you again," and he had such a compassionately sad expression I could only imagine giving a man headed for the gallows.

* * *

The morning was chilly and filled with the scent of cook-stove smoke. I awoke to see we were anchored in the canal that follows Highway 8A between Rach Gia and Ha Tien. It could easily have been a scene from one of the many paintings on lacquered wood sold to tourists in Saigon. Graceful, tall alder and willow-like trees reached down to the water. Ducks swam single file up the canal following their master, slowing only to evade, or ride out, an eddy or ripple in the current. Every once in a while there was the stereotypical Vietnamese pirogue-canoe carrying the gawking passenger. But, while everyone else was in motion, we were stuck: our large diesel engine had died. The sun had not come up yet, so the monster mosquitoes were still prowling, enjoying their bloody feast on two plump Caucasians. As for the Vietnamese, they were either being ignored, or they were inured to being eaten alive.

"Oh man!" I said, and slapped a mosquito. "This is RIDICULOUS! When's the sun going to come up and get rid of these frigging blood suckers?!"

"They are annoying, aren't they?" Knight said calmly, his face pale with the expression of someone having something more pressing on his mind than our curse of a thousand pricks and itches. Popping out of his thoughts he said, "By the way I don't think we should tell the Vietnamese that we met through Everingham."

"I was thinking the same." It definitely wouldn't have been prudent for the Vietnamese to know that my friend and mentor had been brought up on charges of espionage by Hanoi's puppet regime in Laos. What Knight and I should have done was also come up with a believable story.

Our relief from stagnant air and mosquitoes came in about two hours, in the form of a light breeze above the swampy horizon in front of us. And then the hill to the north of us seemed to catch fire with bizarre reds and browns as the sun broke the horizon. The morning revealed the dry soil of the area that looked like dried blood. The reddish-brown of the earth created an eerie feeling, as that earth had been stained by silos full of blood from the millions who had died in this land's thousands of years of war—Khmer, Viets, Chinese, Thais, Degar, Soviets, French, Japanese, North Koreans, ROKs[18], Aussies, Kiwis, Americans.

The temperature soon changed from comfortably cool to tortuously hot. People collected on the northern bank. They sat there like people at a roadside bus stop; but, instead of a bus, another large boat rounded the levee. The boat picked up the people and then our pilot waved it over. Using ropes from both boats, they brought our boat up alongside the ferry and fastened them together.

Passengers on the ferry couldn't control their curiosity no matter how they tried. They sat in their seats, looking away at first, but always returning to peeking at us. Knight tried smiling at all the passengers to keep them from thinking we were monsters. The passengers would occasionally, very cautiously return his smile. Whenever they were caught giving us too much attention, the commander would yell at them to look away. As more passengers boarded, the commander felt we were drawing too much attention. He ordered us down a deck hatch.

Inside, the only light was from a crack in the closed hatch. There were a couple of inches of water inside, through which we splashed in our stumble over the boat's ribs to the driest area. Knight and I thought that the bow would afford some sanctuary from the water, but this turned out not to be true. We tried napping on the boat's ribs after he edged me into the bow. I curled up in the tiny space. The boat started moving again. The humidity inside made it hard to breath. Even though the air was cooler inside, I thought I was going to choke on the musty stink of the swamp water. With a yawn, I tried to stretch out, but had room only to curl up into a ball between the uncomfortable ribs of the boat. Only a little while passed before something was crawling in my hair! I reached up and felt for the movement.

"Yaaah!" Something with sticky little legs crawled its way up the back of my hand. I immediately shook my hand as though it was on fire. The creature took flight and flew back to the stern.

"What—what is it, Fred?" Knight asked, roused from his nap.

"It's a fuckin' cockroach!" I answered and scrambled out of the bow.

"Cockroach?" he squeaked.

I calmed and edged slowly back to the bow. Knight fidgeted restlessly after that episode. Sleep became the last thing on my mind, though I needed it. Instead, I lay motionless, my eyes scanning repeatedly for the telltale, coffee-brown shimmer of their wing cases. I thought about the Vietnamese out on deck. I thought about the cockroaches that would surely try to crawl over me again. I thought about the disappointment of us getting captured, and then I hissed through clenched teeth, "Suckers!"

* * *

Rach Gia is the bustling center of commerce for the west coast of Vietnam. Though the officers would have preferred we arrived in the dark, we arrived in the afternoon. We were the town's latest and greatest attraction. I felt like Elvis. After we moored against the concrete wall, the militia commander ordered us off the boat and up the stairs to the road that paralleled the northern bank of the canal that ran right through town and straight into the Gulf. We weren't ready for the blinding sun when we got out of the hold, so we had to help ourselves up the stairs with one hand, while at the same time shielding our eyes with the other.

"Now this is a town!" I said, as I scanned stucco houses that could easily have lined a Paris street. Looking back at the canal, I took in the cluttered trash of boats at anchor in the sluggish, brown water. Canoes, dugouts, fishing boats, and sail dugouts were everywhere, as though there were a traffic jam on the water, while the street was almost empty of automobiles. Coconut palms stood among the buildings. The heavy odor of fermented urine and fruit rose from the sidewalk along the canal, and had I not been made accustomed to the stench by the hours inside the boat's hold, I probably would have gagged. This was the Vietnam of my childhood, seen in trips up river from our launching point at the Club Nautique, at the end of Nguyen Hue Street, to the Club Nautique Annex for water-skiing. There would have been a warm, fuzzy feeling were I not so unsure of what was about to happen to us.

We were led down some dusty red streets to someone's home. All the while the militia shooed away the many curious citizens. When we arrived at the house, we were ordered through gestures to wait in the garage. The one who seemed to be the homeowner came down after being beckoned by a woman in pajamas—in Vietnam, pajamas and rubber thongs are normal home wear, and neighborhood attire for that matter. After a short conversation, the homeowner disappeared in a mad dash upstairs. In their garage, bicycles were leaning in a row against the far wall on the other side of the car. Outside, the continuous ringing of bicycle bells passing by reminded me of downtown Saigon. Before the man returned with his keys, a middle-aged woman in a flowered sleeping gown walked down the stairs, gasped, turned, and ran back upstairs. The man soon appeared with his keys. He took us on an evasive ride through the back streets of Rach Gia to the prison.

Kien Giang Provincial Prison was yet another souvenir from the French, with security turrets at each corner. Its salmon color made it seem as though it sprang from the earth below it in one seamless growth. They dropped us off in front of a giant green iron gate, which was opened by a sentry with a large, clattering ring of keys. I looked back as he closed it behind us, then forward again to face a wall of green-painted iron bars that separated us from a courtyard. We were then directed left into the sergeant of the guard's office.

They ordered us to sit in opposite corners of the doorway. An old woman then gave us each a small, traditional Vietnamese stool. The three-inch-high seat was designed for someone following proper Vietnamese etiquette while sitting, which is really a squat. Limber as a plank, I sat with legs stretched out in front, my back against the corner.

"So how long do you think we'll be here?" I asked Knight.

"Shouldn't think that it'll be that long. They'll keep us here for a few short days and then release us in Saigon, probably."

He gave me a serious look in answer to my stifled scoff. I looked around at the room. An M-16 above a barred window on Knight's wall caught my attention. It hung there like a hunting rifle over the fireplace in an American home of a hundred years ago. More like a trophy than anything else, it was chrome-plated and even had a silver-colored magazine. A fleeting urge to run and grab it and fight my way out of there like Bonny and Clyde was checked by more realistic thoughts such as, *what are they going to do with us?*

The sergeant's entrance broke my idle curiosity. He went between studying us and writing in a large notebook, while the group of guards stood to one side, chatting amongst themselves, and every so often pointing over at either Knight or me. When the old woman who had given us the stools returned, the sergeant closed his notebook, and left.

The old woman handed Knight a pair of gray pajama pants, and a black pair to me in exchange for our clothes. When I pulled the pajama pants up to tie the draw string, the old woman and two guards laughed. The pant legs ended ten inches above my ankles. Everybody else's large bell-bottoms billowed around their feet, like the cuffs of an ancient Mandarin's costume in a Chinese opera. She motioned, as if to say she would look for a longer pair. I never saw that old woman again, nor did I ever receive a longer pair of pants.

We were then taken into the prison yard. It was full of Vietnamese and Thais, and a few darker Khmer. In the center of the square was a large single-story building with barred windows. Prisoners peeked out at us through the iron doorway and the windows. On our left, in a corner, stood a white-walled Buddhist pagoda, adorned on both sides by round windows, each filled with a large swastika.

Before the methamphetamine addict from Hell, Adolf Hitler, stole the swastika and twisted it, literally tilting it on end to fit his demented race theories and *Final Solution*, the swastika was a symbol that originated in India with the Hindus, sitting straight on its flat edge and meaning "peace and well-being" in Sanskrit. Some say the Cham—who had originated in the area of Danang, flourished in the Kingdom of Champa from the second century to the fifteenth, adopted Hinduism, adapted Indian art into their culture and incorporated Sanskrit as their language of religion—had brought the swastika to Vietnam. Others say it was simply Buddhist monks who carried the symbol to Vietnam from China, where the swastika is called "the footprints of Buddha," in depictions of Buddha with a swastika over his heart.

The pagoda with *Buddha's footprints* was where the prison trustees had the luxury of residing. All around the inside perimeter were wooden doors with numbers on them, like cells. Knight was led first to the left, and then the Vietnamese gestured for me to follow. They opened the third door down and Knight walked in, smiling a good-bye. Two doors short of Knight's was to be my cell. While walking under the lintel, I paused to read the number on it—*P4*.

The guard nudged me forward and slammed the door closed behind me, the bolt rattling as they locked it. In front of me awaited emptiness. Instantly remembering scenes from the gang rape in Oliver Stone's *Midnight Express*, I was happy to be alone. I stood in a cube that seemed endlessly high with a ceiling reaching fifteen feet.

The door opened for a moment, making me think that maybe their successful exercise in intimidation was over and they were going to put me somewhere less bleak. Instead, they gave me an empty plastic bucket and a kettle of water, setting them down in the corner of this rat hole of a cell. I searched the trustee's eyes for empathy. He laughed, then made the actions of wiping his butt, pointed at the bucket and left. I sat down on the cold concrete floor and lay my back against the hard wall. I stared blankly at the barred window ten feet above the door. Barely any light slipped through from the fading sun. Laying on my side, I curled up into a fetal position and shivered inside the cold, cold void of my thoughts.

Chapter 12

"Either that wallpaper goes, or I do." — Oscar Wilde

Madness

Once again, I was haunted by a giant stone head encaged by banyan tree roots, its soulless eyes crying out for rescue, as I awaited the sunrise on my first day in prison.

My father had bought the poster-sized photo from a downon-his-luck French photographer in Phnom Penh, hanging it on our living room wall in Saigon, and later in Singapore. He bought it as a memento of our excursion to Angkor Wat in 1970, but I always thought of it more as a metaphor for my blurred memories of Vietnam.

After returning from classes at the Ulu Pandan Singapore American School (from age eight to twelve) I would run my books upstairs to the room I had to share with my younger brother, and then run back down to the living room to wait for TV broadcasting to start. Not only did we not have color TV until the late 1970s, but Senior Minister Lee Kwan Yew felt that twenty-four-hour programming on the island republic would only destroy the work ethic of Singaporeans. I easily piddled away those thirty minutes before 3 p.m., and the start of programming, by staring at that photo on our living room wall—first one corner of the photo, then another, delving through my mind's eye into the jungle surrounding that stone head. Big as a small hillside, the face was segmented by the original cuts of the stone blocks piled up to make the mass from which the face was carved, very much like the Egyptian Sphinx. It was easy to be drawn into the intricacies of the face imprisoned by banyan tree roots. From shades of gray to darkness. From light to shadow. I was transfixed. That photo and my father's monthly issues of *National Geographic* were to me what a whaling ship was to Melville, offering me the photographer's eye that others normally develop in journalism school.

Maybe it was the shadows, never really hitting white, never really hitting black, always just a mid-tone of gray—or the white discoloration in some spots from hundreds of years of monsoon abuse and Father Time's own brush strokes—that intrigued me. But it was the banyan tree and its ancient roots that imprisoned not only the stone head, but me too. Like long, rough arms they draped from an immense tree trunk to the jungle floor. A fan of the French-language version of Jules Verne's *20,000 Leagues Under the Sea* ever since my parents enrolled me in Catholic kindergarten in Saigon, I imagined the banyan tree a giant squid, its suction cup arms tightly holding the Khmer, like an ancient pearl diver. Some days, I imagined that the stone head was trapped by a curse; a face behind bars, with the total lack of control I felt not only because of my young age, but because of a crippling inability to express myself that many of my parents' friends described as a *cute* shyness.

If I had been frightened by that photo, I'm sure I would have had many nightmares about those scenarios, the way some people do after watching a spooky movie, or eating too much scream late at night. It was the expression on the face of that stone head, though, that fascinated me most. It actually kept me at peace. It was a Buddha smile, divine and content. Historians say it's the face of Suryavarman the First himself, original architect of Angkor Wat—young and enlightened. I'd ponder on such personal observations of Suryavarman's stone face as I sat there, daydreaming of many other famous young men's feats, like those of Alexander the Great, who had not only conquered the known world by his mid-teens, but also was the last great commander to lead his troops from the front.

Those days of deep calm, and the peace, and the meditation of sitting hypnotized in front of the photo were lifted from me when we returned to the US; specifically the Bay Area. For while my silent teacher stood prominently in our living room throughout the 1970s, he disappeared into the garage and collected dust upon our return to the States, leaving me to enter the excruciating and isolating experience of puberty alone. I pleaded with my father to help me dig my beloved photo out of the densely packed garage, but he yelled, "Why would you want to do a fool thing like that? Just forget it!" But I couldn't forget the solace that smiling Buddha bestowed upon me during my prepubescent years of wonder.

Finally unable to fortify myself any longer against the mental anguish and self-abuse, I dragged myself to the tiny escape of the small rectangular cutout in the door that served as my viewport. I had to hunker a bit to get a good look at the prison courtyard. The rising sun was warm and bright, creating a halo atop a coconut palm beyond the opposite wall of the yard. Its light sneaked through the viewport to warm my nose and lips. For a moment, the sun helped warm my deep feelings of cold remorse.

The mass of prisoners in the courtyard reminded me of an old elephant rising after having fallen down. They slowly moved about: yawning, scratching their asses, picking their teeth, taking down their mosquito nets and rolling up their bed mats. When they were done, a commotion broke out on the left side of the yard. A group of trustees had brought out a hose the size of a large python. Steeling themselves against the force of water shooting out of it, they held the hose up so the prisoners could shower under the waterfall. When they were done with the prisoners in the yard, they went over to the circle of cells that faced into the courtyard. I was elated since my cell was one of them, and this would be my first freshwater shower since leaving Thailand. Most of all, though, my genitals were itching—I had no interest in remembering what it was like to be driven to tears as a child, on camping trips in Singapore because I hadn't washed for a week. Washing would have kept me from developing an intensely painful fungal rash. Now in Vietnam, the telltale whiteness of fungus already covered my crotch. Many of the prisoners who walked around the yard already had the dark markings from scars left on their legs and ankles from scratching the areas effected by this Superman tropical jock itch. It was excruciating—and oh, the stench of it! I was already smelling it whenever I checked my genitals to see how much the rash area had grown.

Soon a door opened and closed near me, and then the sound of the spraying water came closer. The bathing prisoners' playing and laughing only added to the revelry and anticipation. As the shouting and laughing came closer to the door of my cell, I stashed my sleeping mat and mosquito net to the side so they wouldn't get soaked. My spirits lifted higher and higher. But then they passed me by. Not so much as a tapping at my door.

"Hey! What about me?!" I rushed the viewport, and pounded on the door. "Hey!"

They opened the next door, and the laughing increased and waned with the splashing. Disheartened, I guessed they were passing both Knight and me, until the cell door closed and the next one opened, and Knight's mumbled voice came in loud and clear. At least he was delighted.

I pounded the door, and shouted, "Hey, what about me? I haven't had a shower in ages!"

They ignored me. In time, I would clearly see how this tool of torture was intended.

* * *

I didn't know whether to be intimidated by the severity of my first interrogation, or in total awe at the view around me that reminded me so much of POW scenes in overly-dramatic B-movies from the 1940s and 1950s. I was glad, though, that my hands weren't tightly bound nor did I have a bruised face, like the prisoners in those movies. My hands lay freely on my lap, slightly trembling. Though many might think it was from fear, I shook because of an inner battle to keeping myself from scratching. It got so bad I frequently had to close my eyes and pray for relief.

It was hard to tell which was worse: the itching that felt as though I been playing naked in a bed of poison oak, or sitting on a tiny, unstable stool that was the first tool of interrogation. In this interrogation room, simply and sparsely decorated by a wooden cabinet, a table, four chairs and a stool, sat an 'investigative board' made up of three officials. A guard sat in a chair next to the doorway with an AK-47 on his lap and a hard, don't-even-think-of-it expression on his face. The three officials in bell-bottom slacks and casual shirts sat across the table from me and had been talking amongst themselves for almost an hour. The interrogators repeatedly punctuated their hour of conversation by looking across the table at me and giving me a stern look.

All of the officials had profound anger issues from combat against Americans, except for one; he was the clerk who wrote incessantly in a notebook, the kind of notebook perfect for bureaucrats, with its pages marked in intersecting lines instead of normal lateral lines, creating perfect little square cages for holding the free letter and word, and in the end, a person's freedom.To others, graph paper, but to me, prison. He seemed ten years younger than the two other interrogators who looked old enough to have been Vietcong. By his pleasant, almost naive expression, I considered him a nice person. Based on how we as human beings are initially more willing to accept those like ourselves—something good negotiators and interrogators learn to use to their advantage—I'm sure my observation was based on how much he reminded me of a Vietnamese version of myself more than anything else.

From the dark angry energy the others exuded, I knew I did not like them, nor would I ever like them. The short, stocky interrogator sat with his back to the window. His face was diamond-shaped and he had skin darker than the other two, leading me to believe he had Khmer ancestry. With his facial shape, darker than normal skin color, sneering disposition, and small stature, he fit perfectly my nickname for him, "Ratface." He also seemed to be the one in charge, as all the conversations in Vietnamese pivoted off him.

On my right was a much older man, who had introduced himself as the translator. An hour ago, he uttered the first and only English word I'd heard from anybody else other than Knight and myself since capture: "Sit!" The tall and lanky translator, whose hair was the color of salt and pepper, wore glasses on a face that reminded me of a frog with a wide upper lip. He also had a mole on his gaunt cheek that had four, three-inch hairs growing out of it. Made him look like a Ho Chi Minh impersonator, though the custom of never cutting the hairs sprouting from a mole is much older than Uncle Ho. According to the Vietnamese, it's supposed to bring good luck.

Their chattering ended and Frogface said, "Let us begin."

By wishing the most grand welcome to you for sneaking into our happy country. A nervous chuckle escaped and I quietly reprimanded myself for my type of satirical humor that always had a way of surfacing, especially during my most serious experiences: Navy uniform inspections; deaths; funerals; hospitals; interrogations. Frogface's eyes squinted, as he asked, "Do you think something funny?"

"No, no."

He paused, as though searching for the right words in English. He then said, "We will ask you questions and you will tell us everything we want to know. You must tell us the truth. If you do not we will find out and you will be punished." *Punishment*, I thought, *Fuck! These guys still whip the living daylights out of their children for small things like being late to school. What do they mean by punishment when they're talking about a prisoner?!* "First you will tell your name; your full name."

Without a pause, I blurted, "FrederickKurtGraham."

"What? How you spell that?"

I calmed down a bit and spelled slowly, the clerk looking up from his notebook at the end of every part of my name, then my age and birthplace. When they asked me my profession, I smiled, and said, "Photojournalist."

And so my second hour of interrogations dragged on. They learned that my mother was from Quito, Ecuador; my father from Chicago; and that my brother had been born in Philadelphia. They then learned Mom was a housewife, Frank was a junior in high school, and Dad was a sales manager in international trade.

"Tell us every place you have lived."

"Trinidad, Pennsylvania, Singapore, Florida, California, and. . . Vietnam."

"Vietnam?!" They all gave each other looks of surprise. "When did you live in Vietnam?"

Why in the hell did I tell them that?! . . . "From 1968 to 1972."
"Why?"
"My father worked in Saigon for AMTRACO."
"What was AMTRACO?"
Damned if I was going to tell the whole truth—Dad had been in charge of radio sales to the Army with Philco Ford before he went to AMTRACO. Part of his job under the Philco Ford government contract was to go out into the field with US Army units and set up remote stations. Instead, I told the guys in front of me, "AMTRACO was a distributor of farm machinery. You know, like tractors and other kinds of equipment used for harvesting rice. You know for the people, the farmers."
There was a silence so heavy it caused me to slouch. "Hmm," Frogface said. "What is your schooling?"
"I went to French Catholic kindergarten and the American Phoenix Study group in Saigon."
"Phoenix Program?" There was a rise in his voice that made my heart skip.
Phoenix, *Phung Hoang* in Vietnamese, was also the name of a counter-terrorist program set up in Vietnam by the CIA. Its whole purpose was to destroy the Vietcong infrastructure which often meant assassinating or kidnapping key Communist party members in South Vietnam. By the last days of the program it was determined that many informers, those who were supposed to be trusted with determining who was Vietcong, were actually using the program to murder rivals and cover their own corruption. It was easy to do, because the ones who decided on who was to be killed were not the ones who actually did the killing. By the time the target was determined, it was the job of a small team of Navy SEALs, or some other type of special forces and their Provincial Reconnaissance Units (PRUs)—the Vietnamese version of the *Dirty Dozen*, murderers and thugs recruited from South Vietnam's prisons—assigned to the program to sneak into the town or village and kill the suspected subversive.
Considering how effective the Phoenix Program was in destroying the Vietcong infrastructure, I quickly did everything I could to distance myself from such an emotionally-charged hot potato: "The Phoenix Study Group was an education program set up for the children of American ex-patriates living in Saigon."
"Continue."

"I then attended the Singapore American School. After the American school I attended West Miami Junior High, in Florida, for six months. I then graduated from Carlmont High, in Belmont, California."

"And college."

"The College of San Mateo, and UC Berkeley," I said, and then with a hope of rapport, "You know, where everyone was demonstrating against the Vietnam War." Berkeley sure had changed since then. When I was there, almost everyone was a Reaganite, and the reason I attended Berkeley was that it was the closest university for me to fulfill my midshipman requirements at a Naval Reserve Officer Training Corps (NROTC) unit. Still, I was searching for anything to get on their better side, short of saying that Communism was great and the whole world should get a taste of the poverty, corruption, and oppression that had befallen Russia and Vietnam.

"Do you know any famous people?"

"Famous people?"

"People in politics," Frogface said. "Do you know the president? Do you know a senator? Is there anyone in your family who is in the military or in government?"

I gulped and told them, "No."

"Are you sure?" Well if I wasn't sure, how in the hell would a question like that suddenly make me say anything more than no?

"Of course, I'm sure. No one in my family works for the government."

"Do you have anyone in the government you can write to?"

"Why are you asking me these questions?"

The translator became out of sorts and then broke into a heated conversation with his superior, Ratface. When they stopped arguing, Frogface said, "We will talk about this later. . . Tell us how and why you came to Vietnam."

They listened intently to my story of leaving California, and continuing on through Thailand. Of course, they heard a story devoid of the events of my trying to find Lieutenant Colonel Gritz. When we got close to the time period when I met Sam and the Hmong, it became hard to redact, like being told not to think of pink, polka-dotted elephants. But, I cruised right through without even hinting that I'd met anyone except journalists, tourists, and a treasure hunting Englishman. I thought I had created a barrier of safety: I assumed that Ti and Pi were in Thailand by now, telling Mr. Muk that we were in big trouble. I didn't know it then, but one of my few smart moves in this adventure was to give a letter to a friend, asking him to mail it to my parents in thirty days if I hadn't returned from this assignment. Basically, the letter told my parents that if they received this letter, I was in a Vietnamese prison.

When the hail of questions moved to the circumstances surrounding my introduction to Knight, the interrogators edged forward in their seats. I remembered Knight's suggestion in the canals, and wished again that we had prepared something to say, instead of what I came up with. What could have been more unbelievable than: "I met Knight through a friend of his, whose name I don't remember." Yep, I couldn't believe I offered that either, but I had nothing else to offer on such short notice. Ever so slight shifts in expression covered their faces, but nothing seemed out of the ordinary considering their overt suspicions: they must have been good at poker. If I had known then that Knight had completely freaked out and had already told them everything during the first interrogation, I would have known that they immediately knew I was lying.

Finally, the questions stopped, and then they said, "Mr. Graham, you will leave, and tell us a better story next time. One that is true. Remember you will be punished."

"But I am telling the truth—the treasure is there!"

"You will be punished!" Ratface jabbed his gnarled finger in my face. "You must tell the truth!"

* * *

"Good morning Mr. Gra-ham," the translator said, pronouncing my name as though doing an exercise from Hooked on Phonics®. "How are you?!" It was a bright salutation, almost hiding the dark hatred in his eyes.

"I'm okay," I lied, drained from the previous four days of interrogations since my arrival and by the fungal rash on my crotch which had worsened and had spread down to the middle of my thighs. I wriggled in my seat, and fought the urge to scratch by curling my fingers and digging my nails into my palms. I looked around for a distraction. The translator noticed; he already knew of my pain because of my prior complaints about not being permitted to wash. He flashed his crocodile grin and then returned to his conversation with the others.

My only distraction was looking around at the furniture in the ten-foot-by-ten-foot room, for the umpteenth time. All the furniture, except for a cabinet, was simple, fashioned from a hardwood. The cabinet with glass doors was an antique, beautifully carved, and of course, French. Dull sunlight, entering through a barred window, left shadows upon the table's surface. Across the table from my seat sat Frogface. He adjusted his glasses.

"Drink," Frogface said, gesturing toward the glass thimble of tea in front of me. I took a sip while he finished picking his nose, bending over to wipe a booger onto the cuff of his bell-bottoms. I sipped tea and scanned the room, my attention falling on the guard who sat next to the cabinet. I had gotten used to the AK-47 across his lap, but his large teeth now bared in a morbid grin and the stroking of his weapon was new: whenever the volume of my voice rose, he'd slide the safety from "safe" to "fire" with a loud click. Melodramatic but effective. I'd quiet down pretty quickly.

"Tell us again, Mr. Gra-ham," Frogface said, "how you come Vietnam, first time."

So I told him again, going through the whole story of my life, and ending in Vietnam, (but devoid of the Hmong). This time, though, the clerk didn't take any notes; he just watched me like a Vietnamese fish eagle up in a tree trying to look past the glare of the water's surface. But before I got to the end, the translator stiffened and his hand slammed down onto the table "—And you go to Thailand, meet Richard Knight through a friend, who you say you don't remember the name. Then you sail to Vietnam with Richard Knight, who you know for only two days to look for buried treasure?!"

Softly, I emphasized that was what had happened.

"We find that hard to believe, Mr. Gra-ham!" He slammed his palm down on the table again! "Let us tell you what really happened. First, you are not photojournalist, but CIA spy-man, sent to join traitors, and instigate revolution against the People's Republic of Vietnam! You used Mr. Knight to sneak into Vietnam, and after you accomplished your objective, you escape by airplane, boat or submarine. We are not sure how. . ."

A throbbing pain engulfed my skull as though my brain was trying to escape through my eye sockets. "Are you fucking kiddin' me?! I'm only eighteen! . . The people you're talkin' about are trained for years. If I was CIA, you'd never have caught me!"

"You were trained for short term assignment."

Ratface, who had been studying me intently, cut in, speaking to Frogface, who then continued, "And the major says, if you do not admit to what you were planning within two months, you will be taken out into the yard and shot!" His wild-eyed expression was deadly earnest.

"What?" I exploded, not knowing whether to laugh or cry at their idiocy. "You can't be serious!"

"We are completely serious, Mr. Gra-ham." He lifted his foot up out of its thong sandal, and shifted as he put the foot under his buttock on the seat. I looked to him for a joking smile. He remained straight-faced as he sipped his tea.

Ratface, spoke to Frogface, who teased, "'Do you want to cry?' he asks."

"You'll never see me cry," I said through gritted teeth, fighting terribly the urge.

Ratface laughed, and I grabbed the AK-47 from the guard. He went down easily with two rounds to the chest, a bloody mist settling over him. The interrogators were beside themselves trying to get out of that room. My decision as to whom to cut down next was easy; I unzipped Ratface right up the spine. Frogface was simply an afterthought who dropped quickly to the floor with three rounds to the chest. The empathy on the clerk's face brought me back to reality, abruptly yanking me out of my homicidal fantasy, a question in my mind: *why can't life be so simple, just like the movies?*

"Do you have anything else to say?" Frogface asked, and drew evenly on his cigarette.

It was clear now, that we were being railroaded—What *could* I say?

Frogface motioned the guard. "Think about your story, Mr. Graham."

* * *

In Asia there are three nasty kinds of malarias—not to mention the other funny-sounding, mosquito-borne diseases with very unfunny effects, like dengue fever, Japanese encephalitis, *filariasis*, and the *Chikungunya* virus. The symptoms of malaria include nausea, chills, fever, vomiting, and terrible headaches. The manner in which malaria kills you is to fatigue your system so much through shifts from fever to chills that your body gives out and you expire from a heart attack. The nastiest form, *plasmodium falciparum*, is not only deadly, but in many cases has become resistant to chloroquine. This is the one that keeps revisiting the victim, the medicine only lessening the severity of the symptoms. While this form of malaria is not very prevalent in Hanoi and Saigon, it is rampant in west Vietnam and up country.

My only respite from the fear of contracting this debilitating type was to watch the mosquitoes above me in my cell being captured in the webs of the large spiders hanging from the ceiling above me. After getting past my sometimes crippling arachnophobia, I soon realized that having a cell with a ceiling covered with spiders was a good thing. But thankfully, now halfway into my fifth day of incarceration, the trustees, under the watchful eye of the guards, had finally brought me a mosquito net. I suspended it like a tent by thongs attached to the wall. Pegs to hold the tent up were fashioned from spent matches and rusty nails and pounded into the crumbling wall; all that I could find in the corners of my cell. They did a pretty good job of mosquito control. The pegs were leftovers from previous inmates who used them similarly, evidenced by the four evenly spaced and well-worn holes in the wall. As for my sleeping arrangements, the trustees also brought me a grass mat like the courtyard prisoners had. It was as thin as rice-paper. Poor cushioning, but at least a barrier between me and the cold, humid concrete floor.

My main problem was the fungus. I screamed at the burning sensation that replaced the relief from incessant itching when I scratched. It felt as though I had cut open my thigh and crotch, and then coated it with sulfuric acid. The area of my inner pant leg turned dark with moisture. Lifting my waist band, I looked at the red, pus-covered flesh from my genitals to half- way down my inner thigh. Pain made me suck air through clenched teeth. I cried out and cursed the Vietnamese officials and especially their ancestors, hopefully something the officials with their ancient customs would take as a deep affront. I wanted to hurt them as much as they hurt me. It gave me a sense of power in my powerless condition. Hands crossed under my head to keep them away from my pleading flesh, my attention was distracted by the movements of my cellmate who hung by a filament twenty feet above. His black legs worked quickly as he wrapped another fly in his silk sleeping bag, twirling, twirling. No TV, no books, no magazines, no newspapers; the spider kept my attention for hours, teaching me much with his successes and mistakes.

By afternoon, the loud clang of a wheel rim used as a gong signaled prisoners to begin preparing their dinner. Crawling out from under the net that easily became stuffy when the temperature rose, I went over to study the Vietnamese names scratched into the walls: *1954* was barely discernible along with an equally illegible Vietnamese name and French cross above it. Even though I assumed mine, too, would be rubbed out when I was gone, I plucked a spent match from the ground and left my mark:

June 16, 1983

Frederick Kurt Graham

American Photojournalist

A knock at the door drew me away from the wall. Two trustees were standing in front of my cell. They had two loaves of French bread, a bucket, and two blue plastic bowls and spoons.

The friendly one, Quan, handed me a bowl, while the other filled it with a steaming broth of shrimp. The pungent aroma was unmistakably *nuoc mam*. To many GIs who were in Vietnam, it was a fragrance they called a stink. They tied it to other ugly smells of their experience, such as the sweet stink of dead and burning flesh, and the scent of halved oil drums that had to be topped with gasoline and lit as part of a grunt's latrine disposal duties. But for me, as for many who had their first introduction to *nuoc mam* in a Vietnamese restaurant or at home, it had always been a favorite. I've also known it as simply the watery brown sauce prepared from the juices of salted and fermented anchovies, then diluted with water, mixed with lime juice or vinegar, and sugar, finally sprinkled with chili slices and served as a dipping sauce for *cha gios*, Vietnamese Imperial rolls, or anything bland that needed a delicious pick me up. It was then no longer just called *nuoc mam*, but *nuoc cham*, or dipping sauce.

"Bon appetit, monsieur," Quan said as he closed the door behind himself.

I sat down on the cold concrete and tried the soup that was fragrantly sweet because of the dried shrimp that had been added. Shrimp, bean sprouts, and chopped green onions floated in the tea-colored broth. It was an improvement over the first two days of starvation. The soup went down well, even the shrimp tails with the shell still on, which I chewed finely so as to get every bit of nourishment.

Cold yet soft, the French baguette was very sweet, complimenting the sweet-sour soup. I began playing with the bread. I enjoyed whiling away the time by tearing out the soft inside and squeezing the pieces between my thumb and index finger. Then, I'd pop the little dough balls into my mouth, and finish off the shiny crust. Halfway into this baguette, though, I noticed some white crumbs moving.

Maggots!

Without a second thought, I ate the rest of the bread, maggots and all, making sure to chew thoroughly. Good protein. Relaxing back against the cold wall feeling good that my belly was full, I wondered how little we would be eating if we were still floating out on the Gulf of Thailand.

The sound of the door opening startled me. Quan smiled and came in to collect my dishes. He said he would like to come back later to practice French. I agreed and, after he left, I looked out through the five-inch-square window in the door. Everyone else had finished their meals, and were cleaning up the dining areas around large wash buckets used as communal containers for cooked rice. Five such areas were visible. There were Vietnamese, Thai, and Khmer mess groups.

    Most of the Cambodians, more properly called Khmer, identifiable by their darker skin color, were most likely Khmer Rouge unlucky enough to be captured during one of their many raids into Vietnam. Still, the Khmer were lucky to be alive. Most of them never made it past the border town of Ha Tien, as the Vietnamese would just execute them on the spot when they captured them, more out of racism than political reasons. The Vietnamese were the ones with the lightest skin color, who looked Chinese, but with much harsher features. They were imprisoned for the same reason as my French-speaking trustee Quan: for attempting to smuggle themselves out of Vietnam. Then there were the Thais who looked like the Khmer, except sometimes they had lighter skin, and almost all had the telltale fishing village tattoos. The Thais' stories of capture were the most surprising. They were unlucky enough to become the victims of Vietnam's boat resupply program. Hanoi would never admit to something like this, but how do you think they replaced all those boats that left carrying refugees?

    In all my time spent at the prison, I never saw the different racial groups mingle while eating. I was reminded of John Carlisle's remark about the cultures; "If you were to put a Thai, Khmer, Vietnamese, Lao and Burmese in one room with a knife, and come back in an hour, they'd all be dead!" Ancient grudges never die in Asia; they just rot people.

    A motorcycle revving up in the courtyard brought me back from my thoughts. With a roar, Quan came into view driving around the yard on a pre-1972 Honda. He cackled hysterically as he tried to keep his balance. Getting up to speed and stabilizing, he then slowed to a putter, as if cruising an American street on a warm Saturday night. Driving up to my cell door, with a proud grin, he asked "Is good?"

    My laughter subsided. "Nice motorcycle," I said with envy and the immense desire to break down the cell door, knock him off the bike, and pull an Evil Knievel over the wall.

    He motioned for a prisoner to take the motorcycle away. "Are you feeling better?"

    "A lot better, thanks. But when can I take a shower?" A very suggestible person, I was believing my newfound optimism as I told myself that I was feeling much better. Yes, it was a lie at first; but it didn't take long for it to be the truth. The alternative would have been too much for me to accept. I was happy that I had a new loop in my mind, other than the crap that I had been running through since we left Thailand, and especially since we'd been captured by the Vietnamese.

"Quan," I said, "do you know how long they are going to keep me here?"

"Who can say, monsieur?" he said as he leaned against the door.

"Do you know if they're going to take us to Hanoi, or Saigon?"

"You ask questions that I have no answer for."

I drew a labored breath and sighed.

"So what do you think of my French?" he asked, evidently trying to raise my spirits by changing the subject.

"It's pretty good, much better than mine. I understand more than I can speak."

"That's all that is needed to learn, *n'est-ce pas?*"

"*C'est vrai*... So why are you here?"

"Oh." He grinned. "I tried to leave Vietnam."

"How?"

"In boat. Government people came to my family's house the night before I was to leave, and took me." He snapped invisible handcuffs on his wrists. His constant smile faltered, "My mother, she cried very much." Waving off the sorrow, his smile resumed. "Bad luck, no? And you? You come by boat, *n'est-ce pas?*"

"Yes, from Thailand with the Englishman."

"You are a journalist, is that not so?"

"Yes, I meant to ask you. Your profession?"

"I am a student of medicine," he said. "I will be a doctor someday." He looked around and then with a wink, whispered, "In Paris."

"Oh, Paris." I smiled, reinvigorated by the knowledge that no matter how much the Hanoi government tried to oppress the Vietnamese people, they couldn't imprison their hearts.

"And you?" he said, "Have you a girlfriend?"

I wished I still did, but said, *"Oui, elle est suedoise. C'est une blonde."*

"Ooh, a blonde from Sweden. Where did you meet her? Is she beautiful?"

I nodded slowly. "In Bangkok." Not wanting to elaborate, I said, "And you want to go to Paris?"

"Oui, for *my* blonde."

"Ooh, la la!"

As our laughter subsided, Quan's face softened, "I wish you quick freedom, monsieur. You are a good man."

The sunset accentuated the moment of peace. Quan and I shared silent admiration of the sky, whose brilliant red glow outlined buildings and a coconut palm. A bare light bulb hanging from my cell ceiling came on. Quan excused himself to finish his prison duties, and I suddenly felt very alone.

A prisoner brought out a guitar, and an audience collected around him in a circle. He launched into a melancholy Vietnamese song and some of the others joined in. Other prisoners occupied their time with board games; chess and checkers. Two prisoners strolled in the yard holding hands, gazing romantically into each other's eyes. Three prisoners looked up from their conversation against the center building wall to point and snicker at the homosexuals. The lovers shouted back angrily in overly feminine Vietnamese. It quickly turned into a bickering match.

An angry shout burst out from the Vietnamese in P3 next to me, and then Quan and a guard ran past my window. They pounded on his door and yelled, as they had done everyday. The prisoner yelled back, but now more in pleading tones than anger. It was awful to listen to.

"This is nuts!" I told myself, and then I leaned back like Charlton Heston's character, Taylor, and yelled, "It's a mad house! A mad house!" I would often play act in prison to take myself away, and what more appropriate entertainment than this short monologue from *Planet of the Apes* to cheer me up? Depending on my mood and what was happening outside, I would be either Charlton Heston in *Planet of the Apes*, Jimmy Cagney in *The Public Enemy*, or, later, Martin Sheen in *Apocalypse Now*, every morning reciting, "Saigon, shit! I'm still only in Saigon."

As if on cue, a trustee walked over to the left corner of the center building and clanged on the wheel rim, calling the prisoners to gather their belongings and prepare their mosquito nets. It was sleepy time.

I spied those in the center building, through their open doors and windows. Each had a light bulb that stayed on all night, like mine. They crawled under their nets after rolling out their mats. The night air became quiet, not even an auto drove by, but then again, I hardly ever heard motor traffic from my cell. Silence reigned until the unmistakable whine of an electric guitar suddenly charged the night, followed by a rock and roll drum beat. And then there would be a whole rock concert going on, and I would think we were somewhere close to some restaurant or bar. I then thought how sadistic these guys were to tease all us prisoners with music and mental images of people having fun.

P3 screamed and yelled again. The heavy metal music was bad, but not worth getting beaten for screaming at it. Thongs slapped the pavement as people ran past my door again. P3 quieted just as the trustees pounded on his door.

A one-sided yelling match conducted by the officials went on for five minutes. P3's actions reminded me of a puppy, yelping to come inside, only to be told to shut up when his master comes to the door. Suddenly P3's door squeaked opened and hit the wall with a loud slam, as though it had been yanked from its latch. Whipping sounds broke the hush that had so quickly followed the slamming of the door. Just as suddenly there was another outburst from P3, but this time it turned into a string of screams that sliced into my very core, much like the scream of a deer or rabbit being mauled by a large predator would curdle anyone's blood. The sounds of rubber slapping against skin and the screams lasted for what seemed like a long five minutes, punctuated by angry remarks in Vietnamese. A final round of yelling and P3's door slammed closed. Low wailing filled the air of the prison, causing all the prisoners who had been staring in the direction of P3's cell to anxiously turn away to try and distract their thoughts through nervous conversation with the nearest available ear.

"It's a mad house—a mad house!" I whispered.

With no one to talk to except myself and God, I looked blankly at the ceiling and clenched my hands together, praying to get out. The fear overwhelmed me, making me shake uncontrollably. And, I guess if my bladder had been full, it would have emptied itself while I listened to the eerie pleading of P3. Somehow I had a feeling that if I didn't get out soon I'd be receiving the same treatment as P3. A rat scurried from a drain on my right, ran across the room, and then squeezed under the door. "Home sweet home."

* * *

"What do you think now, Mr. Gra-ham?" Frogface asked, after threatening again that I would be shot, trying to bolster their attack on my morale. We were already into my second week.

"Your statements are absolutely ridiculous!" I said. "I can't believe you're even pursuing this idiocy. Your soldiers took a coin I carried from the first cache."

"This is not ridiculous! You are in a grave situation, Mr. Graham...If you continue with your *treasure* story you will be punished—tell the truth; you will be free!" He was beside himself, and carried that loss of control into a conversation with Ratface.

I was elated, and thought, *You lost control and showed your emotion, you mutherfucker!* I now understood their mind game, and my sole aspiration at that moment was to beat them at it. My heart pounded, but I kept a straight face. Ratface exploded, yelling at me through the translator, "If you don't take this more seriously, you will be punished!"

The itching sensation returned, enough to make me press my thighs together to keep myself from scratching, but I remained silent and gave them a devil-may-care look. "But I *am* taking this *very* seriously," I answered, fighting with all my might to keep them from knowing how empowered I now felt. I could have jumped up and danced on the table while laughing in their faces, I felt so fortified. But that would have been a reaction, and any loss of control would have had the opposite effect. I wasn't about to lose what I had fought so hard to gain. The stone Khmer head appeared in my mind, and I offered the Vietnamese his Buddha-like smile.

Caught at their own game, Frogface yelled at me, "Go to your cell!"

My spirits were as high as the sun above the Earth. High spirits lifted my feet as the frowning guard walked me back to my cell. I wondered if this was what it felt like to be in Heaven, light, free, and undeniably happy. I could have been dragging around thousand-pound shackles and I wouldn't have even known it.

Quan greeted me at the yard entrance, and read me. "You are going to be freed?"

"No."

"Why do you have such a big smile?"

"I made them angry."

"What?!" He almost tripped over himself. "That is no good!"

"It's very good!"

"What do you mean?"

"I had control of the interview this time. I controlled myself. Didn't react. They did. I don't feel weak anymore."

"I don't see why that makes you happy," he said. "They will only try harder to break you. Your fungus will seem only an annoyance in relation to what they will do to make you admit your guilt. I hope you don't think they are joking about shooting you. They do shoot people here."

Only one time in the period I spent at that prison did the light ever get turned off in my cell. It occurred during the night of the fourth interrogation. Surprisingly, I was already asleep when it was turned off. The previous day's interrogations had been some of the most draining. The questioning had lasted from early morning until well into the night. I missed dinner, which wasn't too much of a loss considering it was only stale bread with a light consommé, something that would be given to someone with a weak stomach. And then, I got a very bad surprise.

Imagine, if you will, a waterfall. And below that waterfall, a deep dark pool. Listen to the sound of the water rushing down, hitting the pool, it's molecules exploding into a spray that lights upon the bare skin of your arm. Draw your hand across the beads of water that have collected on the hair of you arm. Comb your fingers through your scalp as you look back up at the top of the cascading water into a blinding sky. A blinding sky that makes you pass out. That was the place I was launched to for but a millisecond as my mind tried to save me from the lashing I was receiving in the middle of the night. Because I was asleep when they snuck into my cell, I didn't even realize that they had me clipped to a ring in the wall until it was too late for me fight the rubber hose.

The guards were slow and methodical. I would later deduce that they were pacing themselves to keep up their endurance. How methodical they were while I fought: stopping to catch my breath, then spurred on again by the need to avoid pain beyond description, that point just before numbing. They did not want to draw blood and bring on scarring, evidence of their evil deeds. Mostly, though, they needed their stamina, as it takes a lot of energy to really want to hurt another human being; a lot of inner rage and hatred.

"Why are you doing this?" I screamed, even though I didn't care why—I just wanted them to stop!

It wouldn't have mattered if they understood English. They had a mission and it was me. Again. Again. And again! I pleaded for mercy, but it was as though I wasn't even there, even though I was the main attraction. At first, I struggled against the two who held me stretched out on the concrete. Then, in insane desperation, I fought to snap the steel handcuffs. Pain that almost knocks a person out sure has a way of causing that person to make every attempt—though knowingly futile—to evade its delivery.

At one point, who knows how much later, the guards rolled me over onto my back. In that split second, I didn't think they could hurt me anymore. The first slap across my stomach made blood rush to my head as though my brain needed all that blood to comprehend how such a simple piece of hose could inflict such intense, nauseating pain. They beat me at least fifteen more times, only stopping because they realized I was about to vomit. And the vomiting had more repercussions than a rubber hose beating that left only bruises, no broken bones, and if done right, not even cuts in the skin. The vomit could easily have filled my windpipe and suffocated me—especially since I was already about to pass out.

These guys were professionals who knew that rubber hoses leave no marks, especially when used on the fatty areas of the stomach or fleshy bulge of the calf. Maybe a little tearing, but that would heal quickly, and over time disappear. To the best of my memory, I was hit between twenty-five and thirty times, divided pretty evenly between my stomach and calves. If I hadn't pretended to pass out, I don't think they would have stopped. When they removed the cuffs and walked out, I was truly a shaking bag of Jell-O®. If you had asked me even a simple question then about the weather, I probably would have broken down in tears, not knowing what I should say, begging you to tell me what you wanted to hear.

During the next day's interrogation, I asked Frogface as I fought back sobs why he had ordered me beaten. He said nothing. He even went so far as to deny that such an order had been given, and scoffed, saying I was lying about being beat in the first place. *How effective,* I surmised in my cell. *Let the guards do the dirty work. Make no reference to the incident. Really fuck with his mind!* Only remind me that I will be punished if I make an outburst, or refuse to admit to being a spy. No responsibility, no apparent and specific enemy on whom to focus my hate. Just confusion. Whatever ground I had gained in their guerrilla war of the mind, I had lost in the beatings and the interrogations afterwards. I would need to become even stronger inside. Until then, I was very scared indeed!

Chapter 13

"The man who has ceased to fear has ceased to care."—F. H. Bradley

Bullet With No Name

Some surprises nobody should ever have, like the one my father encountered when he arrived home after work one hot day in the summer of 1983. He had been thinking of me on and off over the past three months since our last good-bye. He smiled for a moment, getting a little humor from thoughts of the heat and how much I must have been hating it after having been away from the tropics. That was one of the differences between my father and me. Childhood winters in Spokane had taught him to hate the cold, but his years spent in Southeast Asia had flipped his dislike toward tropical heat. Even though I would complain about it sometimes, I enjoyed the way the humidity kept my skin from drying and cracking, especially in contrast to California, where the dry cold was especially detrimental to my lips, causing them to split and bleed all throughout high school.

Dad grabbed his briefcase from the passenger seat and closed the car door. He headed up our walkway and stopped at the front of the garage to check the mailbox. Ed, our neighbor, came out of his house, said hello, and lit a cigarette; his wife hated his addiction, and wouldn't let him smoke inside. Dad smiled, happy he didn't need to smoke.

He reached into the mailbox and pulled out a jumble of envelopes and magazines. He shuffled through the mail while continuing on his way to the front door. It was Tuesday, so there was his favorite magazine, *Time*. A letter was sticking out from its pages. It was a letter postmarked from Thailand.

"Well, it's about time!" he blurted in a mixed tone of elation. He would have opened it right then, but my father always had procedures.

Dad fumbled with his keys and then unlocked the door. He entered and plopped his briefcase in a chair. After a detour to turn on the television, he dropped himself into his rocking chair. After a quick glance at Dan Rather commenting on the evening news, Dad removed his glasses and tore open the envelope. He unfolded the one-page letter and couldn't believe what he was reading: "Dear Mom and Dad, If you get this letter I'm in a Vietnamese prison. . ."

He read it again, took a deep breath, and sank into an unfathomable depth of despair. "Oh, my God. Freddy! . . What have you done?"

* * *

I wasn't too surprised when Quan came to my door and knocked excitedly on it. He said that I was to prepare quickly for my release. I'd had a feeling this would happen since we'd been in prison for almost two weeks and hadn't even been moved to at least Saigon. Knight was right. They'd ask a few questions and then set us free.

I was ordered to collect not only my clothing, but also the equipment they had given me. I did so while one of the guards checked the walls of my cell. He found my wall scratchings and tried rubbing them out with the bottom of his sandal. While he grunted away in his efforts to wipe me out, Quan smiled and called me out of my cell.

He walked me across the courtyard with my belongings in hand. Around us, the prisoners who normally threw smiles and chiding gestures along my way to interrogations, instead looked at me blankly. They seemed almost sad. They did not keep their gaze on me long, as they normally did. They turned away. Something strange was going on. . .

"Are you sure that I'm going to be freed?"

Quan looked at me and said, "That is what they have told me. You go Saigon and then California."

We passed the giant concrete cistern from which the prisoners took their water for cooking and washing. They looked up at me from their morning bathing and gave me a quick smile. *That's a little better.*

The corrugated metal door at the far corner of the compound opened, and an armed guard stood in the doorway to deliver an empty stare.

* * *

Vietnam has always had a bad reputation for their treatment of prisoners and their continued use of executions as an answer for all types of crimes, even crimes of conscience, i.e. openly speaking your mind. Yes, even in Vietnam, speaking out against government policy will get you shot or, at the minimum, slam you with at least two to four years in prison—and we aren't even talking about how long it might take you to get to court, if you even make it to court. Does extra-judicial execution mean anything to you? It does to human rights watch dogs, like Amnesty International and Human Rights Watch.

By 1999, according to a report by Amnesty International, there were fifty-six prisoners of conscience in the Socialist Republic of Vietnam (SRV)—or, my spin on its name since my capture: the Soviet Republic of Vietnam—along with fifty-three new sentences, and eighteen actual executions. There were people like teachers, priests, and the average Joe, imprisoned just because they wanted to freely speak their minds, and their views differed from those in charge of the Vietnamese Communist Party (VCP). With such a track record, it's hard to believe that on September 2, 1945, President Ho Chi Minh, or as he was called by his father, Nguyen Tat Tanh, started his *Declaration of Independence* with, "All men are created equal. They are endowed by their Creator with certain inalienable rights, among these are Life, Liberty, and the pursuit of Happiness." Extra-judicial and summary executions are the norm: from 1975 until 1983 there were approximately 65,000 executions in the SRV[19], and the real number was thought to be much, much higher. Considering what was about to happen to me, bliss was truly a luxury afforded the naive and ignorant.

Ordered out of the prison yard by one of the two guards who had been waiting for me, I walked through the gate. The gate ground on its hinges, like steel fingernails across a plate of steel, as the door slammed closed behind me. Still wincing from the sound, they blindfolded me and tied my elbows tightly behind my back. My heart raced. This was the first time I had been blindfolded by the Vietnamese since my capture, but I thought it was only because they didn't want me to see anything while I was being transported to Saigon. I was actually comfortable with it, as I thought I was finally, as Quan had said, going home.

Because of my blindfold I couldn't see how many had joined the two men who had initially met me at the gate. I just knew by the added voices that there were more. They led me by a tight grip on my elbow. A nudge to my back felt like the hard surface of one of their AK-47s or maybe an M-16.

After a confusing number of turns, I was stopped and pushed awkwardly against a hard wall. My head exploded in a ripple of pain as they had pushed me too hard; the back of my head had hit the wall with a loud crack. A numbing pain throbbed in the back of my head as they shuffled around.

"Because of the crime of espionage. . ." I did not recognize the voice of the speaker. It added to my fear.

"I told you I'm just a photojournalist!" I did my damnedest to break my bindings. Tears soaked the bottom of my blindfold as feelings of sorrow overcame me. From out of nowhere, I wished the parting with my father back at SFO had not left me feeling so incomplete. I wished that I had lived a more productive life. I wished I had not been scarred by that fucking war! *That fucking war?* I thought. *How was I scarred by that war? Where did that thought come from?*

The voice of my unseen enemy convicting me of espionage continued, ". . . you have committed against the People of the Socialist Republic of Vietnam, your punishment is execution by firing squad."

The action of a weapon slammed closed!

"Do you have anything else to say on your behalf before you are shot?"

For what seemed like a thousand years, though it could only have been a few seconds, I thought, *Oh my God! This can't be real!*

"I told you I'm a photojournalist! You've got to believe me!" My body shook uncontrollably now. I didn't know how much longer I was going to be able to hold my bladder. *I should have taken a leak back in the cell*, I thought. Then I laughed at that ridiculous thought. And then there was silence, and then there was not.

"Get ready."

This can't be real. Please God, this just can't be real!

"Do you have anything at all to say?"

Suddenly, an incredible new feeling overwhelmed me. My tensed muscles relaxed into the bindings. I felt so relaxed that it was incomprehensible as my mind grasp wildly for understanding.

"Do you have anything to say, Mr. Gra-ham?" My mind was in a whirl, not by what to answer, but by a collection of terrifying facts that had trapped my consciousness: the muzzle velocity of an AK-47 is 2300 feet per second; at that speed and at this range of only five feet, the bullet would explode my heart with 1445 pounds of shock. For a split second I understood how my father evaded his painful emotions and that I had the same innate ability; but this skill was not enough to hold me there, far from the stress of impending doom. "What is that?" the voice continued. "I didn't hear what you said."

I had read about this phenomenon experienced by the dying; a surreal sense of peace as they felt themselves leaving their body while clinically dead. The difference was that I was still very much in my body, maybe more so than ever before. As a matter of fact, I'd never felt so alive, so aware of my existence and my existence in relation to everything else. The bindings were cutting very tightly into my arms, yet they did not hurt as much. A scent of mangoes and papayas, carried on a deep waft of air, filled my nose. Off in the distance, perched on some branch, I imagined, a bird chirped as though he was so close; he could have been sitting on my shoulder. The voice that had been speaking to me seemed to be almost drowned out by the chirping. It was a wonderful bird sound,

full of life and joy. The chirping almost obliterated the following words, "Ready... Aim."
So this is what it's like to know you're going die, I thought.
"What was that you said, Mr. Gra-ham?"
A breeze embraced me. I smiled.
"Ready... Aim... Fire!"
The bullet hit me squarely in the chest. I screamed and recoiled from the pain that at once was sharp, yet so dull and numbing. As I crumpled to the ground, someone tried unsuccessfully to stop me from dropping and hitting the side of my head against the hard earth.
Laughter broke out all around me. At first it wasn't my laughter. I was still trying to grasp that the bullet's impact was all in my mind, and that I had heard the firing pin falling on an empty chamber instead.
When I realized why the order to fire had been given in English, I too laughed. *How carefully they had planned this play for my benefit*, I thought, *just to push me past sanity and into an admission of guilt at their false accusations*. I laughed at the madness of this maniacal ploy to harass me. I laughed at them, not only because they were now going to have to help me to my feet because my hands and arms were bound, which meant they were going to get their hands dirty on my urine-soaked pants; but also because whatever fears I had entering Vietnam were now lost completely. They had just freed a part of me without realizing it.

Chapter 14

"We are able to find everything in our memory, which is like a dispensary or chemical laboratory in which chance steers our hand sometimes to a soothing drug and sometimes to a dangerous chemical."— Marcel Proust

Coming Home

"*Vous allez! Vous allez! Vous allez État Unis,*" Quan finally said, two and a half weeks after Knight and I first arrived in this hole. He grinned as he stopped for a moment to catch his breath. *So, that's why they finally took my fingerprints yesterday?* I thought, *I'm going home!* This was the first time an actual record had been made of our arrival in Vietnam, a record that could be traced: until our fingerprints were taken we were officially not in Vietnam. If I had known how long it would be until Vietnam would admit to having us, I wouldn't have felt so suddenly at ease.

Hurriedly, I collected my belongings. They had been gathered three times. False alarms. I almost didn't believe I was leaving, until finally the door opened. Quan entered and said good-bye; there was a sadness in his voice. I said good-bye and good luck, and gave him my khaki military belt. "See ya later, . . . in Paris."

Quan looked around first, then said, "In Paris." We grinned.

Knight was waiting in the gateway with that wide-eyed look he always had when surprised, as if he'd just awakened.

"Hello, Richard."

"Hello, Fred."

That was the extent of our conversation. Chaos ran rampant as the Vietnamese tried to keep our departure eventless and inconspicuous. *The Keystone Cops* must have been one of their military's instructional films. Knight's face remained blank. I grasped for every relief of levity, with a smile or gauged chuckle.

The Vietnamese directed Knight into an old Mercedes Benz, and me to a seat next to the interrogation clerk in the other sedan. Beyond the clerk, through his left side window, I saw Ratface standing, the man who took pleasure in telling me I would be shot. Having learned the day before that the clerk spoke English, I pointed at Rat-face, and asked, "What is his name?"

"Oh, his name is Colonel Uy."

"Colonel Uy, as in 'Pee'" I said, staring at Ratface to imprint his face in my memory.

Colonel Uy mirrored my own glare, and then pointed at me and laughed along with the guard next to him. Our sedan pulled us away, and we followed the Mercedes out the gate.

Our vehicle dodged the bustling bicycle traffic; bicycle bells rung excitedly; women yanked back their crossing children; and old men cursed at us. Soon we were out of Rach Gia, and I was very, very happy.

* * *

Rice paddies stretched across the land, quilted by walls of bamboo and coconut hamlets. We were speeding east. Thirty miles out of Rach Gia, a Buddhist bonze stood, boarded up, with graffiti covering its walls. Strange, I thought, considering the monks who had protested the war by torching themselves. Four religions had shaped the history of Vietnam: Confucianism, Taoism, Buddhism, and Christianity. Now they had all been shoved underground as the Communists effectively imitated the history of Russia's Revolution, a country and government that had been touted as good for the workers and the common people. And it was now 1983, and the Vietnamese Communists still loved Stalin, doing an excellent job of emulating his oppression of religion and free speech.

"My name is Nguyen," said the clerk, pronouncing it *Wen*.

Shy-mannered Nguyen, who worked for the Department of Internal Affairs, had a wife and daughter. His manner and bearing made me wonder whether his marriage and job had been planned by his family. We talked about my interest in re-learning French and Vietnamese. He seemed to take great pleasure in guiding me along in Vietnamese, completely ignoring the French language in which he also fluent.

With no air-conditioning in the car, the sun burned directly through the back windshield, causing me to roll my window down. I had rolled it up to keep out the deluge of dust and dirt that was being kicked up by passing trucks. Our driver cursed, as he barely missed a girl obliviously crossing the pavement that was in much need of repair. Nguyen glanced back at the girl we had almost flattened on the grill and fired his own admonishment at her.

"How much longer, Mr. Nguyen?" I asked, as we returned our attention to the road.

"We will arrive in Saigon tonight." He smiled politely.

"Great," I said, "I'd love to see Saigon again before I go back to the States."

He gave me a weird look as though I was nuts or something—"go back to States?" Then, he said, "We will not arrive until after dark."

Nguyen asked some questions of the driver, and then said to me, "We will stop by the side of the road to eat. We have brought some sandwiches with us. Would you like that?"

I nodded as my stomach was already grumbling. We soon pulled off to the side of the road, and got out. Looking around I suddenly realized that this was a main highway in Vietnam. It was an important part of what the SRV called the New Economic Zones (NEZ). To the untrained eye, this would seem like a normal migration of an impoverished people to a better life. It appeared to be a drive to get people out of the cities and into the country, and in so doing improve the productivity of the land, and therefore the living standard of the population. It was really a forced relocation program that helped Hanoi move its own population into the better areas of Saigon. For the North Vietnamese it was a boon. For the South Vietnamese, it was a loss of everything they had known. First of all, these people who lived in Saigon were people who were more adept at smuggling, stealing, negotiating, selling, and trading than planting and harvesting. It would be like taking a Wall Street trader who had never lived outside of New York City, and dropping him off in Nebraska with a hand plow and no training, ordering him to produce a thousand bushels of wheat. But, the Pavlovian architects of Hanoi forced the people out of Saigon by reducing the amount of food rations available to those in the urban areas, so that they would be forced by starvation to travel.

Secondly, it soon became apparent that the initiative was designed to rid Saigon of what the SRV called *undesirables*, namely those South Vietnamese citizens who had opposed them during the war. This was part of the three-fold plan of the NEZ program; the Provisional Revolutionary Government's de-urbanization of the cities of South Vietnam. Then there was the North/South program that Hanoi had come up with to alleviate the effects of their mismanagement and corruption that would lead to the famine of the 1980s in Vietnam's rice bowl, the Red River Delta, and the rest of the country. Most of these people would be moved from their once fertile lands in the north to the highlands of central Vietnam.

The final component of the NEZ was the relocation of the hill tribes. These were the Degar who had sided with the Americans and South Vietnamese, and who now fought under *Front Uni Pour la Liberation des Races Opprimees*, or FULRO. This was the anti-

Communist guerrilla group that the interrogators had assumed I was sent by the CIA to meet on my "short term assignment," as some type of advisor.

This road through the incessantly rich rice fields of the Mekong Delta had definitely seen quite a bit of that traffic. It also had seen better days; since the SRV's political infrastructure was so corrupt and inept, that highway had seen more rain and warpingly hot temperatures than the money necessary to improve it. Where there were potholes that had been mended, they had been repaired badly and it seemed as though the road workers had only poured on the tar without flattening the surface smooth with a roller. Probably because there weren't enough rollers to go around. Most of the road, though, was untouched, looking like a beggar's clothes full of holes.

One of our drivers and a guard pulled a plastic bag and bundles wrapped in newspaper from the trunk of Knight's car. While Nguyen and I walked to stretch our legs, the three Vietnamese guards and Knight evacuated their car. A semi-automatic Tokarev clattered on the ground as one of the guards got out of the car. He quickly picked it up, fumbled with it for a moment and returned it to its hiding place under his waistband and dress shirt. The thought of running into the jungle had appealed to me, as I've always been good at sprinting and hide-and-seek, especially when driven by fear. And the thick forest of bamboo was so close. Now, though, knowing they were carrying concealed firearms, thoughts of escape faded.

I turned to Knight and asked, "How's it going?"

"They don't speak any English," he answered sullenly, and then smiled politely to Nguyen.

"Stop talking," Nguyen said, "Eat." He handed each of us a Vietnamese sandwich. Knight opened his first. Between the two halves of the 12-inch-long French bread, lay a spread of thin slices of peppercorned headcheese, ham, chicken, paté and carrot slivers marinated in *nuoc mam* and sugared vinegar. He looked at it disdainfully, but took a bite. Forgoing an inspection of mine I took a great big bite. While we ate, Nguyen spoke to our driver, who walked down the road to a small village we had passed. He returned soon, cradling three ripe green coconuts.

"Alright!" I said, grinning to Knight, who smiled a halfhearted smile, poorly concealing his scowl. My eyebrows furrowed, as I thought, *Does he think he's the only one with problems here?! This guy had better lighten up or he's not going to make it.*

"So what time did you say we'd be in Saigon, Mr. Nguyen?" I asked.

Nguyen addressed us both. "Around eight o'clock."

Knight squatted down to sit on his haunches, Vietnamese style. *That's impressive, maybe he is learning.* But, his stressful scowl continued; he wasn't learning anything except how to die sooner. I couldn't wait to jump back into the car and go.

Soon lunch was over and we were back in the cars, moving down the cracked and pot-holed road for Saigon. The sky turned gray as we came to the south fork of the brown-watered Mekong Delta at Can Tho, specifically the Can Tho Ferry. We were the first ones on, but we had to wait as the government ferry employees did their best to pack as many people, cars, and buses on the ferry as they could to gain much needed revenue.

Confined inside our cars, we rode the ferry across the wide expanse of hyacinth-dotted water. At one point, I noticed a Caucasian on the deck walking about and taking tourist shots. I looked at Nguyen, who said, "Soviet advisor." I was surprised that he said it with such disdain. I would later learn that the Vietnamese referred derogatorily to the Russians and Soviet Bloc visitors as "Americans without money."

Street vendors worked feverishly to sell us bubble gum and Coca-Cola through the open windows. A young boy in cut-offs opened a glass, pre-1975 Coke bottle that he kept for refilling at the factory. Its contents went into a small plastic bag, while the bottle went into a wooden shoe-box-like container. Sticking in a straw and tying the bag closed with a rubber band, he handed it to Nguyen.

Nguyen handed the Coke bag to me then paid the boy. He chuckled at how fast I finished the Coke. I declined his offer to have another. Instead, I looked out past the ferry's superstructure.

The Mekong looked like the Lower Mississippi. Silt-brown water stretched almost a mile across. Tall grass, bamboo, and pads of hyacinth bordered its banks. Fifteen minutes passed before we arrived at the other bank. A Soviet jeep next to us kept my attention much of the time. It represented Communism at its best. The jeep was an almost perfect copy of an American Willys. It was widely known that the Soviet Union was stealing a multitude of military secrets from the US. Looking at that jeep next to us, it was apparent.

By the starting of all the engines around us, I noticed that we were about to land. An olive-drab CJ-5, an American jeep left over from the war, carrying four, pith-helmeted military personnel, led us off the ferry's ramps. They sped away, overtaking the Mercedes. Nguyen spoke to the driver who then pushed on the accelerator, bringing us up close behind the Mercedes. Their headlights came on, along with ours. Nguyen's face took on a death-like glow from our headlight's reflection off the pavement. We drove fast, alone, through the dark tunnel of night that was intermittently trimmed by shacks, trees, bamboo, and grass. I tried to nap, my head banging against the window. Forced sleep was becoming a buffer between me and the stress of my predicament, even with bright lights flashing past my closed eyelids.

* * *

"We are in Saigon, Mr. Gra-ham," said Nguyen. "Look."

I looked at the city I had last seen eleven years ago; and in some perverted kind of way, I felt as though I'd come home. But, this was not the city I remembered, this city was blackened by night and the lack of electricity. From 1976 until the late 1980s, Saigon, and for that matter, the SRV, couldn't pay its power bill. The Soviet Union was already feeling the pinch of global expansion and military spending. It was heavily strained trying to support its latest successes in Southeast Asia and Central America. Vietnam would soon have to start looking for loans from other countries, and the United States was a country they had been after long before the fall of Saigon.

We crossed a bridge over the obsidian Saigon River. I could still hear Dad yelling over the outboard of our ski boat to get ready as he then gunned the motor and I rose out of the water, terrified of screwing up and falling back into the water at such speed. I was especially afraid that when my father turned the boat around to pick me up, he would be furious that I had not stayed up on my skis, had not done everything perfectly and up to his standards. It was a confusing memory full of vinegar and sugar.

Streetlights lit the way over the concrete bridge. Beyond the curtain of bridge lights were the black silhouettes of two docked freighters. I could just pick out a giant, gold hammer and sickle painted on the funnel. The weak lights on the ship created long shimmering lines in the river. Coconut palms and tall trees created a black, jagged trim along the slinky lines of what once was Lady Saigon, and what was now called Ho Chi Minh City by everyone except its inhabitants. We crossed the river, and somehow I felt questions would be answered here, not only for the Vietnamese, but for me. Questions that had been plaguing me since my family and I left, like—why did I have such a fascination with Vietnam?

The drive through the streets was fast and furious, making me feel like Cinderella trying to get back home before anyone found out who I was. Even if I knew where I was going, I was sure their evasive route was to keep me from recognizing any landmarks.

Nguyen pointed and said, "There is your embassy." Its dark windows looked out of the past at me from its old white walls behind a wall topped with barb-wire. The Hanoi government had taken it over along with the country. Once an American landmark, it was now just another office building. Unknown to me at the time, they were taking me on a long ride around the city to make it look as if the prison in which I would spend most of my time was far from the US Embassy, long since evacuated. It was actually just around the corner.

Continuing on our tour, I realized with a pang that the Paris of Southeast Asia had turned into a scavenger's cave. Rubble and trash littered the dark streets. Streets that had been brightly lit during the late 1960s and early 1970s were now dark and deserted. There were the slums Dad had described to me as a child. But, the area he was talking about were shacks on stilts near the river. We had left the river, yet the slums seemed to go on forever.

My distaste grew and I saw what Hanoi had done to Saigon. I wondered if Nguyen could see it. Instead, pride lit his face while he acted as guide and made introductions to the hag, once young and elegant, now hiding in the dark from us like a horribly disfigured old woman. *Man*, I thought, *if you're forced to tell yourself enough times that shit tastes good, then I guess it might start to seem so.*

We pulled up in front of a gray iron gate that mysteriously parted for us, like someone had whispered, "open sesame." Nguyen smiled at me as we drove into what had, until 1975, served as the South Vietnamese National Police Special Branch Detention Center, where counter-terrorism interrogations were held against Vietcong prisoners. It had also served as a barracks where the Republic of South Vietnam kept a detachment ready to protect the US Embassy from another take over, like the one that had occurred during Tet, 1968.

Knight and some officials were standing next to their car in the dark, under a corrugated metal-roofed carport. The garage was in the center of the compound, an area bordered on three sides by buildings. While Knight looked around in bewilderment, the others greeted us. One spectacled man, who seemed to be the superintendent, directed us into a room behind him that was lit by a single, bare bulb.

While the Vietnamese chatted amongst themselves near the open doorway, Knight and I sat in wooden chairs and silently drank tea. One of the guards was sent out of the room, returning shortly with a petite young woman clad in the uniform for women working in this prison, black pajama bottoms and a white Brigitte Bardot blouse. She smiled politely at the two of us, and asked us in French to follow her and three other guards. She seemed delighted to be speaking French—as though she hadn't had that many opportunities—and Knight tried to charm her with his charisma, or what there was left of it considering he was bug-eyed terrified.

Nguyen said good night, and we followed the three guards and the young matron past the carport to a doorway that opened to a stairway. The stairway was in the middle wing of one of the large buildings. It had turquoise shutters; very odd against the whiteness of the building. Drab colors would have been more appropriate here. *Maybe*, I thought, *it's supposed to look to the outside world like just a large apartment complex, and draw little attention.*

Walking upstairs was surprisingly taxing after just two weeks without much exercise. I was out of breath by the time we reached the third floor of this three-story building. As we turned left off the stairs, Knight was directed into a cell kitty-corner from the stair hallway. He spun around with a look of surprise, "What's this?"

The matron directed me in French, "You are down the hall."

"See ya later," I said and followed the guard.

A sad look came over Knight's face as he said good-bye again, and then the Vietnamese bolted his metal door shut. The Vietnamese then led me the rest of the way to the end of the hall. A guard dashed ahead and opened a door on the far right end. Incandescent light spilled out into the hall, contrasting with the fluorescent light of the hallway.

The matron smiled and said, "*Bonsoir, monsieur!*" I walked into my new place of residence. The door closed and I glanced back. The latch sliding closed and being locked made a sound that reverberated through the whole cell, reminding me of my spartan bachelor officer quarters (BOQ) room during my midshipman orientation at Pensacola NAS. I scanned the furnishings that left a lot to be desired. Against the right wall lay a rectangular grass mat on a traditional Vietnamese bed, no more than wooden planks to support my back, and four tall bed posts to hold the corners of a mosquito net. Under the only window, which was large and barred, with half-opened shutters, was a rough hewn desk and chair.

I walked past the closet that had no door, to a bathroom that also offered no privacy as it also faced openly to the room. Inside was a toilet with white ceramic barely showing through the dark crust of who-knows-what; only the seat seemed slightly clean. Opposite the toilet was a shower. Instead of a shower spigot, it had a normal faucet, barely three feet above the ground.

"Guess I'll have to learn how to squat Vietnamese style," I said.

I stripped, and after stretching a bit, squatted down like a monkey, which was just low enough for me to get my head under the faucet. At first, the position drove red-pokers through my Achilles and knees, as it does for most Westerners not raised from childhood to sit in the traditional Vietnamese style. But I soon forgot the pain as I was refreshed by the cool water that felt like a waterfall. How well it wiped away not only the dirt of the body, but also the mind. A complete relief from the itching in my crotch. Almost.

My hair pouring down over my eyes reminded me of how grungy I was, and in dire need of a haircut. Not only was the water relaxing but so was the idea of nudity and the sense of freedom with that nudity. Now I knew why as a child I loved to run naked around the yard and inflatable pool on hot days. So many of us never know why we did things as children, we just did them because they felt good and honest. It was nice to know that I could still feel that way after facing a firing squad. I was sure then that even the Vietnamese didn't realize how counter-productive their little execution melodrama would become to their efforts in getting me to do what they wanted. But, these interrogators were good, with the evident skill you can only learn through lots of practice; and I feared that they might actually find another button that I couldn't yet see.

The darkness of the bathroom accentuated the coolness, protecting me from the glaring light in the cell, and the distressing thoughts in my mind. For what seemed an hour, the shower held me in a waterfall of meditation. Snapping out of it, I took a deep breath and turned the tap off with a single loud squeak.

A new man, I patted myself dry with my only towel: a sweat-stained T-shirt. I sang the happy song by the 1960s group *The Flying Machines—Smile a Little Smile For Me.* The light bulb seemed to dry me like the sun as I walked back out in my rubber sandals and black pajama pants.

Five feet away from my new bed I took a deep breath, and blew it out. As a child I had learned that a cloud of carbon-dioxide made a nice mosquito decoy during the quick dash for a mosquito screen door, or in this case my mosquito netting. I rushed to the bed on a held second breath of air and slid under the net.

After tucking in the bottom edges, I lay back welcomed by the pillow. *My God!* I thought, *What an amazing pillow!* Even though it was a garden variety pillow, purchased by many, unique to none. It takes two weeks of sleeping on concrete to truly appreciate a pillow.

I stared at the ceiling for a few minutes. The viewport in the front door slid open. Black eyes peered through. My gaze returned upward to the ceiling. The metal shutter closed again and the light bulb went out. I was almost in tears at the shock and the elation.

For the first time since being captured, I had a night to myself. I sucked air through my grin, clenched my fists and voiced my exaltation in the resulting joy. The excitement of once again knowing just a little part of a whole freedom kept me awake for an hour. Outside, a strong wind had picked up and the resulting sound of rustling leaves lulled me to sleep.

* * *

American Consul Frederick Vogel, a dashing red-headed gentlemen with looks concealing his forty-one years, followed the two Vietnamese to the near end of a glassed-topped table at the back of a room of the Vietnamese Embassy in Bangkok. They took seats in this room sparsely decorated with a long center table, and lacquered paintings on the walls: the Trung sisters riding an elephant against China in an ancient war; peasants working in the rice fields; demure-looking women in *ao-dais (*a traditional Vietnamese dress of pajama pants and a dress with the sides split from the knee to waist, or hip depending on the suggestiveness of the wearer: those in the paintings were almost nuns) and conical hats; and a single portrait of Uncle Ho. A few years older, Vietnamese Embassy First Secretary Tien, whose black, thick-rimmed glasses added to his serious demeanor, adjusted his white dress shirt and black slacks as he sat down on the couch. He said something in Vietnamese to the similarly-dressed, but younger interpreter, and then turned to face Vogel. "Tea, Mr. Vogel?"

"Please," Vogel said, preparing for the never changing procedure Tien had for beginning talks by sitting forward slightly to accept the offering.

Vogel made a mental note to himself as to how the length of fluorescent bars along the ceiling could scarcely illuminate the rectangular room. Tien finished pouring Vogel's tea and reached it over. "So how is your family, Mr. Vogel?" Tien asked as the translator poured tea for the both of them.

"Fine, fine, everything is going good. And you, how is your family?" Vogel sipped his tea, and noticed again, as so many times before, that the long table had been carved in Thailand. The carver had captured well the daily happenings of country life in Thailand, covering it with a plate of glass so that the scene underneath could be admired and also serve a flat surface for thimble cups, thermos, and such. One day he would ask Mr. Tien why Vietnam's embassy had this type of table, especially since there are so many great carvers in Vietnam. Now though, there was a more pressing matter, much more shocking: the disappearance of an American teenager.

Tien looked up from his own sip and answered, "My family is fine, thank you. Did you see that accident on Wireless Road? Horrible."

Vogel nodded, "Very horrible." They all quietly took a sip of their tea, their downward glances looking at nothing in particular, yet on the watch for everything.

"Mr. Tien. There is a matter of great importance I'd like to bring up with you. We have reason to believe that your country is holding a young American named Fred Graham. Do you have any information about this?"

"What?" Tien answered, and then spoke heatedly in Vietnamese to the translator. Mr. Tien had that look as though saying: "Why have I not been told of this?!" The first secretary and interpreter talked rapidly amongst themselves, leaving Vogel to wait and watch, and then remove a sheet of paper from his attaché.

"This is a very important matter," the interpreter translated. "We will have to confer with Hanoi, as we do not know of this matter."

"I understand." Vogel knew that Tien was a man who would tell a lie just as easily for his government as the truth, but Vogel also understood Vietnam has one of the worst intergovernmental communications systems in the world, and that Tien might actually not know. News travels as slow in the SRV as freedom and progress.

"We will get back to you as soon as we get information, Mr. Vogel," the translator said as they all stood and prepared to leave.

Vogel handed Tien the sheet from his attaché as they stood up from the table. Since the United States hadn't had diplomatic relations with Vietnam since the spring of 1975, Vogel could not be in the Vietnam embassy on official government business. As such, the letter was unofficial and had no formal American seal. Typed on the uniquely unofficial sheet was information about me from my parents, so hopefully the Vietnamese would have the facts straight as they investigated. "I cannot begin to tell you the gravity of this situation, Mr. Tien."

Tien nodded.

P 091405Z 83

FM AMEMBASSY BANGKOK

TO SECSTATE WASHDC PRIORITY 2927

UNCLAS BANGKOK 64694

2. Comment: Mr. Tien's reluctance over the past week to even discuss this case indicates that we may have difficulty assisting Mr. Graham in negotiating a release for his son. End comment.

* * *

"*A bien tôt, monsieur!*" the matron said, cheerily, as she shuffled out of the room. She left so fast it seemed a dream. Rubbing the sleep from my eyes, I climbed out of bed and ambled over to the desk. Coffee sat in a thimble cup, on a saucer. Sweetened condensed milk lay at the bottom. Taking the long slender spoon from the saucer, I stirred slowly. A new experience in prison, I debated on whether I really wanted to be totally awake and bouncing off the walls. In the recent emotionally charged interrogations I had been protected by the buffer of sleep deprivation.

A sip exploded my taste buds, its sweetness overpowering after three weeks of a sugarless diet. Bananas supplementing our diet at the end of our stay in Rach Gia had had the sweetness of banana cream pie packed full of sugar. The coffee was so sweet it almost made me nauseous. What seemed like heart palpitations hit me as the coffee kicked in. I gazed out my window, my eyes seeming to jump in their sockets.

Though an out-of-reach, hanging blue blind prevented a straight out view, my window provided a good view of the street below. People were everywhere; walking back and forth down the street, while others sped by on bicycles, motorcycles, and mopeds. Every once in while a car or bus would pass. Not once a new car, unless it was Soviet-made.

Most of the people visible were those who walked on the opposite side of the street. Those who walked on my side were hidden by the far wall, topped by barbed wire. A plot of planted ground separated our building from the wall twenty feet away. A mango tree, over three stories tall, blocked my view to the left corner of the prison.

I crouched to see whatever more of Saigon that I could beyond the blind. Pulling the chair out from the desk, I sat down. The desk made a comfortable platform for my elbows and I would rest my chin on open palms, spending many a day just watching. There were apartments on the other side, most of them four stories. And beyond the line of flats, through a gap made by a couple of apartment buildings that were only two stories high, was a soccer field with children playing. The sight raised my spirits. I thought of old men who smiled as they watched children playing ball games because it reminded them of how young and carefree they, too, used to be.

An old tree, gray patches spotting its trunk, grew out of the concrete sidewalk along the row of apartments on the other side of the street. Three Vietnamese children in pastel-colored pajama suits sat and played on the sidewalk. A wind that had been blowing lightly down the street changed course and blew straight into my room, bringing with it the sweet stench of Saigon's sewage that ran through the pipes below the sidewalk.

A peddler, pulling a wooden wagon, came walking down the street from stage right. On his crew-cut head, the man, who appeared to be in his mid-twenties, wore an old-style baseball cap. It was the long-billed type seen on Ernest Hemingway and Humphrey Bogart in the summer's day photos of marlin fishing during the late 1940s and early 1950s.

The young man had a pleasant, energetic demeanor. His manners were overtly soft and polite, as he set up shop by putting out a sign. I couldn't understand exactly what it said, but it seemed to describe his services. His actions, along with his equipment, soon explained his profession. A child came to him with her bicycle that had a flat tire, and tapped him to get his attention.

He was rapid and meticulous. This was a man proud of his profession. There were no monolithic unions, laziness, or loss of self-respect to get in the way of this man's way of life. He was the common man. What was more impressive was his adjustment to his being a deaf-mute. Fingers and hands spoke for the tongue that could only create a grunt here and there, and every once in a while a high-pitched whine. He was a Vietnamese I would see many times, over many days. He was to become someone in the coming months to whom my empathy would go out to with great reverence, because the streets of Asia are littered with people like him who only beg for scraps. Watching him would lessen the severity of my prison term, because it seemed so trivial in relation to his life experience.

The girl gave him a coin when he was done. He put it in his old, green ammo box. Proudly, he snapped a cub scout two-finger salute, and waved good-bye to her. He smiled as she mounted her bicycle and rode away. The innocent pleasure of the scene caused tears to well up in my eyes. I questioned my reaction, and the only answer was that the scene was so heart-warming and good, so vivid a contrast to my feelings of being in this concrete cage.

A clang at the door brought me back inside to face a young guard. He motioned for me to follow him. The guard's civilian clothing told me something unique about this prison as compared to the others. In the two days, which I assumed was a weekend because we had not been interrogated in that time, I had seen no uniformed guards except from my window.

Two turquoise doors at the end of the hall nearest my cell were opened, revealing a large room with two concrete columns on each side. Lit by sunlight coming through two barred French windows on the far wall, the columns were more for decoration than reinforcement. A large table waited to the right as I walked in. It and five chairs were the only furniture inside this blank white room. I smiled at the floor that had a black and white chessboard pattern on it, and thought of *Alice in Wonderland*. I wondered if the Vietnamese and I were going to play a new game.

Nguyen was the only one who smiled. He was once again the clerk. Two officials sat on his right as he faced me: there was Nguyen; a Eurasian with extremely brown olive skin, with a pudgy French face; and a thinner, balding Vietnamese at the end of the line.

Away from them at the right end of the table, the translator introduced himself as Mr. Le. He was slim, like Nguyen. The fat Eurasian spoke to Le, who asked me about John Everingham.

"Oh, he is the one who got me in touch with Richard Knight." I feigned calm, though bewildered and infuriated with Knight.

My surprise was nothing compared to the look on Nguyen's face, as he realized that the friendly, naive American had been lying all this time. He spoke in an excited Vietnamese. The Eurasian raised his hand and waved back Nguyen's outburst.

"Now Mr. Gra-ham, please tell us about how you came to Vietnam," Le asked, pointing to the Eurasian. "He finds it hard to believe that it took you so long to arrive at Iles des Pirates."

I told the story again as I'd done since the first interrogation, though this time it seemed refreshingly new. They were polite and cordial, always keeping my glass filled with tea. Quiet and expressionless, they learned how we left Bangsare, Thailand. They didn't even chuckle with me when I told them about how Ti and Pi got drunk on Maekong whiskey, and the ensuing confrontation during the stormy start of the voyage. As the interrogation came to an end I sullenly asked, "When are we going to be freed?"

"Soon," he answered as he motioned for the guards to take me back to my cell. Define soon.

* * *

"So, what do you think of Vietnam?" Le asked during our second interrogation.

"The country is very green and beautiful." I gauged my honesty, as back in Rach Gia. Frogface had disliked my straight answers about his poor English. Vietnam and its people are truly beautiful. It was only the parasitic government who merited my disdain. Frogface was a third-year high school English teacher. I had suggested he not seriously entertain the possibilities of teaching fourth-year English.

Mr. Le was definitely carved from a tall and graceful mango tree. While Frogface was chopped out of a poorly cured piece of heavy mahogany, interacting in that crusty old Vietnamese harshness of someone raised during the French occupation, Le had by the third day of interrogations opened up to smirking and smiling. He was intimidating because he was so much at ease, so much like someone who held all the cards or had grown up with privilege, and for whom life was very easy. He sometimes smiled too much, reminding me that they could at times be more smug than me. Le reminded me of Kaa, the python in *The Jungle Book* no one was ever sure about. What a smooth talker. He looked like he did well with the women, really knowing how to nurture and deliver sweet delicious words of seduction.

During the short breaks while the other three conferred, Le enjoyed talking about himself. He was yet another teacher of languages, a French teacher at a nearby college. Teaching, he said, was what he would rather be doing than translating my words. I smiled, and said, "Send me home, then."

Le scoffed. More questions arose about how long I had really known Knight. Again, the truth. Again, they couldn't believe that I had left on such a dangerous venture after knowing Knight for only two days. I almost began questioning my own honesty, as now I too found it hard to believe I had followed Knight, after knowing him for such a short time.

In skydiving, my actions would have been called target fixation. Target fixation occurs when a competing skydiver concentrates so much on stepping on the target, the plate, that he forgets to flare before landing in order to slow his descent. It's a straight line to the plate that can get you the trophy, but it often also results in a broken leg from coming in too fast.

Then the Vietnamese asked me again what they had asked in Rach Gia: "Do you know any famous people?"

I was really confused, but this time they also asked, "Do you know any people in the United States who would be friendly to the cause of the Vietnamese people?"

Taken aback, I asked, "And what cause is that?"

"Your country has promised to give us much money for the repairing of our country. That was the reason we gave you back your war criminals. Did you know that?"

I kept quiet, but nodded that I knew that Nixon had promised reparations at the end of the war in exchange for the freedom of our POWs.

"If you know any influential people, we can have you out very soon. We would just have you sign an agreement to help us, of course." The Eurasian who had been talking looked at his cohorts, and then added,

"You would be free to go as soon as next week." He smiled. "And then you could be home and free to live your life."

He became very serious.

"I don't get what you're saying. I was told that we were going home. Are you saying this isn't true?" I asked, becoming very uncomfortable now, as if an unscratchable itch had overcome my body.

"We have many friends in your country, you know," he said. "We would like very much to add you to that list of friends. Some of them are Vietnamese. But many are Americans. They are very friendly to us, and know how we have been poorly treated by your government. We would just like to consider you our friend. If you were our friend you couldn't possibly be our enemy. A spyman. You are our friend, aren't you? Not our enemy."

"I'm not your enemy," I said, "but, I don't know anyone famous, someone who could be of benefit to your cause."

"Think about it some more," he said. "You'll have time."

After an eerie silence, the interrogation drew to a close with Le asking me if there was anything I'd like. A plane ticket direct to SFO came to mind, but I asked, "Do you have any Vietnamese-English dictionaries; I'd like to re-learn Vietnamese. Seems I'm going to be here a while." The Eurasian took on a stern look of concern, and suddenly tapped the table as though covertly warning me that the clock was ticking.

"Yes, yes, yes, we shall see," Le said.

A guard ushered me out to my cell and lunch. Little Red Riding Hood pranced in, almost skipping. *"Bonjour, Monsieur!"*

I was happy to see her. She was a woman, reminding me that there was some sort of *Yin* in this harsh country of *Yang*. Laying her tray on the desk, she dried her hands by drawing them along her out-turned blouse and supple waist. Quickly, she transferred a metal plate of fried sweet potato chips and beef steak, and a glass of hot water from the tray to the table. Cast aluminum eating utensils were also placed with proper etiquette. *"Biftek avec pommes frites. Bon apetit!"* she said and left with the guard.

The steak was thin, cut with the grain, but full of flavor, like that which has always caused me to prefer free-range beef and wild game. I was fortunate that Socialist Republic of Vietnam (SRV) was on a propaganda kick. I could think of no other moment that so clearly represented how much Vietnam was trying to manipulate public opinion than when they had a prison matron coming in acting as though she was with room service at the Ritz Carlton. As if that's how the SRV treated all its prisoners! I also took it as a sign that they knew they would soon have to let me go—this was the first time I had a strong inkling that my dad had received my letter.

The orange-colored chips were a new experience. They had the familiar French fries texture, yet were very sweet. I learned a new and tantalizing recipe for a vegetable, which up until now, I had hated. I eyeballed everything first, trying a chip, chewing it meticulously, tasting completely this treasure given me; then my next treasure, the small piece of steak. My habit of eating fast that started during our last days in Vietnam had almost disappeared. I pondered my new actions, eating slowly, that had started since the mock execution.

Instead of grasping for quantity, I now reached for quality. To know quality, I had to be able to find it in the most simple things. In Rach Gia, it was bananas. Now, at this lunch, it was the sweetness of the sweet potato chips. I questioned whether I would feel the same about Japanese food, considered bland by many, including me. The question rode in and right out of my mind, spurred on by the enjoyment of my meal.

The whole scenario still seemed incomprehensible—"too good to be true" would be the perfect cliché. It also reminded me of Le's smile. I *really* didn't trust him now. Knight had already lost my trust. I kept thinking of Knight's lie about having the original treasure maps and heirlooms, and Le asserting that Knight said he only had copies. This added momentum to my anger at Knight's untrustworthiness. My anger only served to frustrate me as there was enough stress from being imprisoned. So, I took a long, deep breath and finished my meal. Afterwords, I lay down trying to get comfortable on the boards for a nap.

Napping didn't last long; thoughts of Knight's lies gnawed at my every fiber. I jumped up, punched the wall, and then looked for entertainment at the window. Down on the street, the tire man sat idle next to a wagon under a tall tree. Near him, also on the opposite sidewalk, played two children: a seven-year-old girl and her baby brother.

They were adorable. Both of them had the same haircuts as though they each had coal-black bowls on their heads. They looked like two small dolls, the boy in a T-shirt and shorts, she in pajamas. She played tea party with her baby brother.

The work day must've been over because their middle-aged father was already home and sitting in a chair tilted back against the garage. He was reading a newspaper. Wearing only an undershirt, shorts, and thongs, he pointed his finger at his daughter, and scolded her for pushing her brother around. The girl immediately softened her interactions with her brother. I wondered whether she would be a henpecker like her mother, who nagged the girl's father.

They played, oblivious to the passing of pedestrians and a monk. It was always my habit to bow my head out of respect whenever I walked by a monk back in Bangkok. Monks patrolled the streets of Bangkok every morning to collect alms. I was aghast at the appearance of this Vietnamese monk. He was completely ignored, and most of all his orange robe was held together by patches. Never would this have been seen in Thailand, even in the poorest of areas. Then again, there wasn't any religious and spiritual persecution in Thailand. Many of the other Vietnamese in prison were religious leaders: Catholics, Buddhists, and the like. In the SRV, such persecution was publicly evident by the boarded up temples and churches seen on the way over from Rach Gia. The SRV liked to say that they had religious freedom, and a large number of religious leaders, but the key was number and not independence: into the new millennium, they would continue refusing bishops appointed by the Vatican, because these bishops would likely not give the rubber stamp the VCP expects on all its dealings. I put my palms together and wished the monk well as he continued out of view.

  Suddenly, the girl walked a couple feet over to a drain cover, pulled down her slacks, squatted and urinated. I chuckled at how that would not go over too well in the US, especially since she was right in front of her flat; but here in Vietnam, it was as accepted as relieving yourself by a bush on a camping trip back in the US. Done, she shuffled back to continue playing with her brother. The only disruption was a pedestrian who scowled and dragged his sandal after accidentally stepping on the moist booby trap. I was just about to laugh, when a filthy beggar in tattered rags stopped at the covered drain. He seemed to be eyeing something hidden under the concrete slab. There was such an intense look of concentration on his face, as though he were working on the answer to end all of life's conflicts. Suddenly striking like a cobra, he reached under the slab and pulled out a two-foot-long fish that had the head of a snake and the body of a ling cod, a delicacy best enjoyed as the main ingredient in a clay pot dish, and known as *cá bong* in Vietnam. In the Eastern US, however, the highly aggressive snakehead fish has become an unwanted import in danger of wiping out a number of indigenous fish species, due in part to its ability of crawling onto land and migrating easily from water mass to water mass.

  My surprise was nothing in relation to the excited reactions of the crowd that had been walking around him so cluelessly. Like a true hunter, he quickly stuffed the struggling beast into a burlap bag and went off to eat it, leaving the others to concoct great myths as they gossiped and pointed in amazement at the neighborhood drain-hole. I laughed happily, having seen that contrary to the old wive's tale, you can make a silk purse out of a sow's ear, and pull gems out of rubbish. The laughing agitated an itch in my ear. I tried to scratch it by rubbing my earlobe. The itch was deep inside and unreachable and didn't mean that much at the moment, though soon it would mean much too much.

"*Cuba! Cuba!*" someone on the street said. Crossing the street were three husky Cubans in civilian clothes. They had that serious demeanor and physique that makes it hard for many military advisors to hide their identity in public. But these advisors were hiding nothing. With fingers held up in victory signs, they yelled "*Cuba! Cuba!*" again at the Vietnamese neighborhood.

"Castro sucks dick! Castro bites the big one!" I flipped them off. Embarrassed at such an emotionally charged and automatic outburst, I told myself that my reaction was probably programmed by Mom's story about her father: The day Castro took power, my grandfather heard it over the radio in Quito and broke into tears. Just another childhood story that added to my dislike of Communism.

As the Cubans disappeared, the neighborhood black marketer opened for business. He was a young entrepreneur who wore a dress shirt and bell-bottoms, sandals and a Vietnamese military cap. His horn-rimmed glasses gave him the look of a college student. His wares lay upon a bed sheet spread out on the sidewalk. On the sheet were albums with the faces of singers that I could barely make out to be Frank Sinatra, Nancy Sinatra, and Bing Crosby. The Beatles' *White Album* was easily recognizable because of its jacket. Also, there was a stack of eight tracks and kitchen wares. I wondered if he was a thief like the ones who had broken into our house in 1970.

The man was edgy. His confidence in conducting business directly across from a political prison impressed me: every day an olive-drab uniformed policeman would make his rounds. I realized that one was walking by right now, for the college boy's eyes had suddenly turned wide and he was madly gathering up his goods. Like a scene from the *Bowery Boys*, he stood in front of his covered mound, whistling as though nothing was wrong. I laughed and gave him a thumbs up through the bars of my window.

Prison #2 demolished and being turned into a high-rise in 1995.

My smile faded. In all the times I tried to get someone's attention, no one looked up. Once in the afternoon, there was even a tour bus full of Caucasians, maybe Swedes, but more likely "Americans Without Money." In hopes of recognition, I shouted as loudly as possible. Considering I'd not even had the opportunity to speak with my consulate, even being recognized by Soviets would have lifted my spirits. But they were like the neighborhood, and the pedestrians. They were always averting their gaze.

Reminded of my desperation, I turned away from the window and headed for the hardness of the bed that suddenly didn't seem so hard.

The empty ceiling filled my view. I felt as though I was disappearing into the white wall, like a ghost.

Chapter 15

"Unfortunately, the balance of nature decrees that a super-abundance of dreams is paid for by a growing potential for nightmares."— Peter Ustinov

Escape!

When Barbary pirates stole our vessels and kidnapped their crews we sent the Navy and the US Marines to Tripoli. When the King of England illegally conscripted our sailors, we fought the war of 1812. When Vietnam hijacked Thai ships and imprisoned their crews, ever polite Thailand—actually the fishermen's families—paid the ransoms to these Communist pirates. The fabrication the Socialist Republic of Vietnam (SRV) used to excuse this illegal practice was to say that the Thais were caught in Vietnamese waters: amazing how suddenly Vietnamese territorial waters included half of the Thai Gulf after Hanoi annexed the South.

The families of those held at Kien Giang Provincial Prison in Rach Gia had been trying for months to secure the freedom of their fishermen. Funds had been collected from the fishermens' respective families and now, at the end of July, these families waited with great anticipation for their loved ones to return from Vietnam. Amongst this large group at Don Muaung International Airport were a couple of ferangs.

They were from the American Embassy, two men dressed in polo shirts and slacks. The younger one was in his thirties, with a full crop of brown hair. The older man was US Air Force Colonel Paul Mathers, a man who held well the heavy responsibilities of one working for the POW/MIA Division of the Pentagon.

"So what do you think, Paul?" the younger investigator asked the older.

Mathers reached into his attaché case and removed two photos. "I think there's a good chance; that is if they were taken prisoner instead of killed outright."

The two of them walked up to the glass doors separating the lounge from the tarmac. The airplane, visible through the door, cut its engines and opened its hatch. Thais spilled out of the door, down the stairs, and out onto the tarmac. They ran and jumped in the air, reveling in the sunny day and their freedom as they ran and hobbled straight for their families and friends, who almost didn't recognize them because they were so emaciated.

The two ferangs moved among the families. Rapidly, yet humbly, remembering not to stare them in the eye (a rude invasion of privacy to a Thai), they walked from ex-prisoner to ex-prisoner, asking them in Thai if they had ever seen the two men in the photos.

"Paul!" The younger investigator waved him over, and said, "These guys say they saw them." He then went back to speaking Thai as the older investigator took notes. His concentration almost seemed to cause his pencil to tremble.

In Mathers' mind, there was an American in trouble and he was going to do everything in his power to help him out. He had been here two years, two years of chasing dead bones, and dead end tales of live MIAs. Chasing this young American and the Brit had brought new life and a little youthful adventure into his investigations for the Pentagon's POW/MIA Division.

". . .and both of them had beards?" the younger investigator asked.

The feeble old man nodded. (This is funny, because I've never been able to grow a full beard. The closest I've ever come to facial hair is a mustache, which I grew years later in Alaska.)

"Let's go back and file our report!" They had found the truth, contrary to what the Vietnamese had been saying about Knight and me for the last three months: that we had been lost at sea.

Mathers nodded and turned silent for a moment as they went to the lounge entrance at the other side of the room. "Anything wrong?" the young investigator asked.

Mathers gestured his partner through the door, and said, "Hope that nothing happens to them after we blow the lid on the Vietnamese."

* * *

"Bangkok, Friday Morning, July 29, 1983—Treasure hunters detained, say released fishermen."— The Nation Review

"Saturday, September 3, 1983—On Thursday, Vietnamese officials first acknowledged that they were holding the pair, in a report to British officials."— San Francisco Chronicle

* * *

Screams. Screams filled the complex. My screams. The earache that had been only a mere annoyance three months earlier had developed into a raging infection that had worked its way deep into my ear over the last month. The maddening pain resulted from the pressure built up inside my ear as it tried to flush itself. This was my fourth sleepless night as I tried to lay on my right side to drain my ear.

A warm wetness would pour out, leaving large amber stains on my pillow. And, whenever I happened to fall asleep and roll over, the pressure built up so much that it felt like someone was driving a spike through my ear. (In my life as an adventurer and combat photojournalist, I had been punched in the head, kicked, slammed by a gun butt, wounded by bullet fragments, nearly drowned, slammed by the blast of a concussion grenade, had a rib cracked, suffered through minor surgeries without anesthesia, and tear-gassed with a CS grenade; this earache had always ranked as one of the more traumatizingly painful experiences.) Fed up with the pain, I ran for the door, whimpering, and pounding on it like a crazed animal. A guard looked in, and I communicated my pain by grimacing and pointing at my ear.

Along with the major and Le from the day's interrogations, a white-smocked doctor arrived the next morning. While inspecting my ear, he asked if I had any other ailments. I told him about the fungus in my crotch. The pus-bleeding rash was all the way down to my knees. I rolled my eyes because Le and the major were along, and the doctor took it upon himself to give an embarrassing lesson in epidermal medicine, using my crotch and genitals as the examples. Not only did I feel like a walking botanical garden, I was now the red-faced main attraction of an interrogator's peep show. Insult to injury and very unpleasant indeed.

When he was done, the doctor injected me with tetracycline, gave me a tube of tetracycline cream, and then said good-bye. After he left, Le and the major then went into another repetitious interrogation that ended when I finally said, "Can't we pick this up later?" They left me to my solitude, to finally treat the fungus with the cream, and mull over the previous week's interrogations. I realized how much I'd grown to hate them not out of fear, but out of how much they bored the hell out of me, and were such examples of quintessential bureaucrats at work.

Interrogations occurred regularly every other day, except weekends, which was how I kept track of the days of the week. Days of the week were also evident by the actions of the people in the street. While children were the only ones on the streets during weekdays, their parents were almost always dilly-dallying around and doing household chores on weekends. Some customs were retained from western influence. The neighborhood seemed to be a bastion of the middle-class. They all had their weekend siestas, everyone except the tire man.

"Hey, tire man."

He pulled his wooden cart along as he had done for the last month. The feeling he gave me was still as uplifting as the first time. Months of studying him offered me the realization that we were both prisoners. His imprisonment was inflicted upon him by Mother Nature and genetics; mine was put upon me by a totalitarian state. We even had to use the same sign language to communicate with the world around us. He taught me so much about patience. While I coped with what I prayed was a mere short inconvenience in my life, he had to deal with a terminal condition. One lesson remained constant through the months of observations. Though the children sometimes ridiculed his ailment, his animal-like sounds, and his corny salute, one example remained constant: he always rendered service with a smile. And it was not a business smile hiding greed, but a true heartfelt shine.

I suddenly remembered that today was my clothes washing day, which was every other day. Grabbing my dirty clothes, I went into the bathroom and dropped them in the bucket that was given to me by the guards. They had intended it to be used for scooping the water out of the mini-shower and pouring it into the toilet. A silt had clogged up the drain.

The bucket was also useful for containing the water in which I handwashed my clothes with a bar of body soap. After three cycles of rinsing with water from the spigot, I'd twist them dry and spread them out on top of the mosquito net. The continuous cycle of this chore gave me a muscular tone and definition in my arms and hands I'd never known. It was uplifting. A benefit of the clothes drying was that the evaporating moisture did a good job of cooling the air space under the net, which I always took advantage of by napping under it at that time.

A knock at the wall next to my bed woke me. I rolled over and returned the salutation to my unknown neighbor, met only through my own initial idle and inquisitive tapping on the wall a month ago. I remembered that this was how American POWs communicated with each other in the Hanoi Hilton. Though I wished we both at least understood Morse code, as did the US POWs, my unknown neighbor and I did have a common language; we relinquished ourselves to communicating unintelligibly in a gibberish of taps and scratches. It continued everyday for fifteen minutes. I smiled at how much just the effort to communicate kept me from feeling so alone. It must have provided the same comfort to my neighbor because there was always a return to my tap. When I was done, I pulled away from the wall and returned to thoughts about my previous meeting with the officials. At times, my thoughts turned to prayers that my father had received my letter.

Since it was September, the two month deadline—the one the Vietnamese in Rach Gia had given me in order to force me to lie and say I was a spy for the CIA, or else be shot—was two months ago. I now felt more lighthearted as the chances of execution seemed much more remote. If I knew that they had been telling Dad for those first four months that they didn't have us, even after the investigators had the confirmation from the Thai fishermen, I don't think I would have felt that secure. People disappearing in Vietnam is all too common.

* * *

In his memoir, *Man's Search for Meaning*, Viktor E. Frankl noted that the lack of proper nutrition killed the sex drives of prisoners in the Nazi concentration camps. In the SRV, it was the fear of execution that had removed mine.

Then one night, after an evening of soothing songs rising from the guards' turntable below, I was uplifted by Judy Collins' *Clouds*. Soothed by her as a child in Saigon, from a turntable very much like the one owned by the sentry downstairs, I fell asleep and escaped in my mind to another place, a place so far from iron and concrete, it was as though I was free.

I was with Erika, who stood at the end of a dock in Pattaya, a white sailboat moored next to her. When I came running up, the boat's sails were suddenly full and Erika, magically, was no longer on the dock, but on the sailboat, sullenly waving good-bye from the aft deck. I fell to my knees and dropped my head. And then, I woke up.

With my mind dealing with the tensions at hand, I was surprised by this dream. I guess I didn't hate her as much as I thought I had when she admitted to me that she was already engaged to someone else, and that her Southeast Asian pilgrimage was one last hurrah before the bonds of marriage. The surreal dream of Erika and the sailboat only served to remind me of how lonely I was. Trying to help my mind escape, I took myself mentally to other places. The planks of my bed had a springiness to them that reminded me of the action of my surfboard. Taking advantage of it, I practiced pushing up off my *surfboard*.

Summer at Pleasure Point, Santa Cruz was my daydream. I could see the beautiful six-foot sets coming into the rock reefs below Cliff Drive. It was a clear golden day, so warm, I didn't even have to use a wetsuit. Hardly any surfers out. No need to fight for a wave. A perfect day. My gift came in from the Pacific. I paddled. I paddled harder. *Here we go*. Pushing myself up, I crouched low for balance, writing my name in the imaginary wall of water.

"Wipeout!" I hollered, rolling down onto the bed, laughing, then suppressing the urge to cry that surged up from a quagmire of intense emotions I had until now held in tight. And then I got quiet, and closed my eyes, trying to remember what Erika looked like lying nude next to me in the moonlight, her tanned skin glistening with moisture as we lay on sand at the water's edge.

Suddenly my cell door slammed open. The loud clang startled me out of bed, erasing all thoughts of Erika, but doing nothing to deflate my erection that had a mind of its own.

"*Bonjour, Monsieur! Como ça va, . . .*" the matron said as she walked in, her cheery smile plummeting into a deep scowl as she looked down at my only connection to free thought.

"*Uh, Bonjour Mademoiselle,*" I said, standing at attention and whistling *Dixie* to distract from the obvious, wishing I had the tightest pair of thick denim jeans, instead of the paper-thin parachute pajamas that made everything that much more pronounced.

She wore the same despising look Mom had when she caught me masturbating when I was twelve. Such a scene. She told me that I was damned forever and headed for Roman Catholic Hell. Mom screaming at Dad, and blaming his subscription to *Playboy*. I was excused from lunch that afternoon to cry alone in shame in my bedroom.

An adult now, I realized I had nothing to be ashamed of. I glared back at the matron. While she could only scowl, the guard watched me with a look of empathy, as if he too had been there. They left, the matron offering me no usual, "*Au revoir, Monsieur.*"

I stabbed the curry fried chicken with my fork, forcefully slicing it with a knife. Bringing a piece to my mouth, I relaxed by chewing, and thinking how much easier it was for women to physically hide sexual arousal. I also thought about how we in America are responsible for the continuation of a sexual morality that dates back to Oliver Cromwell, and oppresses men and women alike by placing the Puritan work ethic above the strength of deep intimacy.

Resting my chin on my hands, I looked out the window, my focus going fuzzy, my mind and soul returning to glazed memories of Erika: smiling blue eyes and a tan line peeking over a candy-applered bikini as we played under the sun at Pattaya; nights filled with lovemaking under coconut palms on a secluded beach. A moment of jealousy surprised me as I wondered whether she was now with some Australian or New Zealander down south. Perhaps she was back in Stockholm already, and had read that a request, as Le indicated, had been made of Sweden's Prime Minister, Olaf Palme, to speak to Hanoi on my behalf. Too many months had passed since I'd had the joy of Erika's company. And jealousy was just one of the emotions I couldn't afford. I needed an outlet. I needed a tool. I came up with a letter.

Originally, the interrogators had given me a stack of paper to write out my confession, describing how I had come to Vietnam in order to lead a rebellion within the ranks of FULRO; then later they asked me to compose a contract in which I would be a support to them in the US, either as a spy, or as a contact for one of their spies, or "Americans friendly to their cause." Finally, they just said that I could use the paper as a journal. Journal my ass! More like spill my guts out and then one night they come in and know everything about me: my thoughts and emotions, and how I processed them. It would be a cold day in hell before I'd ever use that stack of lined paper for anything other than doodling: and writing good-bye letters to ex-lovers.

Taking a piece of paper from the stack that was kept in one of the desk's drawers, I wrote to Erika, told her how depressed I had been since she left, how lonely I was in Bangkok after she'd said good-bye, how lonely I was now, and how months now seemed like years. I told her that I was writing because I couldn't afford to have an emotional connection to anything or anyone outside my cell. I wished her all the best, and that in so doing, I would be working with the universal law of mutuality: I would be free, too. I signed with an *I love you*, and then folded the sheet into an airplane. There was no one below in the garden; the area was empty. So, I let it fly. It sailed off, along the drafts that battered the building and signaled an encroaching monsoon. The plane then flew beyond the tree, over the fence, and out of view. With Erika now in the proper place of a deeply fond past memory, I smiled and thought, *at least somebody got out of here.*

* * *

No longer would I be what my Bangkok bodybuilding buddy from Munich, Wolfgang, called the "Ice Cream Baby." No longer would I be the butt of fat jokes. I had become buff! Rising in the cool twilight of dawn to sculpt my body, starting with one hundred push-ups a day against the bed, I would go right into two hundred fast toe-touches, and a hundred sit-ups. Then, the chair held by the backrest served as my weights. Fifty curls with the chair for my biceps; and then straight-up arm extensions, lifting the chair from behind for triceps, I'd do standing skull-crushers.

Tae Kwan Do horse stances almost cramped me up completely as I threw fists and then open hands, releasing the cramps in my legs by directing chop kicks and roundhouses at the walls. Funny that I had hated studying martial arts as a child in Singapore. It got to the point where one day I looked over at my mother, who sat with all the other Tae Kwan Do moms on the bleachers at the Singapore American School, and said, "No more," beginning a quitter's mentality that hounded me through junior varsity football.

To end my daily workout, I would take long calorie burning walks in my cell right after the matron picked up my dishes after lunch. I must have walked more than twelve to fifteen miles a day in that room, from corner to corner diagonally, changing direction every once in a while for variety. When all desperation had been drained from me, I was able to sleep once again. Added to the aerobics and toning were skydiving positions, laying flat on my stomach with my arms, head, and legs raised off the floor. These encouraged me to sit and stand up straighter.

During one interrogation, Mr. Le was suddenly aware of and uncomfortable with my self-confidence gained from the new discipline. For the first time in my life, I was in total command of how my body performed. By contrast, Le usually slumped in his chair, bringing up his feet as though relaxing in a modified form of the more traditional style of sitting on his haunches. When he first noticed the change, he sat up straight like a startled cat. Then, it became a battle with himself to emulate the strength that I had developed, as he tried to keep his spine straight, his chest out. I smiled at him, suddenly even more confident, relaxed in my strengthened new poise as though born to it.

By this time, the interrogations seemed as though they had been going on since the two Trung Sisters led the Vietnamese revolt against China in 40 A.D. By now, Le could probably tell my story better than I. Our interrogations had become so informal, one would think that they were just casual chats, instead of camouflaged efforts by the interrogators to turn me into a "friend of Vietnam."

"So how are you doing today, Fre-der-ik?!" Le asked, still very conscious of his own posture.

"I feel great, how 'bout you?"

"Goot." Le continued, "The major, he would like to know what you think of Vietnam."

The major had a pleasant smile. He was the one who always kept his head covered with a North Vietnamese Army cap to hide his bald head. Nguyen and the Eurasian had stopped attending the interrogations. I had asked for reading materials, only to have received the *Vietnam*

Courier. I was getting pretty frustrated with their thinly veiled efforts to brainwash me, using the more personable tactics similar to those I had read about in reports from refugees who had been detained in Hanoi's re-education camps. Contrary to what many might think, beating someone into submission over ideology doesn't persuade that person to believe that ideology: New beliefs always go down better with sugar.

The *Vietnam Courier* was a monthly English language newsmagazine. An English-Vietnamese dictionary would have been my preference, but they ignored my request; they must have still thought I was trying to instigate a Vietnamese *Attica*. Since reading the *Vietnam Courier*, I was completely astounded that someone would actually pay for it at a newsstand, government controlled or not. Not once was the United States referred to simply as that. Instead, they only used the following to describe America and Americans: Western Imperialist; Yankee Imperialist; and the American Imperialists.

At the start of one feature, I thought perhaps I had found relief from the Communist browbeating. It began beautifully, profiling an old photographer from Hanoi, whose photograph of a mountain in North Vietnam looked just like a grand Chinese rice paper painting. But, then the feature shifted from a description of the photographer and his life into a long diatribe about how the only reason the photographer was distracted from photography in the 1960s, was because of the "American Imperialist aggression," and how this aggression was the reason for every single one of the problems in Vietnam.

My empathy went to all required to read this one-sided drivel. My patriotism to the US swelled, as the Vietnamese continued to persecute me because of my nationality. During one of my earliest interrogations, the Eurasian relished telling me that I would have been freed within the first two weeks if I were from another country, for example, my mother's birthplace of Ecuador. In a blatant effort to annoy me, whenever a plane was shot down by Sandinistas and other Communist forces in Central America, the interrogators would bring in a newspaper and rejoice in reading to me how once again their comrades had been victorious against the *American Imperialists*. When they showed me the accompanying photo, it was of a downed Salvadoran Air Force plane, its circular tail markings clearly identifiable, but to these officials, it was an American fighter or bomber. "One of your planes was shot down," they'd gloat—to think that there are still history and political science professors who actually believe that the "Domino Theory" was only a propaganda campaign designed by Eisenhower to create fear in the American public. Either all that was happening to me was never communicated to the State Department, or it was ignored in the Reagan administration's efforts to concentrate more on the war in Central America, and the hostages in the Middle East; and to stay clear of a politically unfavorable Vietnam/US history. At one point, even my father, who had been approached by Amnesty International to make a trade of me for a Czechoslovakian mercenary captured by anti-Communist forces in Angola, thought that there was nothing political in my imprisonment, and so to attempt a trade probably wouldn't have succeeded. "Oh, Dad," I would later tell him, "I wish you'd known what was really up."

    As for the Vietnamese for persecuting me because of my being an American, I went for every opportunity to play mind games with them. The easiest target was their political arrogance, and their feelings of superiority for having conquered the US and its allies, South Vietnam. I was getting good at mind games; after all, I had the world's best teachers in the SRV. My answer to the major's question about what I thought of Vietnam was one of those opportunities. I retorted by asking them, "How come you have beggars in the street?"

"What?" the major exclaimed in one of his few English words.

    "You still have beggars in the streets. I thought this was one of the reasons you fought the war. You know, so that everyone would be fed."[20]

    The major was not happy. Even though not fluent enough to speak English, he had completely understood my words. I chuckled when Le redundantly translated, and the major impatiently waved him off. The major then said through Le, "We have beggars, but not as many as before."

    The major's anger flared at me through his eyes, even though he tried to cover his emotions with fingers over his mouth. *Less, eh?* I thought. *Probably because you killed so many with unguided rockets fired into Saigon from the surrounding jungle.*

    Throughout the war, the Vietcong in the area outlying Saigon would prop up an 'X' fashioned from bamboo that was almost as strong as steel. In the 'V' of the cross, they would then lay a small surface-to-surface rocket. Since it was aimed using Kentucky windage, it was indiscriminate in who it killed. The principle was similar to what the Nazis used during the Battle of Britain when they fired unguided rockets from Normandy, taking a heavy toll on the civilian population of Britain. It was through this style of attack, along with ambushes, that the Vietcong had gained the reputation of owning the night. Almost all of the rocket attacks occurred at night, after anti-Communist forces had made their evening withdrawal to the safety of bases.

    I sat back contentedly having achieved my purpose. They learned I would never be converted, and I felt reassured that no matter how they tried to show themselves as my superiors, they weren't the powerful and restrained leaders they pretended to be. My posture straightened even a little more, and my gaze met theirs evenly.

"We also have some books that the English consul gave Richard Knight."

"The English Consul?! When am I going to see the American Consul?"

"We would let you speak with the American Consul, but your country will not send one. Your country refuses to have political ties with Vietnam," he said, then after the major broke in for a second, Le continued, "Maybe you can write a letter to your government so that they no longer ignore us?"

I was not going down that road. Every MIA conspiracy theorist used that one to explain why all MIAs hadn't been accounted for. I sat silently, though I wanted to ask them what other venues were available to me to let my government know that I was still alive. I had not communicated with my family since leaving San Francisco, and they hadn't received anything from me since I had left that one letter with my trusted friend, Mr. Bhornchai Kunalai. I was sick with guilt, not only because of my disappearance, but I now understood what the emotional toll must have been for the families of MIAs, and the MIAs themselves: horrible desperation.

"The British Consul in Hanoi has agreed with your government to handle both your and Mistah Knight's case. But, he will only be able to meet with Mistah Knight."

"Why?" I asked, flabbergasted.

"You are not English," Le added.

"Then how is the Consul going to know how I am?! Or if I'm even alive?"

"The Office of Internal Affairs in Hanoi says that Mistah Knight will speak for you."

"What? Are you kidding me?" Knight testifying as to my condition? I might as well have been dead. "Just let me attend a meeting with Knight!" I pictured Knight having a jolly old time with the British consul, having high tea and crumpets, and receiving the latest world news, when all I got was jealous and much more pissed off.

Le shook his head, and I felt as though I was under a surging sea, fighting just to get another breath of air. Le and the major had both taken on that hard look that meant they would not budge. I shook my head and released my tension with a breath that ended in a yell. That flustered them, so much so that they each reached for something stashed under their shirts—*so, they were packing all along!* After they realized I was just letting off steam, they returned to sitting calmly at the table. Le's face softened and he pulled four books out of his attaché, and slid them slowly across the table to me. I grabbed for them, my eyes pouring over the great wealth.

The book on top was *Touch the Devil*; next was *The Eagle Has Landed*, both adventure thrillers by Jack Higgins. One book was a comedy I remembered seeing Knight read on the voyage, *Three Men in a Boat*. The last book in the stack was called *The Seeking*. It was the adventure narrative of a group of ancient Mongolians chasing a white stallion across Central Asia. I liked it because it was supposedly the true story of a vision quest. According to the author, an anthropologist, the story was translated from an ancient manuscript he had found in Tibet.

And then there was the big monster, thick as a brick, upon which all the other books sat: an unabridged collection of Shakespearean plays!

Le gazed at me with admiration. It was the admiration a teacher has for a pupil hungry for knowledge. "We aren't that bad, you know," he said humoringly in a calm voice.

My gracious, over-the-top acceptance of the gifts threw the major off guard. He broke into a bright grin.

"Your lunch is ready," Le said, signaling that the interrogation was over. I was hungry alright, but for the word, not lunch. I couldn't wait for the guards to leave once they dropped off my food.

I finished *Touch the Devil* and *Three Men in a Boat*, each in a day. *The Eagle Has Landed* took two days. It was amazing how vivid the books were: my mind free from the dulling effect of TV, and full of an intense desire to escape. On the fifth day, I felt like a child who had stuffed himself at Thanksgiving. What was worse was the feeling that it might be a long time before I would receive anything new and worthwhile to read.

Richard III was the play that peaked my interest most, starting with reminding me that back in Thailand I had been *running before my horse to market*. And in that play, and the history of that play, I was reminded of how the war in Vietnam was played out in terms of recorded history: they who win decide who was hero and who was villain.

I looked out the window, just in time to see the black marketer whose luck had run out as he was trying to do his escape and evasion. He wasn't paying attention and two uniformed men walked right up to him. The look of resignation on the black marketer's face was like that of a sad Donald Duck. He was definitely terrified because he talked fast and fidgeted. They asked for his pink identification card, for which he fumbled in the manner drivers in the United States do when a cop asks to see their driver's license, and they still can't believe they'd been pulled over for speeding. One official checked the ID card, while the other pointed at the goods and yelled at the black marketer.

The officials were slow and confident in their actions, knowing they had more time than the black marketer. They gave him back his card. Slowly. Ever so slowly. Almost pulling it back.

Frowning, they waved him away. He bowed very quickly and overly humbly, thanking them again and again. He then snatched up the corners of his blanket and rushed away with his goods. The officials grinned at each other as they had enjoyed their little terror trip on the poor guy, and then shook their heads and strolled away.

View of the street from prison #2 site, where my cell was on the third floor. Two young, middle trees, having since overgrown view. Photo circa 1995.

It was getting dark and I realized that I hadn't done my meditations. Al Stewart was a badly wounded WWII Army Ranger who ended up becoming my high school history teacher, and gave me my first lesson in how to meditate. Instead of calling it meditation, he labelled the techniques he taught me during my junior year of high school as self-hypnosis. And along with my calisthenics, I highly attributed my new overall self-improvement to it. I was initially drawn by curiosity when I accepted Stewart's offer to hypnotize me. His goal was to help me with my weight problem that had gotten out of hand. From Mr. Stewart, I learned about Wong Tai, the Father of Chinese medicine and one of the authors to describe hypnosis; Socrates, the Father of Western Medicine and another chronicler of the effects of hypnosis; and Julius Caesar,

Franklin D. Roosevelt and just about every powerful leader throughout history who used the imagery techniques of hypnosis to lull and inspire the public toward greater good. And finally, Dr. John Elliotson of the University of London and his protégé Dr. John Esdaile, a Scotsman who did wonders for surgery without anesthesia. Administering anesthesia during the mid 1800s was often more dangerous than the crude surgery practices of the time!

    I would start my self-hypnosis by counting down from five to one, drawing and releasing a breath with each number, tuning all my attention into my heartbeat as I slipped further into trance. After taking five deep breaths, my heart would be beating once per second. The outside world became non-existent, and I would then leave my body, feeling as though I was rising and the Earth was falling away. The hard bed became soft like water. Waves, actually. Slow, rocking waves, like laying out on a raft at sea.

    A smile graced my face. Warm sun rays alighted down through the roof, and onto my skin, my chest, my body. Free from my cell, the sea opened wide around me. There were no crests on the waves. These were early morning waves, slick as glass. Bright sun, lapping waves; my consciousness was free. Completely bypassing my critical factor, I directed my attention to the blank wall above the cell door and installed a positive hallucination of a calendar, and then I would imagine the calendar becoming a clock, where the twelve months from the calendar had changed into the twelve hours on a round-faced clock. The only problem was that since I had a twelve hour clock, I had programmed myself with the intent of getting out within twelve hours. No one can be hypnotized unless they want to be, and with what I had in that prison, I was a truly enthusiastic sub-ject![21]

    After my three hour trip visit to Shambala, I would surface out of hypnosis by counting up my breaths from one to five, recharging with the revitalizing meditation on *Chi* direction. Then I would go over to the cell window for my physical attempt at escape.

    The concrete around the bars was soft. It came away easily, the result of years of humidity working on the cohesion of the concrete. I had been scraping at it with a tin spoon. I chuckled, remembering that the idea came from a movie called *Escape From Alcatraz*. Clint Eastwood's character escaped by scraping away at the crumbling concrete in his cell.

    The plan was to push out the bars, climb out onto the shadowed ledge, run along it for fifteen feet, then climb over the concertina wire and down the housing on the other side of the wall, avoiding the eyes of those in the corner guard house I assumed was hidden behind the large spotted tree. I already learned where everything else was outside my window by using a hand mirror.

Relying on the Vietnamese assumptions that they were simply feeding my vanity, I was able to convince them to give me the hand mirror but used it as a periscope by holding it out and away from the bars as far as I could reach. With it, I determined the only other obstacle keeping me from freedom, other than the bars and the concertina wire, was the clearly visible small guard house at the corner (the one that hinted at a cousin hidden behind the tree on my left), across the two large fish ponds to the right of my view. Nighttime would be when I'd make my break. The mud-like substance that had collected in the shower drain was perfect night camouflage to be smeared on my white skin, which by now was ghoulish from the lack of sun. Fortunately, the Vietnamese had left me my olive-drab shirt and black pajama pants, or else I would have been forced to paint my whole body like the Picts. Once out, I would climb down into the drainage system, or just walk hunched over and dirty like the street beggars (nobody pays much attention to the poor in any country), and make my way to the harbor, and stowaway on a ship. Swedish cruise ships visited all the time. And if that didn't work, I would steal a boat with a sail and fend for myself.

"Come on, man! Move it." I would tell myself, repeating the mantra I'd been using for the last two weeks. "You've only got a few more *hours* in which to do this, before it turns twelve." I dug deeper into the concrete that so easily turned into powder at the slightest scrape of my spoon.

The initial dilemma had been how to hide my scrapings, and the other evidence of my work. I licked that problem by using water to turn the powdered concrete and stucco into a paste. I then would stuff it back into the cracks. It made the going slow, but better to be safe. At the beginning, the act of digging and turning the result into paste was easy.

The corner pillbox I was sure was there, but couldn't see because of the large tree in the way. Photo taken looking back at where my cell would have been, circa 1995.

The telltale signs weren't too bad initially, but now I was starting to get worried because the paste was brittle and didn't hold well once it dried. I would sometimes wake up in the morning to see that in some places the previous night's patch job had fallen out in little, and sometimes not so little, flecks on my table and window sill. Putting those fears out of my mind, I moistened another anthill of milk-blue powder with spit and mortared the crumbly paste back into the cracks around the bars.

A clang at the door scared me out of my rubber sandals. Scrambling, I scraped the mound off the table and ran to the bathroom. Flushing and acting as though I had just come back from the toilet, I went through the motions of tying the string that served as a belt. Taking a breath to calm my heart that was jumping around in my chest, I smiled at the matron as she entered.

"Bonjour monsieur!" She said, as she walked in with my lunch.

The matron delivered a large bowl of curry duck, with two baguettes. As she left, I broke open the French bread, relishing the fact that the Vietnamese were even more into friendly persuasion now, instead of how it had been back in Rach Gia. But, then I looked down at my loaf. There were dead ants inside. A week before the bread had contained live ones. My incorrect assumption then was that it was okay to ingest the ants as long at they were dead. I would simply kill them by dunking the bread in the hot broth. Because of them I quickly learned the Vietnamese word for diarrhea: *dao bom.*

The matron had incorrectly told the officials I was drinking water directly from the tap again, which was full of parasites. I was finally able to convince the interrogators that the ants were the cause of my super *dao bom.* Roasting them neutralized their toxin and rendered them harmless. The matron, who also played at being prison nurse, was, in answer to her own inability, miffed at my ability to correctly diagnose the reason for my ailment. My *dao bom* stopped after they started reheating the bread to kill the ants. The matron's stuck-up attitude was the reason I waited until she left in order to break the bread and make sure the ants were dead. The bread was warm and the ants were still. I took a bite, enjoying the soft bread, ignoring the slightly bitter spice.

While chewing my bread, I looked down at the far corner of my table and noticed a spot where the leftovers of my scrapings had been. Brushing them away, I smiled the smile of the contented. I was going to be able to make my break in a couple weeks!

* * *

Normally the guards turned the latch over with a loud clang, but that night they must have oiled the bolt and slid it over quietly as they snuck into my cell. By the time I realized what was happening, it was too late: my wrists were held by two guards; two others had already grabbed my ankles. The four of them flipped me over on my stomach. Thoughts of sodomy and rape whirled around in my mind, and just as quickly a third guard was beating the back of my calves with a rubber hose.

As they beat me, I tried to jump to that place that I had escaped to the last time I was beaten, the place where the waterfall soothed the sting of the hose. A slap to the back of my neck sent an explosive electrical charge into my skull and out the top of my head.

One of my hands struggled free and found somebody's balls. His scream filled the room until he got away from my hand that squeezed with a pressure I was sure would make them pop.

A fist, or something of that knuckled consistency, hit me where my jawbone connected to my skull. I felt something give and then my world went black for a moment, a world in which the language was Vietnamese, barely heard above the ringing in my ears. I briefly felt searing pain across the back of my calves and the back of my neck. And then I passed out completely and felt nothing.

* * *

"You have been a bad little boy, Fre-der-ick," Le said, as he sat in my desk chair. "What is the meaning of this?" He had burst in with a little mound of moist powder-blue concrete in his hand. I looked over at the window. The other guards were already chipping away at the area around the bars. One of them I recognized as the guy who had punched me the night before. Driven by a surprising urge for revenge, I jumped up from the bed to return the gesture with fists. But my foot was quicker. The guard clutched his groin and fell to the ground.

Le hit me across the jaw with a slap that was more a blow than a slap, making me see sparkling fairies dance in front of my eyes. I fell back onto my bed, the mosquito netting tearing under my weight like Kleenex. The collection of guards who had been picking away at the bars with chisels stopped and looked over at us as though preparing to jump me. Le raised his hand, sighed, and returned his attention to me. "You will not try this again. You will spend the rest of the day helping them repair what you have done. Do you understand?"

I nodded, and fell into a stifling despair.

As Le left, I felt the need to follow him the way horses do when you break them for riding, but one of the guards gave me a hand trough full of fresh mortar. His smile turned into a mocking grin as he then instructed me through sign language and stilted Vietnamese that I would be holding that trough, adding insult to injury.

Chapter 16

"All the world's a stage, And all the men and women merely players."— William Shakespeare

Going to the Theater

O 301148Z DEC 83

FM AMEMBASSY BANGKOK

TO SECSTATE WASHDC IMMEDIATE 5077

"CONOFF [US Consul, Bangkok] discussed with Mr. Truong Tien, Vietnamese First Sec., the Vietnamese response to REFTEL request for humanitarian release for Graham. Speaking from notes, Tien made several points as follows. First, he stated that the provincial court decision in case was already an act of clemency. . . Mr. Tien pointed out that in the Graham case, the provincial court did not levy a sentence of imprisonment but imposed only a fine, specifically to facilitate the release and departure of Graham and his companion. Tien concluded that in the view of the Vietnamese government consideration of humanitarian concern and clemency had been satisfied."

    A rusted tank here, an armored personnel carrier (APC) there, discarded victory trophies of the North Vietnamese littered the South Vietnamese trail of tears of 1975. Sometimes, children played soldier on the gutted war machinery. Other times, I'd catch a quick look at villagers pulling strips of metal off these beasts, as though they were pygmies butchering a great elephant. Le said that blacksmiths used the metal scraps to fashion just about everything from cooking pots to parts for cars, trucks, motorcycles and bicycles. I smiled at the ingenuity and resourcefulness of the Vietnamese, and looked around at my traveling companions in the Ministry of Interior's version of an APC, an airconditioned white Toyota van partially packed with armed guards.
    Every once in a while, the van bumped over a small concrete bridge spanning a ditch, and we would see a two-foot-high concrete post, marked with the name of the next village or town. We had already been advised of our conviction for illegal photography and for violating

Vietnamese territory. The upcoming trial was simply a formality for the government of Kien Giang Province. The term *railroaded* repeated in my mind as I thought about how the interrogators had already coerced me into writing a letter to my parents on September 24, stating that we had been convicted and to be prepared to send money. Now it was already November 28 and the SRV was just now taking us to our trial!

Packed lazily into our van were the driver and Le chatting up front. Behind them were the major and Knight, who ignored each other as they sat in the second row seat. Next to me was a friendly-looking young woman who had introduced herself as Le's Thai-speaking counterpart for Ti and Pi. She and the guard occupied the third seat with me. The last row held Ti and Pi, with a guard between them. Yes, Ti and Pi had been captured, out of fuel, after having scuttled the fishing boat on some island. Pi sat against the left window like me. We had been traveling for three hours now; the sun sweltered high up in the sky, bringing a clarity to the present scene, as I looked at the two, aware that their interrogators had been amateurs and much more sloppy than mine: Ti and Pi both had faded black eyes and dark bruises under their fingernails.

Pi, whose real name was Aht[22], and I traded the giddy laughter that only an anticipated release from prison can produce. He felt so sure of his release that he now talked freely about how they had been captured. Every once in a while, though, he'd gauge himself by glancing at the Vietnamese. The circumstances of their capture had been a nagging question since I first learned of their imprisonment in October.

Leung sat silent and timid. He occasionally glanced at me through breaks in his stare at the bamboo, trees and waving rice fields, that were like lush green seas due to the current rainy season.

"So what happened to you?"

"Oh, bad, bad. Leung and I come, look for you. We no have gas. We go island, they follow. They chase in fast boat. Big cannon!" Aht looked at the guard next to him for a moment, then continued. "We chased by soldier, shoot cannon, I throw grenade. Water— Boom!" He imitated firing a mortar round and then made the shape of a plume of water exploding to the heavens.

Shaking his head, he continued, "We go island. You no there. We no have gas. They shoot bang-bang! Leung say stop, play Buddha! Play Buddha!"

"Pray to Buddha?"

"Yes!" he said, shaking his head, as though not believing it himself, and continued by pointing at his own neck where there used to be two gilded jade Buddhas. "He say stop! Kneel! Pray Buddha! Pray

Buddha! I scream, no! Run! Run!" Aht punctuated with a strong nod of his head.

I roared. It was one of the best laughs I'd had since being caught. With tears in my eyes, I enjoyed it to its fullest. Satirizing the scene in my mind, I envisioned Leung kneeling, looking up at the sky, pleading, "Buddha save us from evil!" as Aht scuttled around in circles, screaming, "Run! Run!" Even the Vietnamese were jolted out of their seats by my sudden hysterics. Knight tried to stare me down.

"Did you hear this?" I asked, as I wiped the tears from my eyes. Knight smiled politely, the tenseness of his face revealing how much the major intimidated him. The major gave him the same kind of look he might have given something that had gotten stuck on the bottom of his shoe. As my laughter subsided, I looked back at Aht. Aht pointed at Knight then raised his hand and pointed at his palm. Then he punched it, and launched me into another bout of uncontrollable laughter. No love lost between the Thais and Knight, that was for sure.

***

Were it not the site for the main political prison in west Vietnam, Rach Gia would be a town I'd remember as idyllically peaceful, having the romance of Paris in the late afternoon, its central canal not unlike the Seine. Memories of cold concrete and psychological warfare tactics made me anxious being back here. Instead of the prison, though, the Vietnamese put us under house arrest in a nice four-story hotel. It was here that I had my first words with a non-Vietnamese, aside from Aht, Leung, and Knight.

At the top of the stairs stood a Vietnamese woman, and a man with coal-black hair and skin so dark it was hard to even believe he was Cambodian. I found the scene very suspicious, as up until now we had been under tight wraps. Uncomfortable in the stillness, we studied each other.

He opened with a bright smile, and the most eloquent English I'd heard in a long time. "Hello, my name is Abul Kalam."

"Hi, my name is Fred Graham, I'm an American photojournalist." I extended my hand, and hoped he'd memorize my name in stone, and broadcast it to everyone outside Vietnam. "What are you doing here?"

"I am a volunteer with UNICEF and a civil engineer," Kalam said.

"Wow, I was an electrical engineering student." And then, just as the guards demonstrated that they were unhappy that I had been talking to anyone, I repeated, "Fred Graham." Kalam grinned and nodded.

The guard nudged me, whisking me away before I could ask more questions. Abul and his translator waved good-bye, as Le and the major came running up the stairs to see what mischief I'd been up to. They both glared at me. I grinned at them, like a child quickly retrieving his hand from the cookie jar.

"Go to your room and stay there!" Le ordered.

* * *

There was knock at my door. Surprising. Dinner had already been eaten, and I had been locked in for the night. The door opened and a guard motioned for me to follow him kitty-corner to a room at the end of the hall.

In the room, the officials were gathered around a small coffee table on which there were brown bottles of Saigon Export beer and small pastries, white Vietnamese cakes, and sugar-coated lady fingers. I laughed at their reaction to my off-hand remark that they should give me a birthday party. But, I was going to enjoy it. Plus, I had learned that whenever we were expected to do something for them, they always did things like this. The Vietnamese had an excellent recipe for manipulation, knowing when to add vinegar and when to pour on the sugar!

Le stood up from his chair. He had the air of a politician. "Freder-ik, we have brought you here, so that we can all help you celebrate your birthday."

Knight stifled a scoff and glared at me with fiery eyes. I couldn't help laughing at his jealousy. I shook my head worn out from Knight's selfish immaturity, reminded that physical age means nothing other than "older" is a year closer to the grave.

"Please sit down and enjoy." Le gestured for us to take one of the rattan chairs.

We sat, Knight staring hungrily at the Saigon Export. Like a vampire quenching a thirst for blood, he sucked the bottle down, reached for a lady finger, and then asked for another beer. One of the bean paste cakes called my name.

"You didn't give me a party on *my* birthday," Knight sniveled, as he sucked down his second beer.

Le looked at him in disgust, and said, "We will give you one next year." Knight's eyes turned wide. Though Knight had said he was a trained comedic actor, this was the first time I believed him. But, I'm sure humor wasn't his intent.

"So what would you like as a birthday present?" Le kidded.

"A free ticket out of here tomorrow."

He translated my request to the rest of the officials. The Vietnamese all laughed. Knight stared in a stupor at the brown bottle in his hands. Considering how well he had handled himself with so many beers in his gut back in Thailand, I was surprised at how much of an effect that only two beers were now having on him.

"You like Saigon Export?" Le asked. "Brewed right here in Vietnam. We send to many other countries."

"Haven't tried one before," I said.

Le passed one over. I searched through the bittersweet taste for formaldehyde. My Australian drinking buddy, Len Clemens, told me that the Thais put formaldehyde in their Singha beer as a preservative. I assumed it was because of the high temperatures, and guessed that the Vietnamese brewers did the same; I wanted to be prepared for the monster hangover if there was to be one.

"Is there anymore beer?" Knight asked.

Le ordered more and asked me, "How old are you today?"

"I'll be nineteen tomorrow," I answered, feeling the full effect of my emotions, along with the beer that had set my temples to throbbing.

The major noticed. Placing his hand on my shoulder, he spoke through Le, "I hope everything will be good for you tomorrow. Wish you a quick freedom." I smiled.

"And what about me?" Knight sniveled, a perfect example of an alcoholic in desperate need of immediate recovery, he had his shaking hands on a sixth beer within an hour.

Le nodded, "And you too, Mr. Knight."

All the people in the room devoured the tea cakes. More were brought. It turned late and Le ended the night by asking us to take some cakes with us to our rooms.

Knight grabbed two beers and an armful of cakes, leaving two lady fingers and a bean paste cake. Le offered more, but I declined. A guard directed me to my room. Inside, I sat on my bed and stared in silence at the room that was lit only by the bright stars and moonlight sneaking in through a tiny window. Thoughts of tomorrow tightened my stomach even further and all I could manage was a light brush of fingers across the cakes in an effort to eat more. I put them aside, and instead made a birthday wish.

* * *

On our restaurant table was a small chalkboard. Scrawled on it was the Vietnamese word for American, My, a tilde above the *y*, pronounced *mee*, with a rise, and a fall, and a rise again of the *ee*, just like the melody of Lennon's *Mind Games*.

I pointed it out to Knight as we entered the dining area of the restaurant for breakfast. A guard noticed it, too, and hurriedly rubbed it out. There was dissension roiling under the surface in Vietnam during the 1980s, like a powder keg with a smoldering fuse. Any sign to feed the people's hopes that they'd be rescued from the oppressive conditions in South Vietnam that started in 1975, even that of an American imprisoned by the ruling dictatorship, could be interpreted as an invitation to revolt. An American in a Vietnam prison, the SRV feared, could be interpreted by the common citizen that he or she had not been forgotten by the US, and that was much to dangerous for Hanoi. If anyone made comment about our identity that was not expressly towards Hanoi's gain, they would have none of it!

Bowls of *pho*, Vietnamese noodle soup, were served and I was reminded that except for my first two weeks in prison, I'd never had a bad meal in Vietnam. I was famished, and hungrily eyed the floating pieces of sliced meat and wide rice noodles. Knight could have cared less. Hypochondria had convinced him he had an ulcer. But, it was inflated ego that forced a scowl across his face when I asked him about his state of mind and then withdrew to my soup.

Leung and Aht were mirrored images of Knight and myself as they sat at the next table. Aht ate wholeheartedly, while Leung meagerly probed the *pho* with his chopsticks. But at least Leung wasn't self-pitying, he was just depressed. As were we all when it came down to it. Even more so as Le bid us enjoy our soup, and in total earnest said that this day's trial was going to be worthy of any American or British court.

* * *

Knight's hotel room was all abuzz shortly after we returned from breakfast. It looked like a military intelligence operations command center, with uniforms and plainclothes everywhere. Thinking about it later, I realized it was more like a collection of actors getting ready for their performance. Everyone, deeply immersed in their preparations, scurried around like first year drama students. Knight was led away to be briefed on how he was to conduct himself at the trial. I asked why they were taking him away to do that, but Le said not to worry about it, and invited me to sit with him.

"Why are they only talking to him?" I asked, again. Knight read from a piece of paper as if he were auditioning for a play and was so serious, you would have thought he was getting ready to portray Hamlet.

"Knight will speak for all four of you during the trial," Le said and crossed his legs in a manner befitting a debonair gentleman. "That will make things easier."

"Easier for who?" I asked, angered that once again Knight was in charge.

To distract me, Le asked, "Do you know the song *If You're Going to San Francisco*?"

"Oh yeah," I said, still keeping all my attention on Knight, "That's a pretty old song."

Le looked hurt, apparently because he had tried to keep hip. "Many times I sing that song when I was a student at Saigon University."

"Maybe you were a student of my father's. He taught English at the university on the side, as a volunteer."

He smiled. "Maybe. Do you know the other song, *Pallet of the King Parrots*?"

"King Parrots?"

"Yes, it is the King Parrot's song," he tried again. "Ballad of the King Parrots. GI's sing it all the time when they were here."

Amazed, I realized how incorrectly Le had pronounced the title of the song. "Do you mean *The Ballad of the Green Berets*?"

The tone and accent of my voice imitating that of an earthy graduate of the Army Special Forces school at Fort Bragg, North Carolina, flustered Le. "Uh, uh, yes, *Ballad Of the Green Berets*."

For a French teacher, you sure don't know how to pronounce 'beret', I thought. He had pronounced the "t" at the end of beret. Suspicion hit me: was he alluding again to previous charges brought against me in Rach Gia? Did he still think I was spy for the CIA?

"Many times while walking in streets, I would hear American soldiers singing it here."

Not a word more from me. Instead, I was like a Chesapeake Bay retriever amongst people, eyes darting from person to person, loyal to attention. The major called for Le, who quickly rose to confer. He then called me over, and said, "We are ready to go."

Knight and I led the hurried file out of the room, down the stairs, and out of the hotel. Abul Kalam and his translator stood at the hotel entrance. They both smiled to us as we left, and Abul flashed an energetic thumbs up for good luck. I didn't return it as I normally would, because I didn't want to bring anymore adverse attention to him that might risk his getting out of the country and verifying to the free world that he had seen us.

Our short walk through Rach Gia's crowded streets took us to a movie theater just down the street from the central market. We had attracted a crowd of gawkers. A parade. The movie currently showing at this theater was a Russian war movie. Posters hung on billboards against the entrance walls, depicting a World War I scene, two biplanes locked in a dogfight. The quality of the poster reminded me of the nostalgically painted posters for *Ben-Hur* when it showed at the Tan Son Nhut Army theater in 1970. Past the side walls of posters, were two sets of opposing stairs that made the shape of a diamond against the back.

The Rach Gia theater used for the mock trial

"Inside," Le ordered, furious that we had attracted such a cheering and enthusiastic crowd, so big it had filled the street, block to block, shoulder to shoulder. We took the right set of stairs. The mob waved goodbye and good luck, much to the chagrin of the military.

Quite large, the theater sat at least five hundred. Up on stage was a large red banner with white letters. The only recognizable words were those for *English* and *American*, along with our names.

"Always wanted my name in lights," Knight joked.

We chuckled. The officials left, except for the major and Le, who motioned for us to walk down the aisle to a bench just in front of the stage.

As we sat down, Knight said, "By the way, they told me to say that we'd accept the fine of ten thousand dollars and that we'd be glad to pay it."

"Are you kidding me?!" I was floored. I reached to get Le's attention, because I was damned if I was going to take this route. I had until this point thought that we were going to have a trial. I didn't know that the *only* reason for trials in Vietnam was in order to make examples of dissenters, and further Hanoi's agenda.

"Don't worry, it'll be okay. They've given me their word that it's only for show and later they'll let us go free as an act of mercy. Propaganda," Knight said in his weak effort to soothe me. I begged God to save Leung, Aht, and me from Knight's testimony, and then sat trembling, holding my hands in fists out of fear and complete rage.

In the five seats along the long table upon the stage sat officials and bigwigs. Facing the audience, they could have easily popped out of any propaganda film from the Soviet Union, China, or North Korea. They all had the slicked back hair, the white shirts, the dark slacks. I was learning that this was the uniform of the Ministry of the Interior: in Vietnam this means the secret police. On a display table fronting the stage was a table with our equipment and my photographs of Grand Pirate Island. I'd never seen them before.

Leung and Aht made a remark about the number of people in the audience. There was a whole theater full! Suddenly, all my self-confidence disappeared! Not only were there thousands of eyes leveled on us, but they belonged to some very angry-looking Vietnamese.

What a contrast to the people outside!

The national anthem of the Soviet Republic of Vietnam blared over the speaker system, and I chuckled to myself, imagining Stalin walking out onto the stage and taking a bow. Everyone stood at attention, saluting or just standing stiffly. Knight, always the brown-nose, had his hand over his heart. I wanted to throttle him. My hands stayed in the pockets of my field jacket. Leung and Aht stood with their hands hung at their sides.

The music ended and the sham began. The five officials on stage read their scripted accusations. Audience reaction quickly interested me more than the trial itself. The whole front row bent forward in interest, as though watching an exciting play. Had I not noticed that they took on the look of intense interest only when the camera crew light stopped on them, I wouldn't have given it a second thought. A salmon-uniformed soldier glared at me with one thought evident in his mind: *Capitalist Dog!* I grinned back at him. The more he glared, the more I returned the opposite. *No intimidation here, big boy!* As a two-man movie crew made their propaganda film, moving freely throughout the entire event, I wished that I, too, was moving just as freely and emotionally removed on the other side of the camera lens.

The crew moved away from the judges, who by then were vainly aware of themselves, preening and glancing at the crew from the corners of their eyes. When the camera light was on them, they sat up straight, smoothing their shirts and hair, trying to put on their best look of stoicism, as though they were the ones persevering through this and not us. I rolled my eyes with incredulity at everyone and their preening, making sure that I was caught on camera at least once.

Leung and Aht continued to look down at the floor. Knight tried to flirt with one of the women in the front row of the audience. She frowned at him. Knight caught me watching, and self-consciously turned away to look at the prosecutors. I stifled a chuckle. Though this trial was no laughing matter, the sham and hypocrisy of the scene was quickly turning everything into a gigantic farce.

An hour passed as each of the five judges spoke, their words being translated into English and Thai. After the officials on the stage went through their script, Knight began his, translated over the speaker system into Vietnamese and Thai.

"We acknowledge the guilt of our crimes, gratefully accepting this verdict of illegal photography and violating territory. And we are willing to pay the $10,000 per person fine."

I scoffed. The light man hit us again with the hot, blinding light and then shifted the light up into the seats for the audience reactions.

We had to go through another two hours as the officials continued reading from their script: talking about how benevolent the Vietnamese Communist Party had been in leveling such a meager fine on us; how lucky we were to be going home soon; and how all the people should feel proud to be protected by such a powerful government. I was overjoyed when they let us out so that I could get away from all the hot air that had collected in the theater from the heat of the day and the mouths of the windbags. Strangely, I was not angry that we had been given a trial that was no trial, but that we had just been used as yet another tool of propaganda for the Vietnamese Communist Party (VCP). Being such an unwilling tool of propaganda for the VCP left an icky, greasy feeling that made me crave a shower. I was dying to get back to the hotel.

Le, Knight, Leung and Aht led the way up the aisle and I followed. The audience started filtering down to check out the evidence table. My first photos seen by the public and I wasn't even able to check them out myself. How ironic! I grinned and shook my head at the hoax of a trial that had just been performed for the residents of Rach Gia, and on film for the rest of the world. I especially enjoyed that the trial had been held in a theater: there is actually truth in the SRV, if only by accident. A woman tapped her uniformed male companion, and pointed at me, clicking her tongue in a "tisk-tisk." I could just hear the goings on in her Communist-programmed mind: *To make light of such a serious occasion!* I laughed at her the way I did when my mother told me that I was going to get it when my father got home. I grinned a little more brightly and then shook my head specifically for her this time as I walked past and whispered, "Sucker."

* * *

O 301148Z DEC 83

FM AMEMBASSY BANGKOK

TO SECSTATE WASHDC IMMEDIATE 5077

"Summary: The Vietnamese government considers that the humanitarian concerns have been already satisfied in the Graham case. He will not be released until the fine and expenses incurred since the court decision have been paid. Graham is in good health and there are no restrictions on his correspondence. Vietnamese response to talking points on the Glomar Java Sea are reported separately.[23] End summary."

Chapter 17

"We only confess our little faults to persuade people that we have no big ones."—
François Duc de la Rochefoucald

Confessions

P 031223Z FEB 83

FM AMEMBASSY BANGKOK

TO SECSTATE WASHDC

"Lau [Vice Foreign Minister Ha Van Lau] emphasized that Knight and Graham were not held in prison, but in a 'place of detention.' He pointed out that this was because their 'crimes' had been dealt with by the Kien Giang Provincial authorities under their own regulations and not under Vietnamese criminal procedures. Their incarceration resulted from a 'provincial decision' and did not constitute a criminal sentence.Vietnam did not want to take such consular cases to the courts because of 'procedural problems' (presumably a reference to the current lack of penal code)."

    I was more than horrified. I was furious! As I lay back on my bed, my eyes searched our cell for Thor's hammer with which to pound Knight into the ground like a thick fence post. Failing, I surrendered to the headache driving its way out through the back of my eye sockets; the eye movement seemed to help dull the pain. The tiredness in my eyes and inability to focus in the dim light of Knight's cell had, unbeknownst to me at the time, indicated that my eyesight had changed from 20/20 to 20/70. That militiaman on Grand Pirate Island had certainly done some damage with the butt of his AK-47.

    Coming back to the horror at Knight's admission of having been to Vietnam before and was actually detained at the airport, I massaged my eyes and then glared at him. He feigned innocence from the table centering our cell. I was moved into his cell right after our return from Rach Gia. The Vietnamese had said it was because they thought we'd prefer it, but I had learned enough about the SRV to know they only wanted to free up my cell for another prisoner.

It wasn't too much of a change, moving into Knight's cell, other than it was definitely a little smaller and the windows were nailed shut so that you couldn't see the prison main yard and parking lot. The only sunlight that came in was that which reflected off the carport, through the thin slits in the shutters. What with Knight's heavy smoking and lack of natural light and air, my eyes would sting most of the day.

As for the furnishings, the guards moved my bed in to share a corner with Knight's opposite the door. Sharing a wall with the staircase, the bathroom was even darker and dirtier than the one I had left. Lighting consisted of a small light bulb above the center table. It was left on twenty-four hours a day for sleep deprivation in order to keep us groggy throughout the day, and too dull of wit to attempt anything rash or adventurous, like overpowering the guards in unison. That light bulb just added to the stress of being forced into sharing a cell with someone who had few redeeming qualities. Till the day he dies, I'll bet Knight will think that he was the only one who suffered in prison during that time. To get away from Knight's never-ending whine about how this was all a conspiracy to grind him down, I'd spend much too much time in bed with the mosquito net lowered, and my back facing the table, which was where Knight spent a lot of his time smoking. But, now he had my complete attention.

"Well," Knight said sheepishly from the table, "when I visited Vietnam the first time to get an idea of the area and find out if I could get to the island on a tourist visa, I had some letters from the Central Intelligence Agency. They were sent to me when I placed a request for maps."

He stopped fiddling with his cigarette and searched me for a reaction. Afraid I might finally do what I'd dreamed of doing since he spoke for all of us at the mock trial, I shifted my attention and concentrated my anger on the ceiling. My thoughts must have been transparent, because Knight suddenly got up from the table and paced the room.

Much to my vexation, he continued to walk barefoot, even after I told him not to. The humidity and the dirt he picked up off the ground made his feet the perfect garden for cultivating fungus. His paddy foot was not just athletes foot, but something much more contagious. My hands pumped in fists, as my arms lay rigid at my sides and I thought about how I possibly could have followed such an idiot. We were Felix Unger and Oscar Madison in a Vietnamese version of *The Odd Couple*. But, while Madison wouldn't listen to Unger because Unger was neurotic, Knight wouldn't listen to me because he was simply ignorant. After all, what could a teenager teach a middle-aged man, eh?

"They confiscated the letters," he said, "and a few months after our capture, they brought them out. You can imagine my astonishment when they confronted me with them."

"You son of a bitch!"

Knight stopped in his tracks. "Now that was bloody rude!"

"Do you realize they were going to shoot me for being with the CIA because of those stupid letters?!"

"I can't believe that," he said, and looked at me as though I was the idiot!

"I had a diary on that boat, you know! The boat that wasn't supposed to have ever been taken. They kept on saying that I'd used *you* to get to Vietnam and join guerrillas still fighting the Communists."

"You're being ridiculous!" he said. "Stop making up stories."

"I've listened to enough of your shit, you asshole!" I said, as I jumped out of bed and went over to Knight whose eyes were as big and round as the moon. I was hit for a second by how small he seemed. "Your fucking letters almost got me killed!" I pounded an imaginary nail into the table with my fist.

He must have thought I was going to peg him right there because he grabbed one of the steak knives from lunch and brandished it in a wimpy rendition of Robin Hood. So pumped up, I just stared him down. He lay the knife down on the table and said, "Sorry, Fred. It's—uh—the stress you know—I don't know what came over me."

Knight then admitted to having attempted suicide with one of those steak knives. I wished that he hadn't chickened out. At least I would have had the opportunity to sleep peacefully that night, instead of with my own steak knife under my pillow, and jumping at every bump and creak for the rest of my time spent with that egotistical nutcase.

* * *

Having confronted Knight, I covered my back with the wall and held a steak knife under my pillow whenever I slept, but that did little to allay fears that I might one day wake to see Knight imitating Norman Bates, standing over me with a knife poised in his hand for attack. The lack of light and exercise, and the paranoia, all contributed heavily to my increasing depression. Many wishes went out for solitary confinement again. At least in solitary I didn't have a daily reminder of how easily I'd been duped by someone I wouldn't even have given a second thought to under ordinary circumstances. As for his volatile nature, it was much too unpredictable. And his paranoia had gotten the best of him, displayed by the way he went through the day, like a cottontail surround by coyotes.

At least the Vietnamese were serving us soup again, making me feel safe enough to return the stolen knife by hiding it in a soup bowl with the other silverware. I was happy that the Vietnamese, in their usual after-meal collection of our dinnerware, hadn't made a comment to us about one too many knives. I especially didn't want to add to Knight's paranoia. He was already checking the light fixture for listening devices. He said that he had done so since first arriving. But he still did it every two or three days, even though we hadn't left the cell in a week.

Wanting to calm him and myself by feeding my idle curiosity, I asked him, "You know, I've always wanted to know what prompted you to get in touch with John Everingham?"

"I was in Malaysia, just about to leave for Bangkok, and I read his story in *Reader's Digest*. Thought he might still be adventurous enough to go."

I fought the extreme urge to laugh and yell, "No shit!"

Instead, I rolled my eyes closed and nodded quietly at the irony of how we had both learned of Everingham. Knight lit a fresh cigarette with the dying embers of his previous one, and moved away into the bathroom to work on his *chemical experiment*.

Two days after I was relocated to Knight's cell, he had asked me about the fermentation process for preparing alcohol. Thinking back to my high school and college chemistry classes, I told him that fermentation occurs naturally. The next day he pilfered a steel plate from dinner and mashed his portions of bananas.

By Christmas, Knight had his own steel plate banana distillery. Everyday he strained out the floating mold by pouring the creation through one of his dirty socks into another plate. On Christmas Eve, he decided it was time to get an alcohol fix.

Utterly amazed that he would do something this crazy, I wondered for a moment if it would be that bad if he died of alcohol or food poisoning. He offered some, but considering how our damp cell was such a perfect breeding ground for every kind of bacteria imaginable, I politely refused. Bile came up, leaving a tangy aftertaste as I watched him. With a toast to our freedom, he swallowed. I cringed and glanced away.

"What's it like, Richard?" I asked, unable to control my laughter.

He seemed to be getting a high, but then I thought he was in the initial throes of a toxic reaction. And then again a slight smile lifted the corners of his mouth. "It definitely has an alcohol tang to it. Sure you don't want some?"

Dark yellow ooze seeped out of his dirty brown sock and onto the plate. I refused with a furious shake of my head.

"I'm going to make more! " he declared, triumphantly high on the panacea. He'd found his old support system.

In three days he had four plate distilleries operating behind the toilet. While urinating, I found it hard to keep from accidentally spilling on his still in minutiae.

"Are you sure this is the best place to hide your experiment?" I asked.

"Think nothing of it, Fred. They'll never find it there."

"That's true."

I made sure not to take a shower within two hours of his. I had enough problems with the fungusamongus between my toes, and had no interest whatsoever in mixing with whatever was surely crawling through his veins.

* * *

Christmas comes cold in a Vietnamese prison. As there was hardly any ventilation in our cell, the chill of my first Christmas in a Vietnamese prison lingered all too long. Also, because of the stifling quarters, Knight's constant smoking had turned the cell into a stinky ashtray, and I imagined the second-hand smoke had somewhat damaged my lungs. I dealt with the cold by layering my tailored pin-striped Vietnamese pajamas under my good trial clothes and my field jacket.

Le walked in on Christmas morning and derailed my train of thought about the length of time we'd already spent cooped up, and guided us out to the interrogation room. By this time, there were no longer any interrogations: Knight never let more than a couple of days pass without writing a request for audience. Visits were mainly social, and mostly by request through notes from Knight. Le would always come to ask what was wrong, expecting an emergency, only to become annoyed with Knight's constant nagging about our release date.

But today, Le was visiting out of consideration. We were supposed to have been released by Christmas at the latest. I gave Le a look of empathy because I could now see that he and the major were just the ones left holding the bag while all those other officials had gone on to more important business, such as more status building concerns for the Ministry of Interior. By the sad expressions on their faces, it was clear how much they hated coming to tell us the bad news, if for no other reason than they were stuck with us.

"Mr. Lee." Knight often mispronounced Le's name. I'd sometimes wonder if it was because he was trying to insult them, or that he was so self-centered and above everyone else, much as with Aht and Leung, that he couldn't show the respect of at least remembering such an easy name, especially the name of someone he saw just about every week. "You said that we would not have to pay the fine."

"I know. I'm sorry, but that is what Hanoi has said. You must pay, or you will not be freed. You could be here forever." The corners of Le's mouth dropped even further.

"Mr. Le, my family doesn't have that kind of money and you know my financial situation."

"Yes, yes, we all know about it. If it were my decision, I would let you go free."

Knight and I remained quiet, contemplating our dilemma. "Here. We have brought gifts for your Christmas." Le smiled, pulling out four beers and two Vietnamese cakes.

Knight and I both smiled half-heartedly. The Vietnamese tried to continue a conversation with us, but we were completely lost in depression. There was nothing more for us to talk about.

* * *

New Year's Eve, 1984 was just as sorry as Christmas. Knight had written a letter to Le, and Le arrived expecting some important bit of information, or that Knight had completely lost his mind. Knight beleaguered Le with basically one question: would the ransom be paid; or, would the SRV acquiesce and just let us go? The reasoning behind this was that our situation had been outlawed in the United States and Great Britain almost a hundred years earlier: debtors' jail—no money, no freedom.

Still, it was New Year's Eve, and even though Hanoi had no compassion, Le did, for he brought us some candied coconut. And to placate Knight, there was a Saigon Export. A few swigs and he was quiet as a mouse, more despondent, but quiet nonetheless. Matter of fact, whenever we did get booze, I gave all my beers to him, for when he shut up, all was well within my world. In truth he didn't really need the beers, as he was well onto deriving a pretty good buzz off the homemade banana rum. The Saigon Export did have a higher alcohol level, though. It was while Knight finished his three beers, and asked me if I was going to finish mine, that he told me what had happened to him while I was in solitary.

"They took you to the island?!"
Knight nodded, "Yes."
"Did you find the rest of the treasure?!"

"I'd love to tell you what we did find."

"You mean you didn't find the treasure—they let you go wherever you wanted?"

"I'd love to tell you what I did find," Knight said, in that tone that only served to aggravate me because of its condescension. "When we are free, I'll tell you."

"Why won't you tell me?"*Of all the assholes in the world*, I thought, *why did I have to have him as my cellmate?* "You know that they're going to take all the treasure, even with your stalling, and we're going to have to go back into the world saying we found nothing, else be considered a couple of wingnuts?"

He steered the conversation toward a box of matches on the table. "Want see a magic trick?" He had learned the trick during his short entertainment career on cruise ships.

What had been a matchbox holding ten spent matches, soon held only five. But, my curiosity soon turned to disgust when I realized that this was just another one of his games of secrecy and deceit, that he took some twisted pleasure in not telling me how he did it. Alcohol wasn't his only addiction; it sat alongside deceit and chicanery. I would have been even more infuriated, but then I remembered the fable about the frog who offered a scorpion a ride across the river, if the scorpion promised not to sting him. But when they got to the middle of the river, the scorpion stung him anyway. While they were both beginning to drown, the frog asked him why he'd done it. The scorpion, replied, "I couldn't help it; I'm a scorpion."

* * *

In the morning darkness of January 16th, I was roused from a sound sleep and sped to the well-furnished Tan-Binh Hotel. After a shave, shower, new clothes, and a breakfast of fried eggs and croissants, I was led into a meeting with members of the World Affairs Council. Peter Tarnoff was the first to offer his hand. Leader of the delegation, he would become Undersecretary of State for Political Affairs during Clinton's first term. Carter-era Senator Dick Clark from Iowa, and two other representatives were introduced: Linda Hiebert, a nurse with thick glasses; and Anthony Lake, a young, trim professor from Mount Holyoke in Massachusetts, who had camouflaged his smile with a red beard and mustache.

We took seats at the long table that left hardly any room to maneuver in such a small room, with the delegation on one side and the Vietnamese and me on the other. Senator Clark observed from his seat, taking labored breaths into his bull of a body. Like most Americans fresh off the plane, the heat of the tropics didn't seem to agree with him. With a fatherly smile, he watched Tarnoff interview me.

Tarnoff told me they were on a fact-finding mission throughout Indochina. *Good luck!* I thought. The only way to learn about human rights, or lack of them, is to spend time in a country's prison. Not many are willing to bring investigative reporting to that level of truth, especially those broadcast journalists who make millions of dollars a year. I would have gladly given them a tour of the prison in Rach Gia if that's what they really wanted to do. But, clear reporting of SRV police brutality was out of the question.[24]

There was a short silence. I found it interesting that Tarnoff was wearing a blazer. That sports coat must have been hot. Tarnoff began asking questions, after telling me that my parents were fine and very worried for my safety. My spirits that had risen sky-high with finally meeting my countrymen, sank under the weight of knowing in my heart it had been tough on my parents, no matter what Tarnoff relayed.

"But they are fine, and expecting your release soon," Tarnoff said. "How is your food, are you getting everything you need?"

"Oh yeah, everything's A-okay. We're very well fed," I answered, noticing something very interesting to me. It was not so apparent in the others, but in Tarnoff it was clear.

He had the look of a wolf hunting or checking his presence in a new area. His eyes scanned and scrutinized, more keenly aware of everything and everyone than the others. He asked questions, while his eyes looked for answers in my body movements and the actions of the Vietnamese, who were doing the same back to Tarnoff. I would later learn that he had been part of the delegation that went with Kissinger to Paris for the peace talks.

"Do you have any vitamins?" I asked.

"Why? Is there anything wrong?!" Tarnoff asked, his body tensing exactly like that of a wolf who had just gotten on the scent of caribou.

"Oh no; it's just that we'd probably feel a lot better with vitamins. Our eyes are hurting. No sunlight in our cells, you know."

"You haven't had any sunlight?!" Tarnoff asked.

"No," I said, "I guess it has to do with their bureaucracy." I might as well have tossed a grenade. After the commotion quieted, the Vietnamese glared at me. But, I continued looking straight ahead, doing well to ignore the psychic slaps to the back of my head. Tarnoff, whose own eyes lit up as if a hot rock had been dropped into his hands, glanced at the Vietnamese along with the rest of the delegation.

"What's this about no sunlight, Mr. Le?" Tarnoff asked. "We expect them to get more sunlight."

"Yes, there will be more sunlight," Le grumbled. If I'd not said anything, I'm sure that the sunlight we needed in order to keep the skin diseases at bay would have still been kept from us.

"Fred," Tarnoff said, "we have some money here from your parents. It should help you get some extra things, like vitamins." He slid 90 dong across the table. Le took it as the Vietnamese were afraid I'd bribe a guard for my freedom.

"And here." Hiebert pulled a bottle of Centrum out of her purse and gave it to Tarnoff.

"Great!" I said and reached for the offered bottle. But, Le grabbed it and after reading the bottle's disclaimer about overdosing, would only ration one vitamin a day to Knight and me, even after I told him that I wasn't like Knight, that I was far from thoughts of suicide.

"We'd just like you to know that what you've done was a very wrong and stupid thing to do," Tarnoff said.

I grinned, because he was right. It had been a criminal thing to do; but the Vietnamese had so politically charged the situation, I was no longer just some stupid kid who had made a mistake. It was Vietnam trying to grab as much money as they could, if not from the American government, at least from its citizens. Like the Vietnamese said—if I was from my mother's country, I would have been out within two weeks of my capture. My grin faded though, after Tarnoff repeated his statement. He was trying to lead me into an emotional response. I acted full of sorrow, and nodded. Still, I knew that the Vietnamese were going to get their money; sorrows, and apologies, or not.

"We're doing our best to get you out. Your parents have a fund going to raise the amount." Tarnoff turned to the officials. "Hopefully, the Vietnamese government will be lenient and let you go before then." I was starting to wonder about Tarnoff's negotiation skills, because dictators only understand the language of force. Even General Giap, who ordered the murder of thousands during and after the war, admitted that had we continued bombing Hanoi for a few more days, the Communists would have surrendered and we wouldn't have been dealing with the disastrous effects of a loss in Vietnam for the next twenty-nine years.

Tarnoff reached into his flight bag and pulled out a tape recorder. "Fred, I thought it would be a good idea if you sent a message to your parents."

My sorrow was no longer an act as I looked down and spoke into the microphone. "Hi, Mom and Dad. I just want to say, please don't worry, and I'm okay. I love you. . ."

"Great, Fred. Your parents will be very happy to hear your voice."

His words were comforting.

"Have any questions?" he asked.

"How's the hunting and fishing season doing?"

Everyone chuckled, and Tarnoff answered, "Well, hunting season is pretty much over, but trout season should be real good this year." His smile moved his gray sideburns out a bit. We were all relieved by the momentary diversion. "We plan to have you out by Tet. So maybe you and I can do some pheasant hunting."

"That'd be great! We can go to Grizzly Island over in San Pablo Bay!"

"Great, great. . . Well, if you don't have any more questions?" Tarnoff paused, "We'd like to take some pictures for your parents." Tarnoff looked at Le, "That's all right isn't it, Mr. Le? Can we take him downstairs, since we have to leave now?"

"Sure, sure."

Outside, I was directed to stand between Tarnoff and Senator Clark, as Lake prepared to take the picture. Le, who had stuck to me like a wasp on meat, moved out of the way. Always the prima donna, he was now extremely camera shy, leading me to believe he was more than just a teacher and translator. Maybe *he* was the "spy-man."

"So tell us, what's really happening, Fred?" Tarnoff whispered. *Fantastic set up for not being overheard!* I thought, and cracked a nervous smile.

"Well, they said they were going to shoot me after two months, if I didn't admit to being a spy. They kept talking about a South Vietnamese Colonel Vo, who was executed in Hanoi a couple of years ago for trying to start a revolution." (The Hanoi government didn't execute this colonel until the early 1990's. He had spent all the 1980s in prison, with the public thinking he was already dead.)

"They did?" Tarnoff seemed surprised. Disgust hardened his voice. "Well, don't you worry; we're going to get you out. It'll be soon."

"Great! Knight's the one I'm worried about, though. He's losin' it."

"Don't worry about Knight. The thing is to get you out. Knight's rubbed too many people in Thailand the wrong way."

I nodded, relieved that there were other people who had seen through his conniving.

"Keep your chin up, and we'll get you out. Okay?"

I smiled even though I knew that the people who would be getting me out of Vietnam would be either my family or friends, because, publicly, Reagan's Administration wasn't paying ransoms.[25]

After our good-byes, Tarnoff and the rest jumped into the dark blue mini-van. They waved back through the windows and all I could do was wish that I was leaving in the van with them. My wish didn't come true.

I stood alone in the driveway. All the Vietnamese were sitting and talking amongst themselves in the lobby behind the glass entrance. Glancing back over my shoulder, the streets of Saigon beckoned. *Just one step, then another, and then you're gone.*

With a deep breath, I slowly turned. Putting my hands in my pockets, I raised my eyebrows in acknowledgment of Le, who stood waiting in the entrance. The sound of my thongs echoed in the lobby entrance like a slow drum beat.

* * *

Youth's advantage, whether in attitude or actual years, is that a child's mind is an empty cup needing filling. When we get old, our cups fill with stagnant water. Since age is really only a perception, feeling old or young is really a choice. I was now going to see how much my youthful and politically incorrect attitude would turn into our favor. Conditions had improved slightly because of my statement about bureaucracies during the meeting with Tarnoff. They now let us have sun, something they never went out of their way to offer their own people in prison. It taught me a lot about international respect and how even America's enemies listen when the US government makes itself clear: those with the most guns and money run the world; and that the old proverb about the squeaky wheel getting the grease, applies everywhere.

Our solar visits were tranquil, much like a Victorian high-tea, though not as elegant. Never did the Vietnamese take us out in the sun together. It was always one person a day. I found it ironic that the sky was overcast every day we were permitted sun. Still, barely half an hour left my skin sunburned. For something to do, other than sit at a table, sip tea, and watch bananas grow against a concertina-topped brick wall, the guards played chess with me. They always won. Chess was a game I wanted to learn when I was free. Knight enjoyed bragging about how he always won at chess. But, the Vietnamese didn't like that he always won. Sunning suddenly stopped only a month after my visit with the World Affairs Council. It would be Knight's last time in the sun for a while, both literally and figuratively.

By the time Le and the major called us into the interrogation room at the end of the hall, in order to celebrate Tet with us, Knight was beyond broken. There wasn't even a hint of the forceful, arrogant ship's captain, at least with any strength to back up his words. So caught up in his own world, he'd done nothing to work on his inner strengths.

Even with our cramped conditions, I had already begun to feel better. Prime Minister Nehru was once quoted as saying that one of the best experiences he ever had was that of being imprisoned by the British, specifically solitary confinement. Now having had my own experience in solitary, I understood completely how solitary time used for introspection and inner work is priceless. To this day it still amazes me that the American prison system is based on pressing everyone into small cells, that are really just schools for criminals, and putting the uncontrollable prisoner in solitary as a last resort, when the reverse would be so much more productive.

Knight was one who could never find himself without the safety net of others: those whom he cowered behind and those whom he could manipulate. Every day he tried to manipulate my emotions by complaining that he was wasting away and couldn't sleep without sleeping pills. I reveled in my own weight loss. My erect posture was still an indication of my feelings about the situation. *I'll continue to use this experience to build me*, I thought, *instead of destroy me*.

Le brought back my attention with his statement, "We have come here tonight, on our own time to bring you gifts to help you celebrate Tet." He paused and asked, "Do you know Tet?"

"Vietnam's New Year," I answered. Le gave that fond look of a teacher again.

"Mr. Lee! Your government said we would be out by now. Why are we still here?!"

They both nodded at Knight, as Le said, wearily, "We know this Mistah Knight, but we have no control over the situation. The Kien Giang Provincial Court has decided you must pay $10,000 each. You pay, or you will not be freed."

"Mr. Le, we don't have that kind of money. . . " I said, as Knight nodded in agreement.

"We know that, but the court says you must pay."

"Then we're never going to get out!" Knight and I said in unison. Our exasperation hung as heavy as the cold morning fog of the Mekong.

Le offered an expression of empathy, and said, "The court is separate from the government. It is not ruled by Hanoi. Hanoi can say you must be freed, but Kien Giang sets the conditions. They are separate from each other."

"That really doesn't help us does it, Mr. Lee?" Knight sniped. I looked away, bored from the same conversation we had been having with the interrogators for the last three visits. It was so pointless from our financially and physically weak position against the Southeast Asian powerhouse of the VCP. To complain about something that I could not control only intensified my frustration.

"What's in the bag?" I asked.

"Oh!" Le smiled, jumping at the opportunity. "We have brought food. Very special. To celebrate Tet."

Out of the little mesh bag came a small plastic bag of candied fruit, and two large square items bundled in leaves. The candied coconut slivers, ginger slices and papaya cubes were easy recognize, but the small square packages wrapped in tobacco-colored leaves weren't. "Those are lotus leaves, right?"

Le nodded. "That is *banh chung*," he said, displaying it like a piece during Show and Tell. "It is a meal specially prepared for Tet. Inside, is a mixture of glutinous rice, peanuts, soybeans, and meats. All wrapped in lotus leaves. *Banh* means cake, and *chung* is how the rice is prepared to make the cake. Very, very good."

He smiled as though he'd been hit by an earth-shattering realization, and then raised his index finger as though he were in class. "There is an ancient story of twenty-two sons participating in a cooking competition in order to ascend the Hung throne. One of the sons, name of Lieu, was advised by a goddess to prepare a meal of two cakes: one square to symbolize Earth, the other round to represent Heaven. He was then told by the goddess to put peanuts, beans and meat in the Earth cake to represent the plants and animals. The Heaven cake was made with rice. When the King ate Lieu's cake he like so much, that he say, 'You are a great and devoted son! You will take my throne when I die.'—and that is how you get two cakes," he said, and jabbed the *banh chung*. "Earth wrapped in Heaven."

"Good story, Le," I said. *Now if only the cake had a file in it.*

A glutton for anything to take my attention away from concrete walls and bars, I was more than ready to try it. Knight, on the other hand, stared blankly at the *banh chung*. It was all irrelevant to him: he had already made it clear, in private of course, that he despised Vietnam. If he were American, he would have been the quintessential *Ugly American.*

Knight came out of his daze. "Mr. Lee, paper, please! Do you have any paper? I need to write a letter. Can you send a letter for me? Please?"

Have some self-respect, man! A childhood character flashed across my thoughts as I watched Knight: "Precious. . . Sweet Precious." The words percolated up from when my father would read books to my brother and me at bedtime. I could hear slimy, selfish

J.R.R. Tolkien's Gollum as if we were in this Vietnamese cave together. Reading had always been something I turned to in order to escape; I chuckled at how easily the boundary between fiction and non-fiction shifted.

"Yeees, yeees. Mistah Knight, you will have some paper. Here! We also have beer for you," Le answered impatiently. Knight's eyes lit up. Le handed two bottles to him, as if trying to appease the spoiled child with his favorite treat. Impatient to leave, Le and the major tapped their fingers and glanced at their wristwatches.

"Out of the goodness of our hearts, we have come to visit you. Now, we must go and be with *our* families."

"The pen and paper?!" Knight said. Le nodded, and reached into his old leather attaché, withdrew five small pink letter sheets, two envelopes, and two pens and handed them to Knight.

This time was something far from ordinary: after we gathered our goodies and left the table, we all left the room together. Always before, either they would go first, or we would be sent out first. It was very disarming. I would have fallen into the Stockholm Syndrome had I not been very aware of it. But, I knew of how the psychology of a hostage could shift toward feelings of friendliness towards the captor. I would have been convinced that the SRV was a kind, benevolent government that was only keeping us safe, well-fed, and mildly entertained, instead of what I actually thought, and that was that Le and the major were just doing their jobs as lackeys to Hanoi, and that the Communist regime was Satan's kingdom on earth.

* * *

China was notorious during the Korean War for their ability to coerce American POWs into collaboration. Following the KISS principle (Keep It Simple Stupid), their technique was like a drop of water wearing away a concrete wall; it relied on pressure, consistency, and time. First they would get you to agree on one mildly anti-American or pro-Communist statement. Then, they'd build through association, to much more grandiose statements, all the way to the point that even if you were red, white and blue when captured, you would now be reciting statements such as: "America is the birthplace of Hitler, and only Communism can save America and the rest of the World." More importantly, you would actually wholeheartedly believe what you stated. I would never again look at the *The Manchurian Candidate* as fiction. The Vietnamese, though not as sophisticated as the Chinese, had something just as good for their influence: they had Richard Knight.

"Richard. We've already sent a letter to our parents and the consuls. What else can we do?" I said as I stood away from the table.

"We've just got to push."

"You can push your people, but I'm not going to push mine!" My feelings of guilt had ruined my sleep every night since learning about my parents from Tarnoff.

"Please just write a letter to your parents."

"Why do you persist in being so petrified?" I asked as I sat back down at the table. Escape from Knight's cell was definitely not as feasible as from my previous cell where the concrete was in worse shape. But, like the time I lied to myself and said I felt better, and then did feel better, I had to vehemently tell myself I was going to get out. In contrast, Knight could only look at the dark side of life. His sight ended at the wall of the cell, speeding him along on his downward spiral into self-pity and self-destruction. But self-destruction doesn't happen overnight, and it would soon become clear that Knight had been on this downward slide for a very long time.

"Why are you on this idiotic macho kick?" he asked, as he jumped up from the table, pounded his fist on it and glared down at me.

"What are you talking about?" I asked, sadly reminded of the persona I had traveled with from Thailand to Vietnam.

"You agitate the Vietnamese, only creating a worse situation for the both of us!"

I jumped up from the table and faced him. "Get this, Knight! This ain't no macho trip. One of the reasons we've been getting better treatment is that I haven't been kissing ass! They may not agree with my politics, but at least they respect patriotism, Dick!"

He took a swing at me and I ducked, but not in time to keep him from clipping my ear. In the same move I already had my fist coming at him. I hit him with the full force of my weight in that punch. He fell to his knees, out of breath and holding his stomach. He looked up crying.

I stared back, amazed that all of the martial arts learned in class as a ten-year-old still had some use. And the effect of my punch told me that there was definitely something to be said about doing a hundred pushups a day.

"Are you okay?" I asked, bewildered that everything had happened so smoothly, without much more than a slight sting to my clipped ear.

He didn't answer as he grabbed the table and dragged himself up from the floor. Sitting at the table, he looked at me without saying a word, and I thought he was going to cry again, the way he had done a few nights ago. Normally I would have had the compassion to offer words of comfort. But not after his little boxing stunt.

I paused for a moment as hot blood pounded my eardrums. "Have you been aware of how they've been looking at you when you snivel and agree with them all the time? They're not idiots! If you were a true Communist, you'd want to stay here." I searched for more words. Knight stared wide-eyed at me, befuddled. "It's almost like the Allied prisoners in Japanese prison camps during World War II. The Japanese gave the prisoners horrible conditions, because they thought of them as less than dogs for surrendering. Thank god we're not in the same situation!"

Knight nodded, painfully getting his words out, "But you can't keep on doing these things, like you did at that meeting with your people!"

"Man! Have you forgotten our solar visits after that meeting? Do you think the Vietnamese would've given it a second thought if I hadn't brought it up during the interview with Tarnoff?!"

"Okay, okay."

"Would you please just write a letter, then?"

"I'll write a letter, if you'll stop pestering me. But it won't be a demand to my parents."

"Would you also see if they could pay for me?"

I almost hit the floor. "Are you joking?!"

"The whole idea, Fred, is to get out of here, and that means paying the fine."

"My parents, I know, will barely have enough to pay for me; and you're asking me to put another burden on them?!"

"I assure you, Fred, please, there'll be no problem. Tell them I will repay them their money with interest. The money we'll make on the book and movie rights will more than cover it," he stressed, giving me that look of honesty that I was still learning was really just a ruse. He gulped for air and beseeched, "Fred, ask your parents if they can get us both out; and I'll do the same in my letter. I'll be more than able to pay them back with the money from the book and movie."

I sat in my chair thinking about his request, while he bided time by pacing back and forth and sucking his lower lip. After a long while, during which I realized the unstable nut might crack again, I spoke. "Okay, Richard, but I'm not asking them for $20,000. I'm putting your request and offer in the letter, repeating exactly what you've told me. It will be their decision completely." My father had sense. He would know why I was even writing.

Knight paused for a moment and agreed. We both wrote our letters. Knight asked to read my letter. It was just another action in a long line of actions that taught me to never trust a person who acts overly suspicious of everyone else. In a tit-for-tat manner, I asked for *his* letter. I was surprised to read that he was keeping up his part.

We went to our cots, and I asked, "Is your father still alive?"

"Yes, why do you ask?"

"Well, you've never talked about him."

Knight sat up and walked over to the table. The harsh light from the bulb hooded his eyes in a scowl of darkness. "He divorced my mother when I was young. We haven't kept in touch. He's remarried and has another family."

"Do you think he might help you out at all?"

"Absolutely not." He hardened more, as though he was holding an old pain. Knight changed the subject by asking, "Did I tell you that there's a treasure site in the Caribbean?"

He had them all lined up, but I was not interested. I'd had enough of treasure hunting to last a lifetime.

"Did I tell you that I lived in Brazil?"

Knight had said that one of the reasons he couldn't get a loan from the British Embassy, in order to get out of Vietnam, was that he had already done so before. The loan had been to get out of Brazil when he was broke. I was surprised that the British government had given him back his confiscated passport. He was supposed to pay back his loan in order to get it, but he never did.

"I've got a child there you know."

"You do?!" I said, truly happy for him. *Maybe he isn't such a scum, after all*, I thought.

"I haven't seen her in a while." He waited. He gauged me, watching my expression in order to decide what to say next, something else he could use on me.

"You see, she's illegitimate."

"That's okay; I think it's great that you have a child." I said, and thought, *Maybe, if he had spent more time with her, then he might not have turned into such a self-serving son-of-a-bitch.*

His manipulative attempt was so naked, I wanted to turn my head. Instead, it was Knight who spun on his heels and sulked over to his bed. I closed my eyes, promising never to let anyone else read the word "sucker" on my forehead.

The stress of our situation was beginning to have an effect on me on a subconscious level. I was now having a recurrent dream that I hadn't experienced since my family and I left Singapore. The images had started coming back infrequently in Bangkok, but now these images haunted me every other night. They always started with a white screen across my mind. Then, just as suddenly, the whiteness morphed into a surreal red. The redness drew much of its grotesqueness from its resemblance to blood. Shapes appeared in the blood, looking like entrails. And suddenly again, the scene would change to pink, like strawberry syrup dizzyingly swirled into vanilla ice cream.

But this was no sweet dream. It was a nightmare that until now had meant nothing more than time spent as a child waking up with a question of what it meant to sleep peacefully. It would be a few more months before I'd understand why this nightmare had plagued me throughout my childhood, and was again repeatedly rousing me from my sleep, only to awaken in a sickening sweat.

Chapter 18

"A sound mind in a sound body, is a short, but full description of a happy state in this World: he that has these two, has little more to wish for; and he that wants either of them, will be little the better for anything else."— John Locke

"All the wrong people remember Vietnam. I think all the people who remember it should forget it, and all the people who forgot it should remember it."— Michael Herr

New Digs

P 031223Z FEB 83

FM AMEMBASSY BANGKOK

TO SECSTATE WASHDC

"[Vice Foreign Minster Ha Van Lau] seemed to be trying to propose some kind of (undefined) face-saving solution now that the Vietnamese realized that neither Knight/Graham nor HMG/US were able (or willing) to pay US dollars 20,000 for their release. If neither are released this Tet, and the requisite cash is not subsequently found (if it is, they will most certainly be released), the Vietnamese may put off a decision until May. . ."

  Desperation had wrapped its coils tightly around Knight and it was only a matter of time until he would finally pop. Until then, we had an opportunity for travel that carried with it the release from this pressure, but Knight was reading more into it than I thought possible. It didn't help that the officials had been so cryptic in their notification yesterday: we had to have all our belongings ready to go by this evening. Even when we pleaded with them to tell us what was up, they said nothing other than be ready. And now Knight, full of visions of disembarking to the lights of London's press corps after a freedom flight out of Vietnam, rushed around madly collecting his belongings that had been strewn all over the place in some subconscious, primal attempt to mark his territory. I quickly finished stuffing my pack and sat down to watch his antics. I was mesmerized, yet perplexed by his excited dance from one personal item to the next.

Sadness overcame me, even though his exaggerated, jerky movements would have been considered by many to be humorous.

"Now don't get excited, Fred, don't get excited, let's not jump to conclusions."

He wasn't even aware of what he was doing.

"They haven't exactly said we're free."

Having my own frustrations put upon by Knight, I sighed and then answered, "I know that, Richard. But we're moving and any movement in this incarceration is good for the mind."

"Yes, yes, but we shouldn't jump to conclusions," he reemphasized, as he grabbed his little flight bag.

There was a knock at the door. It was Le. "You are ready?" he asked.

We both nodded, and were then taken downstairs to wait in the guard room next to the front gate. A beautiful Vietnamese woman in a pink *ao-dai* teased us with a smile as she gazed down upon us from a calendar on the wall of the guard room. Taking seats that faced her, Knight, Le and I waited quietly, until what Knight had tried to hide by donning a calm façade, erupted. "Mr. Le, where are we being taken? To a hotel?" he asked, and then smiled expectantly.

"We are taking you to another prison. A better prison. Where you can have sun all the time," Le answered, with a polite smile.

"Uh-huh." I said, and then chuckled, remembering a Russian idiom from one of Le's books: "Do not divide the skin of an un-killed bear." I smiled, secure that I had finally learned the difference between optimism and false hopes. While Knight's delusions repeatedly dragged him deeper, my optimism lifted my sight toward seeing the sun rise on the day of my freedom. I had shared this with him once, but he cold-shouldered me the way a dark cloud does the sun. And now as we waited to go to the new prison, I wondered how much longer it would be until Knight would again put the blade of a steak knife to his wrists.

We were loaded into cars that shot out through the gates, spending the next ten minutes or so banging shoulders as we sped through screeching turns and down dark, not always empty streets. Countless men and women would have become statistics had the driver not been as good as he was in dodging pedestrians.

"We are almost there," Le said, as we made a sharp right off the large boulevard of D Ton—called Hai Ba Trung when I lived in Vietnam as a child—and on to Duc Thang.

A large barbed wire-topped wall on our left separated us from the Saigon River and a docked ocean freighter. We arrived at the mint-green iron gate of the former South Vietnamese and American Central Intelligence Agencys' interrogation center, at #3 Bach Dang (after the fall of Saigon, Bach Dang was renamed Duc Thang).

Fortified like Kien Giang Provincial Prison, just a little smaller with walls not as high, it was evident we were about to be locked in a *real* prison once again. As we walked briskly across the red earth lot I looked up and noticed blinking red aviation warning lights on top of the broadcast tower jutting into the heavens. The guards took us to the right of the entrance and into a hallway cordoned off by yellow, inch-thick bars of two large gates.

Entrance to Bach Dang #3

Vietnamese prisoners lay in sleepy disarray in the tiny courtyard. Jumping to attention, they gawked guardedly at us as we entered. One of our entourage, yelling and waving, withered all curiosity that had greeted us. The prisoners about-faced and returned to their grass mats and whispers. Passing a second gate, we went through an open wooden door to a small hallway. Mounds of bricks, bags of concrete, and wheelbarrows along the unfinished walls immediately compelled me to wonder what our cells would be like. They stopped us short of the full length new and unfinished rooms, and directed us into our new cell. Just inside, on the right, was a concrete bathtub. In the opposite corner was a small round table with two chairs. In contrast to Rach Gia this was the Ritz-Carlton of SRV prison cells; the bathtub was our penthouse Jacuzzi.

I shifted my attention across the mini-yard to an open metal door. We all walked through the door, and watched as two guards wasted no time preparing our sleeping quarters in this cell within a cell. Two wooden pallets would be our new sleeping arrangements, spaced parallel, with a mosquito net over each. I imagined if we weren't being good little boys, all they'd have to do was close that door that separated the sleeping section of our cell from our mini, private sunning yard, and it'd be just like our cells at Rach Gia. Except that now, because there were two of us and this cell was smaller than our last one, it would really be worse.

"This place has sun all the time. It's much better, don't you think, Fre-der-ik?"

Aghast, I stared at Le but couldn't think of anything to say, other than what I had been saying all along about putting us on a jet plane out of here. He walked around the cell repeating over and over that this was a new cell, and a good cell, as though having a good cell made up for our still being stuck in prison. Le had his own memories of being locked up for demonstrating against the South Vietnamese government; he should have known better. I wanted to grab him by the shoulders and shake him, yelling, "This doesn't make up for freedom!" He must have been reading my mind for he evaded my gaze. While Knight walked around the cell in a state of numbness, Le herded me back out toward the mini-yard for a little fresh air.

Outside, he grabbed my shoulder and pulled me close. Whispering in my ear, he said, "We will have another cell available tomorrow. Would you like your own room?"

Even acknowledging how much a pain in the ass Knight had been, I also considered how hurt he would be if I moved and left him in solitary. Stockholm Syndrome had infected me alright, but not for the SRV. Surprisingly, it was Knight I had hated more than the SRV, and yet, I was trying to be considerate of his feelings. But, then I questioned how much longer I would last if I had to keep bolstering not only my own emotional state, but his too—a lesson in what substance abuse counselors call co-dependency, where the compassionate only
become the abettor in an addict's twisted cycle.

"Sure, Mr. Le," I said, knowing that my lesson was over.

"It will be done." He nodded as though he had known all along the dynamics, and I wondered whether our shared cell had been bugged.

When Le and the guards left, Knight and I traded a weak smile as we scanned our bleak surroundings. White-washed walls again. Instead of a bathroom, a toilet surrounded by a three-foot concrete wall. Knight sauntered over to his pallet, and rolled the grass mat out flat. I wanted to go out for air. Fresh air. Free air.

Instead, I walked over to my bed and crawled under its mosquito net. A guard returned, and peered through the viewport in the door. Knight glanced over his feet at the guard, then stared at the blinding light bulb above, as though trying to cauterize all of the evening's events from his memory. The guard continued staring. Looking over my feet, I pointed up at the light bulb, saying to him what my mother always said to me whenever I left a light on in our home: *apaga lo!* As if resulting from my order given in Spanish, the light went out. The viewport closed shut. My stare held to the white ceiling, barely visible in the darkness.

Knight rustled as he rolled over on his side, and I heard a sound I remembered from eight years ago, the first time I knew my parents were having marital problems. It was a man's long, low sobbing: and it disturbed me as much as it had when I first heard it from my father. Back then it terrified me, especially since the only stable part of our lives as globe-trotting ex-patriates was the family dynamic.

Gripped by a sudden case of panic, I reached over to where Knight had left his pack of cigarettes. Striking a match, I lit one and swore it would be my last. The drag made me nauseous, causing me to almost pass out, but I continued and slowly, much too slowly, the smoke carried away the emotions that had so tightly knotted my stomach and pained my chest.

* * *

"You mean, you want to go?"

Becoming defensive, I answered, "Yeah, I do." What did he mean, that I should stay and help him keep it together? I refrained from expressing my contempt, but had nothing more to say.

"My things are ready, Mr. Le," I said.

Le waved me out the door.

"Well, go then," Knight fired, and then went off in a huff into the back room of the cell.

My cell was right next to Knight's, so the trip was short, and the cell was the same, except my pallet that had been moved from Knight's cell was now centered in the sleeping area, under the light bulb.

"This is where you will stay until you are freed," Le said lightly. "Any questions?"

* * *

People from all over the United States had donated to the "Free Freddie Fund" my father had set up at Eureka Federal Savings in San Carlos. But by April 1984, the fund was $8,000 short of the mark. At the rate it was taking to reach $10,000, I would have stayed in prison for ten years. So, my dad, diabetic, and in poor health, took a risk: he cashed in his life insurance policy and combined it with the fund money. That was why Consul Frederick Vogel was able to have a briefcase full of cash. Always suspicious, the Communist government of Vietnam wouldn't accept a banker's check. Vogel cashed the banker's check at the US Embassy and made the short walk, accompanied by an embassy armed guard, down Wireless Road to the Vietnamese Embassy.

"Here you are Mr. Tien, the $10,000 for Fred Graham's freedom." Vogel said as he opened his brief case, revealing American bills.

Tien smiled, and said, "Very good Mr. Vogel." The translator, Tien, and Vogel then stood in silence, a heavy silence, brought on by something Vogel couldn't quite understand until Tien spoke up. "There is one matter more that must be cleared up. Hanoi requests that an extra $1,800 be paid for room and board."

"You can't be serious!" Vogel felt his heart beating faster as it sank. So much time and energy had been put into negotiations, and now to have this unforeseen element?! "Here is the money Hanoi has been asking for. When will Mr. Graham be freed?"

"Please, Mr. Vogel, sit down with us and have some tea," Tien asked and they sat.

"What is the meaning of this Mr. Tien?" Vogel asked, feeling heat rise to his neck.

"Mr. Vogel, Fred Graham was free to go when the trial was over. Since he stayed, and had room and board, the Vietnamese government is charging him for these services, at $300 a month, for the six months that he has stayed in Vietnam since the trial. It is a good price for rent, don't you think?"

Vogel stood up from his chair and shook his fist in the air. "You say he was free. Yet, he was not able to leave until $10,000 was paid to your government. How can you dare to suddenly, without any indication whatsoever, start asking for $1,800 more?! His parents do not have the money to pay this ridiculous room and board charge! If your government does not honor its previous agreement and take no more than the $10,000, *and* free Fred Graham immediately, a greater embarrassment will befall Vietnam. He does not have the money, and according to this new charge, he'll probably stay in Vietnam for the rest of his natural life!" He pointed the finger of his other hand directly at Tien for final emphasis. "If you do not stick to the prior arrangement and free him immediately, you and your government will be completely responsible!"

Tien raised his hand to pacify Vogel. "Please, please Mr. Vogel, I will ask Hanoi and see what they say."

Vogel closed the briefcase, took a deep breath, then said, "Good day, Mr. Tien."

* * *

An official I'd never met before displayed a gold right front incisor with his wide grin. I glanced at his olive-drab Vietnamese Army cap, and noticed there was no usual insignia above the dark brown chin strap. He turned to look down into his briefcase under our table. Quickly, he brought up my Canon F-1 with motor-drive, and lay it on the table between them and me.

"Where's Mr. Le?" I asked as I sat down in the chair pointed to by one of the two officers. We were alone and the whole bleak room smacked of the days during my first interrogations. It felt really surreal and creepy.

"Mr. Le? I don't know Mr. Le," said the translator, who I'd never seen before. "Please sit."

We sat quietly for a long moment. The translator looked at the official next to him, who I also didn't recognize.

"He is a representative from the Kien Giang Province," the translator said, gesturing to the official seated next him.

"He has come all the way from Kien Giang with a question," the translator said.

"What's that?" I asked, hoping for the return of my camera.

The representative spoke with the translator, and they turned their attention to me. Their insincere smiles were unsettling.

"He would like to know why it works without the battery. But, when the battery is put back in, it does not work."

It had been a while since I had handled that camera, or even read the instruction booklet, but I did a quick inspection: shutter release, lever, all the mechanics were in order. The light meter on the New Canon F-1 served two purposes: when the light meter button was pressed, the light meter read for the ASA of the film; when the battery check button was depressed, the light meter pin was supposed to rise all the way up to an f/16 reading, at least. The pin didn't even flicker.

"Yep, the battery sure is dead."

"But why does it work when the battery is removed, yet not with the battery in?"

"It's made that way." Built like an AK-47 or M-14, working always, short of being stuffed with mud and sand, the Canon F-1 was the camera choice of experienced combat photojournalists, after the Nikons, of course.

The representative stared at me suspiciously, as my words were translated, and then he spoke back to the translator. "He finds that hard to believe," the translator said, smiling like the representative.

At first annoyed with their suspicions, I prepared to get up from the table. But, I relaxed back into my seat, intrigued and entertained by how much the surrealness made me feel as though I was once again in a Rach Gia version of Alice's Wonderland. I offered my own rendition of the Cheshire Cat, grinning as I said, "I'm telling you that all you have to do is put another battery in it, and it'll work."

The translator spoke to the representative, who then picked up the camera. The representative still didn't believe me. So incredibly suspicious, the truth became irrelevant to them. Barred from the conversation by language, I stared blankly out the window, while my inner howling at their ill-serving distrust peeked out through the upturned corners of my mouth. *Not only do you get the treasure without any public recognition to us, but you're also going to steal my cameras—fuck you guys!*

"Mr. Gra-ham." The translator brought me slowly back from my gaze. "You may go back to your cell."

"Do you know when we're going to be released?"

"You may go to your cell, Mr. Gra-ham."

After the guard left me in my cell, a trustee arrived with my lunch. He returned shortly with a big pitcher of water. Putting it down on the table, he tilted the tan baseball cap on his close-cropped head and looked around to be sure we were alone. In a flash, he gave me the "number one," thumbs up sign, delivered to his countrymen by American servicemen during the war. It caught me off guard. One of the guards returned and berated the trustee for his lagging behind. They both left, with the trustee glancing back at me. Flashing my own thumbs up, the trustee and I traded a grin.

USA all the way!

* * *

The large white hospital's infirmary reminded me of the Tan Son Nhut Army Hospital where so many wounded Vietnamese gawked at me when I had surgery there as a child. At least there wasn't as much blood all over the place as that time during the war. I turned serious, recognizing the doctor who had put me through so much pain almost a year ago.

Well-fed and arrogant, he was the doctor who had been so deficient in his skills treating the fungal ear infection I had suffered through in the first Saigon prison. The ear would have been cured in three days if the doctor had simply given me cotton swabs and hydrogen peroxide. Instead, he exploited me by shooting me full of tetracycline and probably just about every Vietnamese drug he could find, as if trying to say—"Our drugs are just as good as yours."

In the end, the doctor finally gave me the swab and hydrogen peroxide. The ear infection disappeared within a couple days. Looking at him now, I ignored his feeble attempts to ignite a smile in me. When he did his check up, I noticed that he not only checked out my ear, but paid special attention to the parts of my body that had been hit during the beatings I had received in Rach Gia, namely the backs of my legs, and my stomach. He also examined my scalp, feeling for bumps and looking for hidden scars. At one point, he noticed a section of skin that had actually been ripped open by one of the blows, but was now only a small line of pink on the back of my calf. All the bruises were long gone. But, concern shrouded him when he noticed the thin scar. He and the guard went into a slightly heated argument, but his poker face quickly returned when he noticed me smiling with a knowing look. He quickly finished with a rather cursory check of the rest of my body. I wondered what they would say had they found something really damning: "Oh, he just slipped while taking a shower in his excited expectation of freedom."

Satisfied that my ailment had been cured, and pretty sure that any hints of abuse were gone, he told the guards that they could take me back to Bach Dang #3. On the way to the car that waited in the crowded hospital's empty parking lot, the translator told me that my freedom might arrive soon. I was elated, sure that this was so considering they'd never taken me to the hospital before. Waiting at the car for the guards who had gone off to flirt with some nurses, I asked the translator his name.

"Quan," he said and grinned. "It means 'Spring Day'!"

I looked up at the bright sun, smiled, and said, "Indeed it is!"

* * *

"Graham's father said last week he had paid the $10,000 fine Hanoi demanded for his son's release, a sum western officials have labelled ransom."— UPI

* * *

In the afternoon of the next day, Le led an entourage of smiling guards, carrying my cassette player and Halliburton case in their hands. Also with them was a colonel from Hanoi, who had attended a few interrogations, a likable fellow, with a round, balding head and skinny frame, wearing a khaki short sleeve uniform.

"May we sit down?" Le asked, suspect in his overboard politeness. They had never asked before; they had always just burst in.

"Please," I said, pointed to the table and then joined them in our new, oh so new, demeanors, *and would you like cucumber sandwiches, some crumpets, and a smattering of Earl Grey?* The guards took my things into the other room, smiling brightly as they went.

Le baited well. "Why we have come?"

"Yes?" I tried like mad to conceal my excitement. They, too, remained smiling silently in our tug of war.

"You are going home tomorrow!" Le slapped me on the back.

I jumped in the air. "Awright!"

Flustered, they both jerkily shook my hand. Le spoke, "You must have all your things ready to go, as we will come to pick you up in the morning."

"And my camera?"

"Kien Giang Province has confiscated it," Le answered, treading lightly back from the confession.

I frowned, and said, "And what will happen to the treasure?"

"—What treasure?" Le said, looking at me as if to say, *you're getting out alive; count your blessings!*

His face brightened again. "Everything will be okay, my friend. You go back to the US and make much money. You go on TV, write book, make movie. I am happy for you."

Everyone grinned and then the colonel, grinning widest, drew a cigarette from his olive-drab shirt and lit it. After a long drag, he spoke to Le.

"The colonel says that hopefully you will tell people in America how well we have treated you."

"There has definitely been good food."

"And we didn't beat you."

"Are you kidding me?"

Scowling, the colonel, replying to my statement through Le, said, "Of course, you know of all the good treatment we gave the American prisoners of war during the war?"

"What?!" I had read about the POWs in *Stars and Stripes*. I didn't know the names of the POWs then, but out of respect here they are: Capt. Humberto "Rocky" Versace US Army SF, publicly murdered; Sgt. Kenneth Mills Roraback, US Army SF, held for two years, then shot in the back of the head; Capt. Orien Judson Walker, Jr., MACV, died of starvation; Sgt. First Class Joe Parks, MACV, died of starvation; Lt. Lance P. Sijan, US Air Force, died of starvation; and though I don't have the full list, they were all prisoners murdered and tortured in face of the rules of the Geneva Convention:

Article 3
(1)

Persons taking no active part in the hostilities, including members of armed forces who have laid down their arms and those placed hors de combat by sickness, wounds, detention, or any other cause, shall in all circumstances be treated humanely, without any adverse distinction founded on race, color, religion or faith, sex, birth or wealth, or any other similar criteria. To this end the following acts are and shall remain prohibited at any time and in any place whatsoever with respect to the above-mentioned persons: (a) violence to life and person, in particular murder of all kinds, mutilation, cruel treatment and torture; (b) taking of hostages; (c) outrages upon personal dignity, in particular, humiliating and degrading treatment; (d) the passing of sentences and the carrying out of executions without previous judgment pronounced by a regularly constituted court affording all the judicial guarantees which are recognized as indispensable by civilized peoples.

(2)

The wounded and sick shall be collected and cared for.

Considering also that the SRV is a member of the United Nations, and how they had treated me without any regard to Articles 3, 5, 10, and 12 of the *Declarations of Universal Human Rights*, you might understand why I was getting hot under the collar at the colonel's sloppy attempt at manipulation. The membership rules of the UN were respected by the SRV only when it meant money from which the VCP top officials could graft.

Declaration of Universal Human Rights:

Article 3 Everyone has the right to life, liberty and security of person.

Article 5 No one shall be subjected to torture or to cruel, inhuman or degrading treatment or punishment.

Article 10 Everyone is entitled in full equality to a fair and public hearing by an independent and impartial tribunal, in the determination of his rights and obligations and of any criminal charge against him.
Article 12 No one shall be subjected to arbitrary interference with his privacy, family, home or correspondence, nor to attacks upon his honor and reputation. Everyone has the right to the protection of the law against such interference or attacks.

Le's knowing smile told that he, too, remembered how tortured and deprived the POWs were when a majority of them were returned to the US in the early 1970s. The difference between the colonel and Le was so apparent now, like north and south. Saigon fell after the POWs were freed, so Le had the benefit of American journalism. He had at least read the *Stars and Stripes*. The colonel was still blinded by the propaganda that had influenced him since his Hanoi childhood. He was distressed, but let it go. The colonel grinned selfconsciously at his poorly veiled propaganda attempt. We then all broke into laughter. If only Hanoi could have seen it. And I was damned if I was going to go back to the States spouting like those idiots who have excused Hanoi's actions as "growing pains." I sure wasn't going to tell everyone how wonderfully Vietnam treats its prisoners, and that maltreatment of prisoners was just a propaganda tactic of the US government and its UN puppets.

"Mr. Le? "I asked. "I need to talk to Knight, as I've got to get a letter from him stating that he is completely responsible for the dinghy and fishing boat, since I was only brought along as an observer. Don't you remember what Mr. Tarnoff said?"

He gave me a questioning look.

"After I told him that we had left the bargirls just around the corner in Thailand, he said that there was a chance I might be arrested and held responsible for the boats. Knight promised he'd give me the letter."

Le spoke with the colonel, then turned back to me. The colonel nodded affirmatively, as Le spoke, "He says, no problem. The guard will let you into his cell this afternoon, after we leave."

* * *

"Really?" Knight seemed faint as he looked around and then sat down in one of his cell chairs. "When did you find out?" he asked impatiently.

"Just now," I answered slowly, treading carefully. "I came over to see if there are any people you want me to contact, and also to get the letter you promised to give me. The one exonerating me of responsibility for the two boats?"

"Sure, Fred, no problem. I'll get a piece of paper, and give you some names and addresses." He got up weakly out of his chair.

Knight shakily scribbled a few names down on a lined piece of paper. He slid it across his dining table. I studied the names for a while, trying to decipher them.

"So, you must be extremely delighted that you're going to be freed?" Jealousy turned his voice heavy and squinted his eyes. "I still can't believe they're letting you free without me."

As though the whole fuckin' world revolves around you! "They just told me."

"Well, good then, I'm happy for you."

Yeah, right! Why don't you lie a little better next time? My eyes slitted in anger for a moment.

"And the letter?" I asked, while doing my best to hide my feelings about him.

"No problem, Fred. I'll give it to you tomorrow just before they take you," Knight said, matter-of-factly.

"Is there anything you'd like me to tell your mother?"

"No." He looked up at the barbed wire-diced sky, and said, "Did they tell you how much longer they might keep me here."

"They didn't say. They just said that your family hasn't been able to raise the money." Actually, no one in the whole wide world trusted him, or wanted to give him money. Pretty poignant considering what he would try to do to me the next day.

"That's no surprise." He took on a wry smile.

"What about your mother?"

"She won't come through, she never has before," he said. "I've already received a letter from her stating that she doesn't have the funds. All she's able to do is beg the Vietnamese to let me go." Knight quickly swept away his dark scowl with a quiver of his eyebrows and a deep sigh. Whether it was because of the idea of her begging, or her not being able to get him out earlier, I did not know.

"And you've never even tried to contact your father?"

He looked across the table at me as though hit by the greatest insult. "My father has another family now. He was never there for me in the first place."

Knight had once told me that his parents, especially his father, had been against his following the arts. They had wanted him to enter college and become something other than an entertainer, which he was in his early years as a figure-skater touring across Europe. Figure-skater, combat photojournalist, doesn't matter. It's all the same when the career choice is one that a parent happens to be against, especially when the career is the choice of the child who wants so much to break out and succeed in the eyes of his parents.

He sat there against the wall for what was the most uncomfortable moment I have ever shared with another person. It was not that he was so quiet with an apparent pent up anger; it was because I had delved into my own thoughts and realized how different yet so frighteningly similar we were, considering what I had felt about my parents before I left California.

* * *

In my dream that night I was running up and down bleachers at a football game. The game was held at my intermediate school—the Ulu Pandan Singapore American School. Though I had met all my schoolmates during my years from nine to thirteen, all my schoolmates in the dream were now as old as me at nineteen. They all intensely watched a football game, and ignored me. But there was no one on the field. Anxiously, I ran up and down the bleachers calling out, "Have you seen Keri? Where's Keri?"

I searched and searched. Suddenly, in a most macabre manner, they answered in unison, "She's dead." They bowed their heads. I bowed mine, covering my face with cupped hands. The dream grieved me heavily.

And surprised me greatly; I hadn't thought about her in years. But, I guess she had made enough of an impression on me. When we all played the game of "prisoner" in the school yard during lunch break back in 1972, my first year in Singapore, I was so incensed by the adrenaline of the game and my crush on her, I caught her by the wrist and dragged her to the top of an old British Army log steeple that had been used by soldiers for physical training.[26] What with the excitement of the moment, I announced, "I love Keri! I love Keri!"

"No! No!" she cried, as the rest of the students giggled and chortled.

Within a few years, the crush subsided as they usually do when we realize that the targets of our adoration are just people, and not objects to be placed on a pedestal. What had started as an infatuation soon developed into a good friendship in middle school, even to the point that I no longer even thought of her romantically, even when given the option in middle school of going steady as the result of the match-making efforts of a mutual friend.

Why, after so many years, would I have had a dream about a girl who had nothing at all to do with Vietnam? But then I remembered that her last words to me in 1977 were that of surprise that I was so elated to be returning to the States. She said that soon she and her family would be returning to the States, too. But, it left her very depressed because she would be leaving all her friends behind in Singapore. That would be the case for me, too, but I couldn't wait to get back to the States, because like so many American Third Culture Kids (TCKs), I wanted so much to know what it meant to be American in lifestyle, not just citizenship. What I was not prepared for was the culture shock of being American, especially with a lingering political and cultural environment that still forced many veterans and expatriates to omit on job applications and in conversations that they had served in the military or lived, in Vietnam just to avoid the stigma.

As I analyzed the dream, I initially took the easiest interpretation: it was the proverbial "you can never go back." That Keri being dead was actually my past being dead. For that matter, as time moves along, the present dies and *becomes* the past in that very millisecond; it just takes our psyches and emotions time to accept it as quickly as events occur.

Hmm, I thought as I lay back on my bed pallet from which I had been disturbed by the morbid dream. I had become very good at using meditation to clear my thoughts and really get some really clear introspections. I was left with only one question: *Why did I really have this dream, right now, in Vietnam?*

I relaxed my body by breathing deeply and letting myself enjoy the sensation of sinking. I noticed that I was suddenly keyed in on the smells and sounds of Vietnam, sensing stimulants that made me feel as though I was a little kid back in Vietnam. But then, thoughts about Knight's emotional antagonisms against his parents hit me and I almost recoiled. I hypothesized that one of the reasons why he had become such a vile, manipulative, and selfish person was because of the anger and feelings of victimization caused by the dynamic of his relationship with his parents. And what terrified me most was that if I didn't do something to change my own parent/ child dynamic that was so similar to his, there was a strong possibility that I would be stuck just like him in middle-age: spiteful and thinking that everyone owed me.

Taking an added deep breath, I let myself float and trail further into my meditations, and then I remembered my father, my rabbit, my mom not protecting me, and even those pink, blood-red, and white nightmares that were once again stalking my sleep. My meditations carried me all the way back to Saigon, 1972.

* * *

Seven jets flying in tight formation left trails of red and yellow smoke, creating a Republic of Vietnam flag across the haze-filtered sky above Saigon. A sudden wind from the north quickly wiped away one of the many last ditch efforts by South Vietnam to rebuild its people's confidence in the government. President Nixon was making good on his electoral promise of getting the United States out of Vietnam. That slowly disappearing wisp of smoke represented not only the pulling out of American troops and lost hopes of victory, but also my family's own departure.

Only eight years old, I was too young to understand any of the history of this time period by which I would be so traumatized. I was more interested in playing under a bright sun and holding my best friend's soft fur to my cheek, than philosophizing about the rockets the Vietcong had fired from two crossed bamboo poles, aimed blindly into Saigon the night before—rockets whose only effect was to throw slicing shrapnel into displaced Vietnamese, too impoverished to live in the safety of a brick house—and bombs dropped by jets within clear view of our house during Little Tet, four years earlier. Holding my white rabbit in my arms this calm day in May, I looked into his pink eyes and shared that quiet time so treasured by the shy. Snoopy, my other friend, a little brown puppy saved from the meat market, tugged at my shoelaces. I reprimanded him, then laughed as he again pulled at my laces with his teeth. Snoopy and Bunny were basically my only friends; the dangers of kidnapping and stray shrapnel and bullets kept me from the usual casual visits to friends' homes.

Along with Snoopy and Bunny, I once had five Rhode Island Reds and three Pekin ducks. Only two hens survived, pecking the earth, just moistened by a sudden shower that had come and as quickly gone. Our yard was surrounded by tall brick walls, topped as in many Asian homes by shards of broken bottles planted in a thin crown of concrete. The chickens loved pecking for bugs and worms in the far corner of that front yard.

But that ghastly deterrent of sharp glass wasn't enough to keep brash thieves from repeatedly vaulting the wall at night to steal our chickens and ducks, along with whatever other belongings they could sell on the thriving black market. So brash were they that a year earlier they attacked our amah and held her prisoner while they ransacked our house. We had been out at the Tan Son Nhut Airbase, enjoying the latest showing of *Ben Hur*. Long scratches down the amah's forearms marked her futile efforts to escape the burglars. The scratches so disturbed me that for weeks after I had nightmares about being chased by long-nailed Vietnamese ghouls in black pajamas, characters much like those I had seen in Asian horror flicks filled with swashbuckling vampires and sorcerers. While my mother consoled our amah, and bandaged the wounds, my father called the cops and looked through his wallet for the expected bribe. Usually no better than the thieves, and because of their white uniforms and cowardly behavior, just about everyone called them by the name coined by GIs: white mice.

So angered was my father by the attack, and the ineffectiveness of the corrupt Saigon white mice, that he took matters into his own hands and fashioned a billy-club from a baseball bat. Positioning himself in his favorite living room armchair, he waited up at odd hours of the night, but to no avail. Finally, after four days he surrendered. But two nights later, while taking a shower in our bathroom that opened to the second-floor balcony, he caught the shadow of a crouched figure shifting across the bamboo blinds. Summoning up the nerve to deal with an unknown number of intruders, he tore away the blinds and yelled, with the same fervor he'd been taught by the Marine Corps during the Korean War. Screaming back in his own terror, the thief escaped my father's lunge and scrambled to the roof top of our home—a two-story French Colonial that had been a kindergarten run by nuns before we moved in. But, the thief tripped on one of four guy wires that held up the chimney. The stack of bricks toppled, snuffing out his life with a sledgehammer-blow to the skull. The teenager's death would be my parents' secret from my brother and me for years. It served us well: no more thieves harassed us. Ghosts were better deterrents than police when dealing with superstitious thieves.

A robust man, my father intimidated me like large animals do some people. Still, when he returned home from work that day I was playing with my pets, I plucked up the nerve and walked over to him as he said good-bye to the departing company chauffeur. I gave my father the kiss on the cheek he expected. He smiled but there was something reserved in his expression as he made his way up from the driveway to the porch. It was unusual and unsettling; a stern look that in the past only preceded spankings. Confused, I followed cautiously as he carried his briefcase into the living room.

"Maritza?" my father called out.

"Si?" she answered. Coming in from the kitchen, she cocked her head forward, smoothed her beehive hairdo with a quick brush of her fingers, and finished primping with a wipe of her flour-dusted hands against her apron.

"I'm going to take the rabbit now."

"Where are you taking Bunny, Daddy? Spokane?" The naiveté in my voice would be stained forever in my memory by cynicism.

Cold as stone, he stopped at our fat lounge chair, removed his gold engineer's tie clip, and placed it on the chair along with his leather briefcase. He adjusted his unflattering, horn-rimmed glasses. They were those nerdy, black ones that engineers wore during the '50s and '60s. I hated them because they were an instant give-away to the true identity of Santa Claus during the previous year's Tan Son Nhut Airbase Christmas party, destroying any belief I had that there was a Santa.

Pulling a three-inch wooden dowel and a white cord out of his trousers pocket, my father walked out to one of our mango trees standing in the middle of the front yard. My rabbit hopped around on the muddy lawn at the base of one of the two stunted trees whose mangos were pockmarked and rotten—fruit bats always knew before us when the mangoes were finally ripe—and nibbled contentedly at a small mound of carrots I had set for him.

I was my father's jittery shadow now, moved by the dancing light of curiosity. But, I was also darkened by dejection from my father's failure to answer my questions. From the same pocket he drew a red Swiss army knife and sharpened both ends of the stick, now resembling a very sharp pencil. Cutting a notch around the middle of the dowel, he tied one end of the cord around it.

"What are you going to do?" I was in awe of my father's deft use of the blade, which reminded me that our leaving for Spokane would finally give me the opportunity to become a Cub Scout.

Silence. My father tied the other end of the cord to a wrist-thick branch of the tree. He bent over and scooped up Bunny. I repeated my question.

"I'm going to have to kill him, son." No anger in his words. Just a wall reaching up to the heavens. I could only shriek. Bunny was yanked out of my reach.

"I have to, Freddy. The Vietnamese will eat him if we leave him behind."

"I don't care! Don't kill him! Leave him alone! Give him back! Give him back!" My father's obvious height advantage thwarted my rescue attempt. My friend's hind legs bounced up and down as he tried to catch ground and bound away. His efforts to wriggle out of my father's beefy construction-worker fingers clutched around his ears seemed so pointless, but I fought on to free my buddy. Suddenly, Bunny emitted a sound, a cross between a bawling lamb and a screaming baby, a sound so unnatural it was fit only for a horror film or the most terrifying nightmare. A sound so shocking I was paralyzed.

Frankie and me in the driveway with the Toyota. On the right, in front of the main entry, is the mango tree.

"Maritza!" my father yelled, as I screamed in the same pitch as Bunny. I was empowered by unrestrained emotion and the launching of my fists against my father's leg. In truth, I was only a light wind across a flat ocean, stirring barely a ripple to signify passing.

"Fred, don't kill his rabbit! It's his pet," my mother pleaded as she ran towards us from the house. But, instead of aiding me, she grabbed my wrist and yanked me all the way back, my heels dragging in the barely dried soil, and then knocking against the marble stairs. Tears soaked my cheeks like rain. No one could be trusted. No one.

My father's punch to the back of the rabbit's neck stunned me as much as my rabbit. Disbelief clouded my eyes with hope: I imagined that my father had missed his mark. Bunny's convulsions did not lie, though. After what seemed like a long while, Bunny stretched out long and dead, a limp length of white fur in my father's hands. Hyperventilation dropped me to my knees, numb and unmoving, except for sobbing and scraping tears from my cheeks.

I looked at my rabbit. I looked at my father. I knew even then that my father had broken a promise, a promise all parents make to their children. It's that promise God made to His children when He created Eden and invited His children to live unharmed, physically, spiritually, and emotionally. And I hated my father like I'd never hated anyone before.

* * *

My memories all sent me falling into the most painful, wrenching abreaction I had ever experienced. I was left shaking and trembling as though I had been electrocuted. I must have cried for a half-hour straight, with many realizations about how deceptive my childhood experience had been. My brother, who lived in Saigon with us, hadn't been adversely affected by Vietnam at all. He was always a wonderful student, never felt alienated, and was able to read for hours, having a level of concentration I found amazing! I had asked him once what he remembered of Vietnam: he remembered nothing. Only three years younger than I, his first memories began at age five, in the utopia of Singapore.

After I stopped crying, I held my hands to my stomach and solar plexus, and regained some control over my breathing. I again delved into the traumas of what I had experienced as a child. And then I realized that in coming back to Southeast Asia, I had recreated everything that I had experienced as a child: the trauma of incongruity; being witness to horror; feelings of helplessness and guilt; and constantly trying to regain the inner and outer control of my reality that had evaded me ever since those traumatic experiences of my childhood in Vietnam. I was a walking textbook of post-traumatic stress disorder (PTSD). But, I didn't realize then what my subconscious drive and the power of coincidence had done (remember that old Native American saying that there is no such thing as coincidence?): it had brought me back to the place of trauma, and in so doing, created the conditions that trauma counselors strive for in the safety of an office.

Witnessing Lor's death on the Mekong had recreated the trauma of my rabbit's horrific death—the interpretation of trauma is relative; what traumatizes an eight year old, may have to be amplified in severity to affect an adult. Feelings of guilt toward how I could have better aided Lor, or kept my parents from going through the pain of having a loved one in prison reminded my inner child of how helpless and guilt-ridden I was when I couldn't provide comfort to the African American with the amputated leg at the Army Hospital, or stop my father from killing my cherished pet rabbit. And the red, white, and pink nightmare that had come back to me since my return to Vietnam was the key, to all of it.

Mentally, I remembered a lot about Vietnam, but emotionally, I'd forgotten many things. My emotional interpretation was very clouded by contradictions, for instance when my parents would publicly reminisce about Vietnam, they did so in a politically correct manner. Living in Vietnam was a safe and idyllic experience, like the "Paris of Southeast Asia." However, if they reminisced privately, the truth would come out. Their memories reverted to "having lived through that terrible war." Remembering facts is great, but hiding from painful memories is horrible, which is why before I was imprisoned in Vietnam, I would envy those who so easily forgot their personal history: those whose catch-all answer to an emotionally traumatic experience is to *forget about it*. These are the kinds of people who jump from one romantic relationship to another as though evading the raging current of a river by skipping from one rock to another. Some people survive quite well with this tactic; until one day they step on a slippery rock and they fall into the river without having had the practice and the knowledge of how to swim with the current and work their way over, much like Knight, who had fallen into prison, and was now constantly rolled and tossed violently by the shallow waters of his emotions and psyche.

That would have been me had I not made an early decision that my life was too precious to waste, and that every experience offered was for my personal growth. In prison, I now realized that I had to ride this painful roller-coaster through to the end. My optimism that had carried me through my search for photo assignments, and now my eleven months in prison, was going to help me get through this journey without a psychologist. I adhered to the old belief that whatever you need to fix, you can pretty much fix yourself. But now it was just a case of survival, and so I started my own age regression therapy, having my adult psyche communicating with my child in a kind and caring parental voice.

As I relived events in those fully realized memories, I had my myself as an adult supporting and educating beyond the pain the child that I was. I first told myself to feel all my emotions. It was very cleansing, and would take a few more sessions to clear out all the emotional garbage, at least to where it was no longer detrimental. In the position of the adult, advising my childhood self, I grasped the many possibilities for my father's ignorance of my feelings: he was always traveling, he had never really been a father figure, much like his own father who was always away from home, fixing pipe organs in churches across the Pacific Northwest. Instead, the US Marine Corps became his father figure. His mother—though very kind, heavily spiritual, and financially supportive—never impressed me as someone who had the emotional wherewithal (because of inadequate parenting skills from dealing with her own post-traumatic stress after her parents' shooting accident and suicide) to provide the connection that would have nurtured my father through his youth into becoming an emotionally aware and responsive parent. And finally, since he was a child of the Great Depression, he raised rabbits for money and food for the family, and didn't believe in turning a food source into a companion or a pet.

I finished by forgiving not only my father for his violation, but also myself for not having fully experienced my life by holding such a grudge. I had cheated my father of a loving son, and myself the opportunity for a much fuller life. One of the easiest signs to recognize in someone who deals with post-traumatic stress disorder (PTSD) is the look of disassociation, or as I've called it since the World Trade Center attack, the *CNN look*. These individuals would not pay attention to what they were doing to themselves by watching hour after traumatic hour of broadcasts of the attack and their reactions to the attack. Their expression of disassociation was the same that a sufferer of PTSD wears when they go through their daily lives, trying to put back the pieces of a reality that has been shattered by a traumatic event, like a rock through a plate glass window.

I had walked through my life from childhood on trying to glue those pieces of glass back together, but while I was so preoccupied with that task, I had ignored all that I was experiencing in Vietnam, and in California. Because I had my hands full with reorganizing my childhood in Southeast Asia, I wasn't emotionally aware of the great experiences I'd had living in the States, and Singapore for that matter. That was why I was so taken by the "grass is always greener" mentality, or as Martin Sheen's character said in *Apocalypse Now,* "When I was here, I wanted to be there. When I was there, all I could think of was getting back into the jungle."

I'd had enough of the quagmire in which I had found myself. I walked out by finishing off my age regression sessions, taking it through to the experience of complete forgiveness. Where my father was unable to be there for me, I forgave him. Where I couldn't be there for my rabbit, and the black soldier, I forgave. And one by one, even Richard Knight, because I was damned if I was going to carry his baggage with me, I forgave everyone. As I did so, I remembered that for dinner that evening my family actually did eat my best friend, the rabbit. My mother kept telling me, "Eat more Freddy. It'll make you feel better."

Even though I knew better back then, I submitted to my mother's pleas and ate my friend, with the same guilt that the Apostles would have felt had they known that the flesh which they feasted upon would soon be sacrificed on the cross, paying for their sins. The more I ate, the better it tasted, and the more guilty I felt. After that I turned to food the way others turn to heroine and cigarettes. My jaw would have dropped had I not been in trance. In that enlightenment, I saw that all the reasons for my being overweight, introverted and unable to enjoy life as a completely happy child and teenager was destroyed by that moment—I had been a thin child until we left Vietnam. What's more, I knew it not only as a mental note, a fact, but I *knew* it, emotionally.

gnosis \'no-ses\ n [Gk gnosis, lit., knowledge, fr. gignoskein]: esoteric knowledge of spiritual truth held by the ancient Gnostics to be essential to salvation. knowledge : recognition : as in <psychognosis>—Webster's New Collegiate Dictionary, Copyright 1975.

I had reached the complete state needed for healing. Without this complete multi-level understanding of my subconscious, conscious, emotional and mental parts of my psyche, I would have continued through life like an obese person who knows how self-destructive overeating is, but continues to find themselves searching a refrigerator for food, even when they're not hungry.

And when all this healing was done, I finished with a promise—because the universe hates a vacuum—that I would never again be afraid of my emotions, and that I would live every pain and pleasure with an equal level of intensity. I would not cop out.

Taking myself out of trance, I suddenly felt so light, a lightness I had never felt before. I was Atlas, with my shoulders free of a World of garbage. Unbeknownst to me, because I was not a trained psychologist, I had gone through the experience that mental health professionals who work so effectively with PTSD patients strive for. I had gone back to the moment and place of my trauma and re-framed it so that those traumas would no longer adversely effect me. Not only had I done this mentally, but also physically by being back in Vietnam, which made everything so much easier. I rejoiced in having gone back to the place of my trauma: physically, mentally, and emotionally. I walked on air around my cell that night, my mind dancing around, anticipating my freedom and the opportunity to look at the outside world through a new set of eyes!

Chapter 19

"Life, liberty and property do not exist because men made more laws. On the contrary, it was the fact that life, liberty and property existed that caused men to make laws in the first place."— Frederic Bastiat

"If you understood what Communism was, you would hope, you would pray on your knees that we would some day become Communist."— Hanoi Jane Fonda

Freedom Bird

O 210637Z JAN 84

FM AMEMBASSY BANGKOK

TO SECSTATE WASHDC

". . . Tarnoff informed Graham that it would be a serious mistake on his part to try and capitalize on his ordeal, that publicity of any kind would be bad for his parents, could have polemic overtones and that he should 'keep his mouth shut.'"

    Freedom trickles so infrequently through cracks in the wall of secrecy of Vietnam, that when it does happen, whether political, religious, physical, or even psychological, it's truly a treasure worth a double helping of joy. With my release from the chains of my past, a quadruple offering of gratitude was in order to Lady Luck, providence, and meditation, for without them I'm sure I would have died of a drug overdose or put a gun to my head in my later years. Never again would I be tormented by surreal dreams of pink, white, and red. What had festered as a mysterious collection of grotesque and upsetting colors, had been clearly revealed as subconscious metaphors for my rabbit's fur, the blood upon that fur, and the memory of his bloody entrails, sterilized of its full emotional impact by my conscious mind's need to survive. What had initially been just a teenager's effort to escape and become an adult, had become an adventure in order to heal, an opportunity to finally come home.

    And home was where I was getting ready to go. Ten thousand dollars would have covered my rent in Thailand for a year. But now it secured my freedom. Considering the Vietnamese had not only gotten $10,000, almost a year of my life, and had taunted me with $1,800 for room and board, I was going to make sure that I got my money's worth. I would do everything in my power to remove their veil of secrecy, if only minutely. I would bring back some information that could be used by the UN, or at least the Pentagon and CIA, whose necessary human intelligence had been lacking since the mid-1970s. For years, they'd been smarting from getting their hands dirty in Vietnam and snowballing toward relying too heavily on satellites and other remote technologies.

Using my body parts as scales of measurement, I paced out the dimensions of my cell. The same procedure had revealed the dimensions of my previous two cells, but now sure of departure, I wanted to have a written record. One inch equaled the one-and-aquarter-inch middle knuckle of my right forefinger. A foot scaled to my shoe size, ten inches. Marking down the measurements on a piece of paper, I also wrote a book outline: thin so that if they found it, I wouldn't be held forever. On this, I scribbled notes of dimensions memorized from my previous cells.

Now, I thought, *how am I going to sneak this out?*

My belongings had been returned, minus the $2,000 worth of confiscated cameras, even after I had pleaded with them and reminded them that they'd gotten a good chunk of change for my ransom. Back in Thailand, my tennis shoes always carried safety money in case of robbery. Here in Vietnam, though, the idea didn't give me the same feeling of confidence. Searching through my pack for a hiding place produced nothing. Glancing a couple times at the cassette player, while searching through the other articles on the bed, I picked it up. "This'll work!"

Four Phillips screws secured the back of the cassette recorder in place. I bent open one of the clips from the nylon carrying sling, fashioned it into a make-shift screwdriver, and removed the screws. Folding the diagram and outline into a small thin square, I laid it against the back of the recorder and put the cassette player back together. Because it no longer worked, I was sure the Vietnamese wouldn't give it a second thought. *Cheap bastards!* I thought when I realized the only belongings I was getting back were those that they couldn't use. I would have traded all my belongings in return for my cameras.

"Call me Bond, James Bond." I joked, imitating Sean Connery's Scottish accent while screwing the back onto the cassette player.

My next worry was the cigarette lighter that was my own special souvenir: the inscription read "Airmen's Open Mess, Tan Son Nhut Airbase, Vietnam." There was also a "7" inside a circle: Seventh Squadron out of Tan Son Nhut. I had haggled in broken Vietnamese with a guard for it. In trade, he got my Casio G-Shock. Terrified of what might happen to him, he had me first write a letter saying that I'd left the wristwatch as a gift to him "because he was such a good guard," and then he would tell anyone who asked that he had come across it while cleaning out my cell after I had left. He then wrapped the G-Shock in the letter. We shook hands to close our deal, and then he left.

My last dinner as a prisoner was sweet and sour prawns, with a side of rice and bananas, laid on the table by guards, who acted as though they were all my best friends. In the quiet that followed, I savored my meal and chewed on what might occur the next day. There would be the reporters, the questions, the return to California. *What to do?* I thought, suddenly hit by the fact that I was going home. *What should I say? What will I say to Dad?*

To distract myself, I went over to the wall and inscribed the same mark I had left at the second prison. I scrawled my Kilroy-like insignia, a 1970s Happy Face with a camera around his neck. The bottom left said "Copyright 1983 Saigon", and at the bottom right was— "Freddy ~~Kilroy~~ was HERE!!"

* * *

Anxiety held me in insomnia all night, waiting dressed and ready to go in the same slacks and shirt worn at the trial. When the officials arrived they were smiling. They were always smiling. But this time, as they walked in, it was honest.

"This is the big day!" Le said. "Are you ready? . . Follow us."

Caught up short by the realization that I'd not gotten the letter as promised from Knight, I said, "Mr. Le! I've got to get a letter from Knight!"

"No problem. I'll go back after we check you out."

Check me out?!

They took me to a room near the center parking lot. After dropping my pack and emptying the Halliburton and handbag on the bed, the guards and colonel stood and watched while the major and Mr. Le sat down on the bed next to me. I did my best not to pay too much attention to my belongings.

"Take off your clothes," Le ordered.

"What?!" I said. *Why are you doing this?! You never checked my clothes before!*

"Gift from the Peoples' Republic of Vietnam," he said and tossed a newspaper-wrapped bundle of clothing, and a pair of Bata basketball shoes on the bed. I was very happy that the map was hidden in the cassette player and not in my pocket, as I'd originally planned, and that I was wearing the boxer shorts they'd given me for the trip to Rach Gia. As my pants slipped down below my knees, laughter erupted from the crowd.

    Le pointed and snickered like the rest of the Vietnamese. "You have such white legs!"

    "You would, too, if you'd been in prison for the last eleven months." I smiled and changed into the new white dress shirt and brown nylon slacks, and prepared to put on the shoes. Le and the other officials rummaged through the belongings at my side, as I sat, tying the laces of my new sneakers. Le reached into his attaché and withdrew his old copy of *Kim-Van-Kieu*. He had loaned me this very special personal copy when I told him I would go mad if I had to stomach one more piece of propaganda they called news. Captivating and full of romantic daring-do, with a sprinkling of *Romeo and Juliet* and all the Asian martial arts movie sword fighting I could imagine, it told the saga of the female title character, *Kieu*, who lost in love and fell into prostitution in order to save her jailed father. It all took place during the wars between two families ruled by the Le Dynasty of the 17th Century: the Trinhs who controlled north of the Ginh River (basically the 19th Parallel), and the Nguyens who ruled the south— kind of like had Scotland been split up the middle, the Campbells controlling the west, and the Grahams the east, all under the House of Stewart. Lauded in Vietnam to this day as its true literal masterpiece, written completely in Vietnamese, it was penned by the poet, Nguyen-Du, who lived from 1725 to 1820, and had originally titled it *Doan-Truong Tan-Thanh*, which means: *New Accents of a Heart-Rending Song.*

    "This, my friend, I dedicate to you."

    He scribbled, "To Graham, Le 17. 5. 84." on the first page, and then handed it to me.

    "Thank you, Mr. Le."

    The major, who had been all smiles like everyone else, suddenly had a dark scowl as he handed Le the Seventh Squadron cigarette lighter.

    "Wh—where did you get this?!" Le asked.

    " Uh, I got it as a gift from one of the guards back at the second prison."

    "Who?!"

    "Oh, I'm not sure who he was," once again, poorly covering my tracks as I'd done in Rach Gia. "I didn't know their names. I just showed interest in the lighter."

    "Your watch, where is your watch?" Le asked and then gave me a knowing smile.

"Oh, I just threw it away. It stopped working."

"Where did you throw it?"

"In the toilet."

Le and the two officers scoffed. "Do you think we are idiots?"

"Wait here," Le said as he left, speaking to the colonel and pointing at me. They all gave me a stern look.

The colonel picked up my cassette player. I looked down at an imaginary bug on the ground to camouflage the fear I was sure everyone could see, though they probably didn't notice anything. When I looked up, the major and the guard were looking at the knobs on the cassette player and talking as though they wished they had one, too. *Please don't look at it anymore*, I pleaded in my mind. As though reading my mind, they laid it down.

Le returned and sat next to me on the bed, with a smirk on his face. "Hold out your hand."

He dropped something small and wrapped in newspaper into my hand.

"Open it," Le said as it unfolded slightly on its own. In the center was my Casio. They all laughed. Embarrassed, I grinned and then nervously licked my lower lip.

"We go," Le said, furiously wiping away the laughter with a wave of his hand.

"Wait!" I said. "Mr. Le, the letter?!"

"Okay, okay. You go with them," he said, pointing towards the carport.

Le went off and I was escorted to a Mercedes Benz by the colonel and the major. We waited in the car for a few minutes, until Le came running out, and we all piled into the vehicle.

"Here is the letter," Le said as we pulled up to the large mint-green gates.

It read:

"To whom it may concern, I, Frederick K. Graham, am completely responsible for the taking of the 15-foot dinghy and Thai fishing boat. I had planned the expedition along with Knight from the very first day. We had agreed that any funds derived from the adventure would be split, 40-percent to myself, 60-percent for Richard Knight... signed_____."

I was sick to my stomach, hoping that I had misread the letter. When it finally hit me what that nut had done, I screamed "No!"

The Mercedes shot out the gate and onto Bach Dang. "I can't believe that mother-fucker!" The driver recoiled, and glanced at his rear-view mirror in answer to my punch against the back of his leather seat. "Take me back! Take me back! I'm gonna rip that motherfucker's head off. Take me back, Le! LE!"

The Vietnamese must have thought that freedom was too much for me and that I had finally lost it, as I tore up the letter in a last fit of rage, I handed it back to Le. "Please Mr. Le, take me back! If I don't have that letter, they're going to put me in jail in Thailand! You might as well keep me here."

Le translated what Knight had done. The Vietnamese laughed and shook their heads. They weren't going to take me back. And then I thought about the scorpion and the frog, and shook my head.

Richard Knight, circa 1985.

I looked back at Le, and then said, "Mr. Le, please give me the letter."

"Oh, no, no," he said. "You don't get letter back. You get letter, maybe no one help Knight. Maybe he never get out of Vietnam— we don't want him here anymore!"

* * *

There was no normal airport noise. No squadron of passenger planes taking off, or landing out of Tan Son Nhut. Except for the whine of a distant propeller plane, only people waiting for tourists could be heard. I had been dropped into a scene from *Night of the Living Dead*. In all my visits around the world, never had I encountered an airport so devoid of machine noise.

Le directed me to a souvenir shop at the back of the lobby. "We still have money left from the funds from your parents," he said. "Is there anything you'd like to buy?"

I felt so out of place in that airport considering all the Soviet and European tourists who were there. Only last month I was going to be spending the rest of my life in a box of concrete and iron, and now here I was shopping for souvenirs as though I was just returning home after an extended vacation. It was almost too much. I pointed to a fine carving in ebony and bamboo. Too expensive, Le said. An ebony fan, inlaid with a demure Vietnamese lady, hanging on a wall intrigued me. Too expensive.

Exasperated, because the last thing on my mind was a knickknack, I rolled my eyes and finally asked, "Okay, then, what can I afford, Le?"

Le motioned towards a glass counter. Little trinkets, rested on its three levels. "You have enough to buy one of these."

His long bony finger pointed to a row of dark-amber colored paper weights in the display case, rocks painted with lacquer and etched. My mind racing towards my flight, it was all I could do to show interest of any kind for an expensive river rock, albeit lacquered and engraved. He asked the attendant behind the counter for one. I inspected the paper weight that she handed me. The case's fluorescent ceiling light bar gave it a wet shine. There was one with a large mausoleum on it. Ho Chi Minh's tomb. It would make a good conversation piece, something I could at least drop on the bottom of an aquarium for guppies to defecate on.

With my new pet rock, we went up a flight of stairs to the second floor, to a room directly above the airport entrance. Inside the airport lounge, Le told me to sit down on a black vinyl couch against the back wall. Passing two black lounge chairs, I took a seat under one of six windows that looked out over the airport entrance.

I was soon shivering from the air-conditioner that was on full-blast. The Vietnamese went into friendly conversation amongst themselves. Their conversation permitted me to play a solitary game of picking out the recognizable Vietnamese words. It made me feel as though I were part of the conversation, and not ignored.

A knock at the door stopped the chatter. The major, Le, and the colonel resumed their chat, until they recognized the man in the doorway. His entry stiffened everyone in the room into the back-straight rigidity demanded by a person known for power and intimidation. He wore the same nerdy, horn-rimmed glasses my father wore during the 1960s. Mr. Importance walked over to sit in a lounge chair on my right and made a few comments to the rest of the Vietnamese.

The conversation that was previously loud and raucous, turned into a barely audible whisper. A deep, dark empty look filled the eyes of the Vietnamese chief as he glanced over at me; it was a look that my friend Sam took on whenever he talked or thought about those he had killed. Flashing a nervous smile for the Vietnamese chief, I quickly turned away.

Another knock ushered in a husky Caucasian, who ran his hand over his wavy black hair as he walked in. The thirty-five-yearold was accompanied by a young Vietnamese. "Hello, Freddy, how are you doing? I'm Tom Doubleday." A slight Boston accent sprinkled his voice as he offered his hand.

God, all these people I've never met in my life, calling me Freddy.

Le made the rest of the introductions, and then everyone sat down. Mr. Importance began speaking to Le. What he translated would have made me laugh at its pomposity were it not for the stress of still being under their control: "We are here, out of the goodness of the Socialist Republic of Vietnam, to give you Mr. Gra-ham."

"We feel that you have been well paid, and we're very glad to take him," Officer Doubleday of the Orderly Departure Program (ODP), retorted. His double-edged words forced me to bite back a smile.

The Vietnamese official spoke through Le, "Your government has dealt quite unjustly with us in the past, but out of our justness, and the betterment of relations between our two countries, we do this."

"And we thank you," Doubleday restated as he was handed forms to sign. He, too, hid his emotions behind a forced blank expression.

After he and the high official signed the documents, the Vietnamese gave him a copy. "Now if you'll excuse us? The plane should be leaving in a little while, and I'm sure Freddy would like to go."

Le and the major shook my hand, and I had the honest feelings that I would miss them much in the same way I would miss friends.

Doubleday led me out, and past the crowds of people preparing to leave, saying good-bye to friends and relatives. Le and the major followed. At the x-ray machine, after Doubleday had passed through, a navy-blue uniformed customs officer halted me.

Doubleday turned around. He looked back at Le, who waved off the sentry. Calming my nerves, I continued through and looked back to see Le and the major smiling and waving good-bye. One last wave from me sent them off.

"Can you believe what they were saying?" Doubleday whispered, from the side of his mocking grin. I raised my eyebrows and smiled.

"Just grab a seat, Freddy." There were eight lines of yellow plastic bucket seats in the waiting area. He pointed to the last row against the wall, and led me to sit down in one that was right next to his briefcase.

"We'll be done processing in a few minutes," he said while collecting some papers from his briefcase, "and then we'll take you on the plane with us." He gave me a reassuring smile and then left me to turn my attention to the tarmac outside, visible beyond the wall of glass.

Vietnamese walked out the door onto the tarmac, and up the steps to a waiting Aeroflot four-engine prop plane. They were the last passengers boarding a flight to Hanoi. The hatch closed, and the engines coughed and started. Ready, the plane turned and taxied away, revealing the nose of an Air France Boeing 747. My heart danced in anticipation.

David Cardwell, a tall and lanky, African-American ODP officer, came over from the processing table and went through his attaché. "So, did they treat you badly?" he asked, refraining from talking directly to me and flustering my gaze.

"Oh, it wasn't too bad." That's the way I always used to address my uncomfortable emotions.

"We thought you were going to leave with us last Thursday."
"Really?"
"Yes, your ransom was paid a while back."
A deeply drawn breath dulled the spike of my anger.
"Don't worry. We'll be finished in a few minutes."

Five minutes passed as I stared at the tile floor, completely oblivious to all that was happening, doing my best to remain patient. Freedom had been such a constantly teasing mirage on the edge of time, that I couldn't yet get my trust around it finally being real.

A commotion of disappointments and anxieties drew my attention to the ODP table as those Vietnamese who were being processed for emigration asked for more time, and those who hadn't even reached the table threw their hands up in the air. More time, more time! But, today, there was none. The ODP officers shuffled papers and collected belongings: ODP officers had to commute from Bangkok two days a week, the way someone might do a business day's flight from San Francisco to Los Angeles.

Doubleday smiled at me as he grabbed his briefcase. "Ready to go?"

I nodded with gusto, feeling as though my heart would explode from all the excitement of finally jumping on that bird out of here.

European travelers, who had been sitting in the waiting area, began walking out on to the tarmac. We waited for a few to pass the glass gate; then, on Doubleday's orders we stepped forward.

One last look at the crowd of Vietnamese, and I gazed out at our plane as we passed through the door. The 747 Air France, flight 175, Ho Chi Minh City to Bangkok, sat on its wheels, wings outstretched magnificently—never before or since have I looked at an airplane with such equally intense feelings of elation and trepidation. Paranoia hit me hard as we walked. *Let's walk faster, man!* I gave Doubleday a look of concern and after the seventy-yard walk, I looked down to see my knuckles had turned white from fingers wrapped too tightly around my Halliburton's handle.

Because of the angle of the stairs, and my emotions, the hatch looked so far up and away. Doubleday politely touched my shoulder and urged me towards my first steps to freedom. Up, up, and away we stepped. A beautiful and petite flight attendant, with sparkling blue eyes and blonde hair tied back in a tight ponytail, smiled and guided me in.

"We're up front, Freddy," Doubleday said, bringing me back from Heaven. *No tickets checked, wow! VIP treatment!*

Sitting down in my chair, I realized we were in First Class. The first starboard window seat was mine. Great leg room when you're just behind the nose.

The ODP officers talked amongst themselves, as they stowed their briefcases in a closet. While remaining quiet, I looked through my window, and glanced at the in-flight magazine. Neither registered in my thoughts. The hatch occupied my mind. *Close it!* Anticipation wreaked inner havoc, making me restlessly tap my fingers on my knee.

Finally, the captain's voice came over the PA system, asking everyone to take their seats. Doubleday took his seat next to mine. Taking a comb out of his shirt pocket, he drew it through his hair.

With interest, he asked me how I had been treated. While the flight attendant went through emergency procedures, I described some of the events of the eight months in solitary, and found myself laughing during my recant of the three months I shared with Knight. The rest of the ODP officers sneaked an ear to our conversation as they read their *New York Times* and *Newsweeks*.

Halfway through my account we began taxiing down the tarmac to the runway. I turned to have what I thought would be my last view of Vietnam. Funny, but it almost felt like leaving home.

Voices behind us faded as we turned and bounced, waited a moment; and the engines roared. I sank into my seat, the force of take-off pushing me back. Outside, old war birds flashed past the window. Camouflaged, torn and tattered, two DC-3's sat fallen on the tarmac, long since gone to the "elephant grave yard."

We lifted off! The world spread out into a carpet of green jungle and rice paddies, as we rose in a wide spiral, up and away from Saigon: emerald jungle, sapphire South China Sea, jade Thai Gulf, and back to Vietnam's jungle, the view slowly revolving.

I finished telling Doubleday about the rest of my incarceration, highlighting the colonel's sheepish attempt at propaganda just before leaving for the airport. We laughed, mine turning slightly hysterical.

Through the crack between our seats, a fortyish-looking brunette had been eavesdropping. Her accent was French as she talked with the other ODP officers. She sat looking forward at me from her aisle seat. The distressed expression on her face told me she must have thought me mad. It stopped me for a moment.

C'est vrai, Madame. I grinned; for I was madly happy.

The view out my window caused me to quiet down and embrace the gulf that had turned an intense opal-emerald by the sun beginning to peek through the gray clouds.

"You know that there's a lot of interest back in the States about your adventure?" Doubleday said.

"What do you mean?"

"Sure! There's been lots of press coverage. Quite a few people are interested in what happened to you." Fame would soon become a high-carb meal, lacking in long-term sustenance, but leaving me wanting more. Until finally, while dealing with more pressing matters, like fighting for my life in a Central American jungle, I'd kick the addiction.

I turned introspective and thought about the press and what a pressure they must have been on my parents, as my parents are people who basically keep to themselves. I then thought about what prison-earned, sage insights to share with my father upon first seeing him, ones that would make him think of me as no longer a boy, but a man. But, I couldn't think of any.

I satisfied myself by looking out at high-floating, light gray clouds. Below, was a structure recognized from a trip Dad took us on while vacationing in 1972. The gray and tan point of Angkor Wat's tallest temple stood out from the dark Cambodian jungle. The immensity of the building, visible so far below, was awesome. Remembering the photo of the stone head that started me on this voyage, I smiled.

Our plane began its descent barely an hour later. Such a short flight for two countries so ideologically apart. Having entered Thai air space, I was suddenly at peace, having remembered that in their language, *Thai* means Free People.

© *AP/WideWorld Photos* *Graham flanked by a US Embassy official (l) and Vogel (r).*

* * *

United States Department of State

Washington, D.C. 20520

March 13, 1984

LIMITED OFFICIAL USE

MEMORANDUM

TO: EAP – Mr. Monjo

FROM: EAP/VLK – M. Lyall Breckon

SUBJECT: ABC Plans Re Release of Frederick Graham

ABC News San Francisco has called to say that their local station has begun broadcasting appeals by Graham's father for funds to pay the $10,000 fine that the Vietnamese have set for Graham's release. They expect to raise the money in a few days. This has prompted many press calls to the consular officer handling Graham's case.

ABC proposed to the father that he and an ABC television news journalist go together to Vietnam to pay the fine and pick up Fred Graham. The father declined to go but is willing to travel to Bangkok to greet his son.

With regard to possible ABC travel to Vietnam we advised ABC that there are no US restrictions on travel to Vietnam but that we cannot provide any consular protection since we have no diplomatic relations. We advised that they could ask about visas either at the Vietnamese Mission New York or at the embassies in London or Paris. We also cautioned them to take into consideration in their proposal to the father any negative impact that publicity might have on the release.

* * *

According to Buddha, "Kinsmen, friends, and well-wishers salute a man who has been long away, and returns safe from afar." With my return these words rang wonderfully true. The dark sky, broken by glimpses of blue, above Bangkok's Don Muaung Airport reflected my mixed feelings of elation and terror. Freedom from prison was the experience of ending a long, terrible relationship and graduating from the school of life collected up in one moment, all full of hopes and uncertainties.

The captain's voice over the intercom prompted me to disembark first. It was a nice gesture, especially since the flight attendant addressed me as "*Monsieur Frederic Graham*"; it made me feel kind of special, something I needed after having gone through the Vietnamese wringer. Just as I reached the hatch, the *chef d'escale*, Christian Mermet, handed me his business card, and said, "Good luck, *monsieur*."

He and the smiling blonde flight attendant waved good-bye, giving me one last moment of calm before leaving the safety of the plane. Even though they and Doubleday stood by me on the stairway, I felt very alone looking down at the waiting group of reporters. My entry into Thailand almost started with a fall down that steep staircase, as stage fright tripped me on the first step.

At the foot of the stairs, Consul Frederick Vogel also waited in a Nehru-style safari suit, and wavy red hair. He greeted me with a heartfelt handshake and smile, happy to meet the man he had worked so hard to free. Trying to shield me from a rapid fire of questions, he briskly walked me to an awaiting white mini-van.

Vogel sat facing me in the parallel seat. As he briefed me on the itinerary, reporters continued their volley. 'Caution' was the word, as Dad had received offers for a book.

One question, too good to pass up, was shouted at me: "What are you going to do when you get home?"

I gave them a shining smile and said, "Surf!" And they all laughed.

"*Surf!*" © AP/WideWorld Photos

* * *

Seated in a semi-circle around me, in a refreshingly cool airport waiting room, was the entourage of embassy people from Bangkok, with one man from the British Embassy. Vogel sat on my left, and to his left sat British envoy A. E. Jakeman, a man with slicked-back white hair, and wearing a gray suit. He looked as though he could easily have popped out of a Graham Greene novel. He laughed and nodded knowingly when told about Knight's final letter and my tearing it up. To Jakeman's left, sat Colonel Paul Mathers, a man with close-cropped graying hair, and wire-rimmed glasses who looked like a teacher as he took notes about the places I'd been in Vietnam. He looked up from his pad and asked, "Do you mind if one of our people from the POW/MIA Division at the Pentagon calls you for more details? Most likely they'll fly you out to Washington D.C." I agreed.

"We're so happy you're finally out, Fred," said Vice Consul Patricia Langford, a pretty, fashionably dressed, middle-aged woman, whose smile had me put at ease when she first introduced herself a half-hour ago. "We didn't know what to expect about your condition."

"What do you mean?"

Jakeman fidgeted slightly in his seat and then said, "None of us had ever had the chance to meet you prior to this time, and the report on Knight from our man in Hanoi definitely did not sound good."

"Frankly, we were expecting someone completely broken and out of his mind. We thought that because of what little we knew of your situation, you might need psychological therapy," Langford said. "I'm glad to see that you've come through the ordeal so well."

"Here, here," everyone chimed in.

Later, I'd be told that after my departure, they would talk amongst themselves, expressing their surprise, "How could something like this happen to such a nice young man?" I'm sure they didn't look at my experience the way I did. Errol and Sean Flynn's spirits must have touched Langford, because she would later be quoted by a journalist from the *Oakland Tribune*: "We had expected a frazzled, wigged-out ex-prisoner, but we were greeted by an Errol Flynn." That statement would have made my day right then, let me tell you.

Vogel moved forward in his seat and said, "You know, Fred, we expected you out earlier."

"I heard."

"Yes, we had the money about four weeks ago, and then the Vietnamese suddenly told us they were again going to charge you for room and board."

I nodded, knowing what the SRV had said to me. What I hadn't realized was that after the ransom was finally paid, they had behaved like cheap, unscrupulous street vendors, trying to renegotiate a done deal, which postponed my release by almost two weeks!

"Incredible, I know," said Vogel. "Well, I yelled at them the way I had when they first brought it up, and created a stir, and then they called us back a week later and dismissed the added charges."

"Thank God." Everyone smiled at my blurb.

Vogel then advised me that it would not be wise for me to stay in Thailand, something they had assumed I might try according to the interview by Tarnoff. They were delighted that I intended to go straight back to California immediately. A customs official rushed in and told Vogel that my plane was boarding.

* * *

The Grand Hotel glowed with luxury in the Hong Kong night, its bright lights embracing me as I left the taxi and entered its lobby. At first I wasn't sure how to react to spending my first night here after eleven months in a concrete box. There was a reassurance in the hotel having changed little from my childhood, when Hong Kong was a stopover between Southeast Asia and the States, and a main vacation destination in itself. Mirrors and mother-of-pearl walled the lobby. I felt like a castaway entering the Taj Mahal. Though the city street lights were so inviting, I spent the whole evening in my room relishing its modern comforts, and looking in awe at the lights outside. To think that the power needed to light two Hong Kong street blocks could light all of Ho Chi Minh City at that time.

A message was waiting for me from Dad to call Mom. There was an uncomfortably strange feeling as we talked. My last memory of Mom was of her saying good-bye and not even turning to face me. I had yet to learn that she didn't turn around because she just hadn't wanted me to see her tears. I wished she had been strong enough to have shown me this softer, human side of herself. On the phone in my hotel room, Mom asked how I was doing. Not ready to share deep, painful emotions, we talked on the phone about the weather and what kind of shape I was in. She worried about my weight loss. I told her I was more or less at a healthy weight.

A sleepless night was spent thinking about my conversation with Mom, and how I really didn't want to tell my parents of my undeterred interest in combat photojournalism, or how bad Vietnam had really been. I thought it was enough for them to know that I had been imprisoned and now I was free. End of subject. Feelings of guilt towards my parents were still very strong, as it would be for a while.

I felt so torn. Part of me wanted to run out into the night, and announce that I was free—free—FREE! Another part had no idea how to greet my parents. And yet a third part was amazed at the shape of my body. Standing in the light of the bathroom, I looked at my naked body in a mirror large enough to give me a full head to knee view. A friend would later comment that the "Jane FondaWorkout Camp" had been a good thing for me.

"Damn!" I repeated for the third time that night, once for each visit to the bathroom to view what seemed unbelievable. In the mirror was a frame almost completely unrecognizable. What had gone to Asia a one-hundred and ninety pound, pudgy-faced, *ice cream baby*, had returned a six-foot man who weighed in at one-hundred and forty-eight. All that meditative walking had sure worked.

* * *

United Airlines flight 18 from Hong Kong to Seattle was on time, and I was happy to see snow covering Mount Rainier. Not many passengers disembarked from the continuing flight, and I found myself walking alone off the ramp. Silence engulfed me during my saunter, my pack on my back, Halliburton and flight bag in my hands. My thoughts dashed around as I deliberated on what I would tell my mother, so as not to hurt her with the full reality of my imprisonment. And what would I tell my father? Would he understand that because we had not healed, years ago, the emotional impact that living in Vietnam during the war had taken on all of us, that all this was inevitable? That even though prison had been horrendous, only because of that experience could we now truly be father and son?

The carpet muffled my steps and amplified the quiet. Rounding a corner, a lone man with white, slicked-back hair, parted on the right, stood waiting at the ramp bottom. Behind him was the airport tram that had just arrived. I would need to take it to the next terminal for my continuing flight to San Francisco. The man unbuttoned the top button of his shirt, the collar resting against the V-neck of his sweater. He shifted his overweight frame and smiled. He kept smiling which made me look to see if there was anyone behind me. When I saw no one, I became uncomfortable with this stranger who just kept smiling as I drew closer. The man pulled his right hand from the pocket of his slacks, and he shifted the weight of his attaché. Feeling as though I'd stepped into a scene from the *Twilight Zone*, I became more and more unnerved as I drew closer, still working my way toward the waiting doors of the tram.

"Oh, my God! Dad?" In only a year his hair had turned white, and his face looked so weary; I was shocked that I hadn't even recognized my own father, and grieved that I had been the catalyst to all that had hammered him.

"Hi, Freddy." His eyes, like mine, shimmered with emotion.

I offered my right hand. He pushed it away and drew me into a hug that told me he understood everything. It felt good, the first hug in a long, long time. "Glad you're home, son."

Epilogue

"No event in American history is more misunderstood than the Vietnam War. It was mis-reported then, and it is mis-remembered now."— President Richard M. Nixon, 1985

"They [the French] have robbed us of our rice fields, our mines, our forests, and our raw materials. They have monopolized the issuing of bank notes and export trade. They have invented numerous unjustifiable taxes and reduced our people, especially our peasantry, to a state of extreme poverty."— Nguyen Ai Quoc (Nguyen "the Patriot," aka Ho Chi Minh) reciting the Vietnamese Declaration of Independence, Sept. 2, 1945

Coming Back for the Treasure

Vietnam, as my friend Sam said back in Bangkok, was a state of mind. It was a state of mind he escaped only to bleed to death in my arms while we waited for a medevac to pull us out of a mangrove swamp in El Salvador. On that too-late medevac back to Ilopango Airbase, that morning in 1986 after I almost met the same fate as Sam, I never thought I would, in the following decade, once again set foot on Vietnamese soil, or for that matter revisit my childhood home in Saigon and listen to a ghost story.

In September 1999, that was exactly what I did. My girlfriend and confidante, Robin Hale, accompanied me on this trip. She had her own peace to make with Vietnam after having lived through the pain of witnessing older friends and classmates during the war, being called up for the draft and never coming home again.

The new renters of my childhood home in Saigon were a French couple, an import-export executive and his wife (for convenience, I will call her Mme. Dupont) with one son who was a little bit older than I was when we left Vietnam in 1972. They had rented the house from a woman who had been a commander and hero of the North Vietnamese Army during the war. The commander got the house as her portion of the spoils of South Vietnam during the takeover in 1975. This was the real reason for the NEZ relocation program; to move the South Vietnamese populace out of their homes and into the country to work, while the northern invaders, under the cloak of "brotherhood," disarmed the Vietcong and took up residence in Saigon and other South Vietnamese metropolitan areas. According to Mme. Dupont, the house had been in shambles at the end of the war, and had to have a lot of repair.

    The restoration was so thorough, that at first I was confused by the layout of the house. From the street, Robin and I inspected the area where the original driveway had been, and I explained to her that this two-story house near the corner of *Phung Khac Khoan* and *Duong Nguyen Thi Minh Khai* couldn't be the place that was my home from 1970 to 1972, as the house was so much smaller and the original driveway ended in a garage. Then, I realized that the driveway that led to the neighbor's house behind *was* actually the driveway my father had driven up many times: the new residents of the house behind ours had knocked out the back wall of the garage, turning it into a roofed throughway, and also built a brick wall, separating their driveway from the yard that held our mango trees, taking the place of the metal railing in the old photo of my brother and me in front of the company Toyota. What confirmed that this driveway was actually the original carport to my old house were the easy to recognize separations between the old concrete slabs where tires had rested, and where the new concrete had been poured to fill in a deep rectangular oil well. I immediately remembered how scared I was as a child that I might one day fall into that dark hole, and I was amazed at how big everything had seemed back then. It was an impression that hit me again and again after we met Mme. Dupont and she invited us inside our family's old house.

    "Speak English. You know how to speak English," Mme. Dupont said to her young boy, who looked strikingly similar to me when I lived in that house. I chuckled not at her remark, but at how much it reminded me of my parents when we lived in this house, and we had French visitors. "*Parle français*, Freddy," they'd say.

    Mme. Dupont was very curious about the history of the house. Nobody in the neighborhood knew anything about the house pre-1975. Even the commander who owned the house was unable to find out much about the previous history. Mme. Dupont was especially interested because she had heard many bumps in the night when they first moved in, and had sensed a distinct presence in the back patio, surprising for someone who labelled herself a skeptic.

    Taking the suggestion of a Vietnamese friend, she called on the skills of a local spiritualist who told her that there was indeed an angry spirit loitering around the back patio. In order to appease the ghost, Mme. Dupont was to set a sand-filled pot in the patio at the back of the house, place lit incense into the sand, and pray for the peace of the spirit and the repose of its soul. She was supposed to do this on a daily basis, but she admitted that since she was Catholic, she only did it on Sundays. She took Robin and I out to the site where she was guided to put the pot. It was on the side of the patio near the downspout, exactly where the teenaged thief's blood had pooled out. A chill absorbed me like a thick and cold Northern California night fog.

    She showed us the rest of the house, and I just could not get over how much smaller everything seemed. What had confused me when we first entered were the missing yard and mango trees that by now should have dwarfed the house. But now, in place of the yard and young trees, was a well-kept swimming pool. A slight envy touched me; I had always wished we had such a pool, like many of our friends and neighbors in Southeast Asia, something cool and refreshing. I smiled at how nice it was now to see that pool, recognizing immediately what was occurring: a new psychological anchor was replacing the previous one of the mango trees and the yard, and the traumatic memory of my pet rabbit being killed. I was now amped to go and revisit my prisons!

* * *

    The ghost story had been creepy, but it was not as unsettling as learning that my second prison, the one that was just a block from the pre-1975 American Embassy, was also just a few blocks from our house. Vietnam was working hard to erase its great shame of the last thirty-five years in order to make itself more attractive to American corporations for the money it so badly needed, and would never again get from the Soviets, and so the SRV destroyed my first prison in Saigon and turned the site into a business office and apartment complex called the Regency Chancellor Court, right there on the corner of *Duong Mac Binh Chi* and *Duong Nguyen Thi Minh Khai*. Considering how much the Vietnamese and Chinese believe in geomancy and feng shui, and how many angry spirits of starved and tortured prisoners surely haunted that plot of land, I was pretty surprised that B & B Far East Limited out of Hong Kong would put a high-rise there. Maybe, like parachute journalists who rely on government press releases, they just hadn't done their research.

    Within a week of my release in 1984, the POW/MIA Division of the Pentagon flew me to Washington D.C. to debrief me. They learned from me about the prisons where I had been held in Rach Gia and Saigon, in order to check against reported sightings of MIAs. What they told me was that there had been a Caucasian in cell number seven, right down the row from mine in the Kien Giang Provincial prison in Rach Gia, as reported by a Mr. Papat, one of the many Thai fisherman in the prison:

O 290952Z JUL 83

FM AMEMBASSY BANKGKOK

TO SECSTATE WASHDC IMMEDIATE 8044

AMEMBASSY SINGAPORE

UNCLAS BANGKOK 40647

6. Papat [a Thai released from Rach Gia] also volunteered the information that there was one other Causcasian prisoner at the facility. This man was "tall," blond, in [his] 30's, and according to Vietnamese prisoners had been there for a very long time. Papat saw this foreigner only once, and never heard him speak. Vietnamese in the prison said he was an American. This information has been passed to the JCRC official in Bangkok.

  MIA, drug runner, castaway from the Glomar Java Sea? Nobody ever gave me a worthwhile explanation of the identity of this mysterious prisoner at the POW/MIA Division. What they moved onto was telling me the original names and locations of my prisons, which was how I learned that my second prison had been the South Vietnamese barracks turned North Vietnamese political prison; and that the third prison had previously been the South Vietnamese and CIAs' interrogation prison along the Saigon River, at *Bach Dang #3.*

  By 1999, the Vietnamese populace was turning sour on a government that had promised so much to them back in 1995, when relations were normalized between the US and Vietnam, but now the only ones benefitting from that promised better life were the top 100 VCP officials. But, for me, it was turning out to be a fine year, what with not only finding my way back to the second prison, but also my old home. Both of those experiences left me with a weird feeling: my home, because in my memory it had been so big, and now seemed so small; and the second prison, because it had been turned into an office-apartment complex. It made Vietnam, covered in the new bright lights of commercialism, like a Las Vegas in the jungle, or like an old woman attempting to regain her lost beauty by wearing big, gaudy jewelry, while her children could barely get enough to eat, trembling in fear at the skyrocketing cost of living. I'm sure Uncle Ho would roll over in his grave if he knew that instead of the French he had referred to in his

Declaration of Independence, it was now the VCP robbing Vietnam of its rice fields, mines, forests, and raw materials; that they had monopolized the issuing of bank notes and export trade, and had invented numerous unjustifiable taxes and reduced the Vietnamese people, especially their peasantry, to a state of extreme poverty. Then again, he might have just joined in with all his old cohorts who had become some of the richest in all of Southeast Asia.

* * *

In a couple of days, Robin and I would be transported by a hired car and driver across the Mekong Delta to Ha Tien, where, hopefully, I would finally be able to land on the island where I had been captured. I had felt so cheated by not being able to do so on my last trip in 1995. Today, though, was a Saigon history lesson. Leaving our room at the Bong Sen Hotel, we walked to the Saigon River, and the statue of the General *Tran Hung Dao* that sits in the middle of *Me Linh* Square. *Hung Dao*, brother to the king and the warrior who had beaten back the Mongols, was part of the *Tran* Dynasty that had ruled from 1225 to 1400, when Vietnam was called *Dai Viet*. Over the last 4,000 years, depending on the latest dictator, foreign or domestic born, Vietnam has been called *Van Lang*, *Au Lac*, *Nam Viet*, *Giao Chi*, *Van Xuan*, *An Nam*, *Dai Viet*, *Dai Co Viet*, *Dai Ngu*, *Dai Nam*, and of course *Indochine*. With a history like that it's easy to see how simple it was for a government to take power under a new name, with nothing to offer but a new dictatorship, promising freedoms to their people that we in the Free World would consider an insult, like little appeasements offered to children to keep them quiet.

Robin and I continued on our history lesson, moving northeast along the river, to the main drag that used to be called *Bach Dang*, but had been renamed *Duong Ton Duc Thang*. Along the way, we passed the construction site of the new Marriott Hotel. Earlier, at *La Fourchette*, a marvelous French restaurant that served the best *biftek avec pommes frites* and was coincidentally right next door to my father's old AMTRACO office address at *10 Ngo Duc Ke*, we had learned that the Marriott was months behind in construction because the SRV wouldn't budge on a common contract clause. The negotiation had been classified as closed, and there would be no hotel. This should not have been news to any corporation doing business in Vietnam, as the VCP had always been good at working public opinion towards its own selfish interests. In *The Wall Street Journal*, August, 3, 1995, Bui Tin, the NVA colonel who received the unconditional surrender of South Vietnam on April 30, 1975, was asked whether the American antiwar movement was important to the success of the North Vietnamese. He answered: "It [the American antiwar movement] was essential to our strategy. Support from our rear was completely secure while the American rear was vulnerable" and that "Those people [the American peace movement] represented the conscience of America. The conscience of America was part of its warmaking capability, and we were turning that power in our favor. America lost because of its democracy; through dissent and protest it lost the ability to mobilize a will to win." But then, Vietnam has always been very good at saying one thing, while doing another—something innate in any political structure that has set itself above the checks and balances of its citizenry. Or as one US official was quoted, about awards for change in Vietnam, "Sometimes I get the impression the Vietnamese government looks at these [only] as if they were plaques on the wall, which make Vietnam look good."

I would later read in a newspaper article that the new Marriott hotel—which still hadn't been completed—was an $80,000,000 US venture set up by the Vietnamese Navy: I guess *Doi Moi*[27] had served as an excellent opportunity for the SRV military to learn that there was more profit in demolishing political prisons and then renting the property out to large American concessions. Not far after the hotel, just before *Duong Ton Duc Thang* ends and becomes *Dinh Tien Hoang*, moving directly away from the river, we stopped walking.

"Where is it?" I asked, as if Robin knew where my old prison was simply from having listened to my previous descriptions of my adventures. When I realized that the open-air restaurant in front of us *was* the old prison, I couldn't help but laugh at the irony. We went in and when the concierge told us that it was one of the best restaurants in Saigon, and that on Friday nights it drew large crowds, it was hard to stifle another chuckle. Now if you want to have a really weird experience, sit down at a table and order a meal, knowing that the site at which you're about to dine was a prison where you wondered heavily if you'd ever see daylight again. Actually, our table was exactly where the car had been parked that took me to Tan Son Nhut the day I was released. Add to that bizarre feeling the fact that only *half* of the prison had been turned into a restaurant, and the back half was still very much a political prison. Now that's not only bad feng shui, it's just plain freaky!

What if my family and friends weren't able to come up with the money to pay for my ransom? The thought cut straight to my center being. I might still be rotting away behind the walls of this new prison, and on Friday and Saturday nights, I'd have to listen to all of the fun, music, and carousing, amplified by the new radios and stereos coming in from the outside. I would have had to endure a torture that would be far and beyond a mere beating. I thought about the poor souls on the other side of the wall, still quietly hidden away from the unknowing tourist's eye—it's anyone's guess how many are still in there, because Vietnam still doesn't allow any human rights organizations into its prisons (even into 2004, the demands by human rights watch groups got louder, as the meager reports of violations got worse). I immediately thought of Richard Knight and Aht and Leung.

During our side trip to Thailand, I introduced Robin to Captain Muk, now the mayor of Bangsare, and he regaled us with the exploits of Aht and Leung. They were released three years after Knight and me, in pretty bad shape after having been almost starved to death. Their treatment had sharply turned for the worse after the trial, and they had resorted to eating scraps and weeds that grew through the cracks in the concrete yard of Kieng Giang Provincial Prison. As for Knight, an English adventurer and Bay Area taxi cab driver by the name of Kenneth Crutchlow—who would be instrumental in gaining Aht and Leungs' release for a few hundred dollars each—interviewed me a few weeks after my release and then got some investors together from the tight San Francisco community of British ex-pats to pool their funds for Knight's ransom. When Knight was released three months after me, Crutchlow had thought that he and the investors would be repaid with at least a partnership in a movie and book deal. Knight made no effort whatsoever to repay Crutchlow. The two-thousand pounds he was paid by *The Sunday Time*s of London was pissed away on drink. According to Captain Muk, Knight was last seen traveling in Denmark or Holland, up to his old tricks, trying to get travellers headed for Thailand to go in with him on a scam of finding buried treasure! Captain Muk was still furious at Knight, who still owed him for his fishing boat that had long since joined the Vietnamese fleet. *Old dogs die hard*, I thought, as I remembered that the macabre prison-turned-restaurant was the last place of my interaction with a species best forgotten—It should come as no surprise that I would learn years later that Kidd's treasure took Knight to his grave: dead in a ditch, drunk as a skunk, still in search of treasure hunting investors.

In awe of Sir Richard Francis Burton's epic adventures and total immersion in a variety of cultures and languages, I've always done my best to emulate that special quality of "going native," part of which is experiencing all indigenous cuisine. In Thailand, it's scorpions fried in oil—bitter-tasting and smelling of fish. In Vietnam, it's the rubbery chicken texture of cobra in a fragrant and sweet curry sauce, or the honey and pork quality of barbecued porcupine; and Robin, quite the trooper, tried them all with me, short of dog—which she flatly refused to try—whose flesh tastes like gamey goat when stewed and served with mounds of sweet basil and a French baguette. But, at Bach Dang #3, the prison-turned-restaurant, even though I had ordered something as common as *cha gios*, Robin did not eat with me, and we did not linger there. The energy she felt in that place was so depressing, she spent most of our time at the table in tears: especially when she thought of me imprisoned in that awful place. After shooting some more photos and video of the back end of the restaurant, we left. I didn't want to spend too much time there, because the owner of the restaurant had told me that when they were creating the wall that separated the large courtyard, kitchen and restaurant—based on a jungle frond and bamboo theme—from the back prison, one of the construction workers had fallen over the wall. He spent two days being interrogated by the secret police and navy!

* * *

We had to leave before dawn the next day in order to make it to Ha Tien before dark. I was damned if I'd put Robin through the danger of driving down cratered jungle roads in the Mekong without any streetlights. In a rented sedan with a North Vietnamese veteran of the 1980s Cambodia War at the wheel, we left Saigon just as the first streaks of purple and orange painted the sky. By the time we hit My Tho, for a quick lunch of beef noodle *pho*, the sun was high and the heat unbearable.

From ferry to ferry, we moved across the Mekong Delta. At Vinh Long we stared in awe at the giant My Thuan Bridge that was being built to span the river at the southern branch of the Mekong. The populace would soon be able to drive straight across, and that I found absolutely amazing considering the immense distance between the two banks. A joint venture between Australia and the SRV, the bridge was late in completion because of Hanoi's see-sawing unwillingness to open itself to scrutiny on human rights violations.

Every once in a while, I'd get a little laugh from the Vietnamese who would stare at Robin through the car windows because of her blue eyes and blonde hair, bequeathed to her by her English and Lithuanian ancestors. At first it was surprising to have the Vietnamese children come up to her and touch her light skin, and act as though they'd also like to reach up and grab her eyeballs, but Robin started playing with the children by touching their hair and skin back in return. Someone once told me that it wasn't necessarily that they were touching you for luck, but that by touching you, they were giving you some of their bad luck. I couldn't recall whether my informative friend was talking about Vietnam or Cambodia. Finally, I just said to hell with it, because I had been in enough tight situations to learn that luck is what you make of it.

Vinh Long, Can Tho, Long Xuen, the names of cities no larger than towns, marked our dash across the Delta. Soon, we rolled into Rach Gia and crossed the canal that points out from An Chau, straight into the Thai Gulf. This was the massive canal that Knight and I were ferried into just short of Rach Gia, after having been towed all the way down the intersecting canal from *Ba Hon* Bay. I could see the banks, manicured in rock and concrete, with that River Seine look, and the row after row of steps that offered an opportunity for boatmen to dock and easily walk right up onto the road that paralleled the bank.

After stopping to shoot some video, we asked to be driven past the prison. Our driver refused because even in Saigon he had heard about that place, and how one should keep as far away from it as possible. It almost surpassed the prison that was kitty-corner from the new American Consulate.

I chuckled as I remembered an Army Corps of Engineers captain who had come into one of my debriefings at the Pentagon. He had a satellite picture of the Rach Gia prison. If I'd been in the courtyard at the time the black and white photo was taken, I would have easily been picked out. What they wanted to know was the identity of a collection of half-circle ports in the side of one of the buildings. The captain had assumed that they were being used for storage, rice, tools, et cetera. "Yeah," I said, "storage, alright, but not rice." The SRV had prisoners crammed in there, like pickled herring in a jar.

* * *

My camera bag was all I would take to Grand Pirate Island. Robin and I thought it safer that she stay behind on the mainland with the driver, with the understanding that if I didn't return, she would immediately contact the new US Consulate in Saigon. Who knew what could happen? I'd already had to bribe the captain of the ferry to even take me to the island, because, even in 1999, no one else was willing to take me there.

Robin watched me through the back window of the car, as I quickly tagged along behind the first mate who had been the negotiating translator for the ferry captain. A wave goodbye and I was gone on the boat. For a moment, I wanted to stay behind with Robin and just enjoy this exotically beautiful mix of Cambodia and Vietnam, called Ha Tien, and partake of the delicious salt and pepper crab promised at the hotel; but, if I had to spend a cold and drenched night on a beach, or in a ship's hold, I was willing to do that if only to regain the peace of mind and spirit I had lost over the last ten years.

I had experienced an adventure that many people, even to this day, find hard to accept, or believe: heaven forbid ever mentioning Knight and I found that first cache. It got to the point that I'd either no longer talk about my experience, or talk about it in a manner that lessened my emotional interpretation of the traumas. When asked about my experience, I'd say "it was just part of the job." When asked if I'd been tortured, I'd either say no, or soften it further with a joke: "I used to speak in a lower voice," meaning they had castrated me. And then, after the laughing, there were no more questions. Case closed. But, there is no such thing as a closed case until after a true making of peace, something that cannot occur through forgetting, only through forgiveness. And forgiveness has everything to do with honesty of memory and the refusal to be hindered by past trauma.

In time, it was as though I had not only dulled the pain of my emotional experiences, but I was also beginning to question whether I had actually experienced being a political prisoner in Vietnam, or for that matter, that I had lived a life most people only read about in adventure books: being a combat photographer in the Central America War; CIA paramilitary officer and the second American trained at the Salvadoran Naval Special Forces School created by the US Navy SEALs at Punta Ruca (In 1983, I told my interrogators in Vietnam, if I was CIA then, they never would have captured me—in Central America, the communist guerrillas never did); a long-line fisherman in the Bering Sea; a subsistence hunter and fisherman in Alaska; an apprentice to Native American healers. Whenever I encountered people who were just so ignorant that they would think I was lying about what I'd been through, because they could only view what I said through the myopic lens of having lived in a world too small to accept a full life, I, too, began questioning whether I was telling the truth. Belief and self-confidence have no loyalties; if you don't believe in yourself, no one else will.

So, by the time I had put myself on that boat headed for Grand Pirate Island, I was beyond compulsion. And the conditions were perfect for recreating the experience, though, of course, nowhere near as dangerous considering the SRV was finally starting to wise up to the idea that they couldn't live without the rest of the world, and that especially meant tourism. Tourism would be my cover when I arrived at the large concrete jetty I recognized as the one at which I had received such a prophetic *"au revoir"* from the old man. As if that wasn't enough of a memory jog, the commandant of the village militia came down to greet me, angry and yelling orders, confiscating my passport before I even had a chance to step foot in the quaint fishing hamlet. Through the postal clerk, who seemed to be one of the few people on the island who could speak English, he told me that I was under house arrest in the home of the ferry captain, one of the many homes on stilts that stood at the water's edge. As I was led away by the first mate, I looked back and saw the commandant and the ferry boat captain launch into a verbal battle as they walked up to the only concrete building in the village, the militia's quarters, I assumed.

El sargento hondureño y el enfermero americano. (The Honduran sergeant and the American corpsman, El Salvador, 1986)

There wasn't much to do for a while, so I took a nap on a bed that reminded me of my prison bed: a grass mat on lumber. It wasn't long before the villagers learned that a foreigner had arrived on the island. I guessed that they hadn't seen one in a while, but I would start to question that by evening.

Once it was dark and the mosquitoes had started their patrols, I was taken up to the militia headquarters to explain why I had come to the island. Though I had the credentials to get a journalist visa, I didn't want to bring attention to myself, and the only reason to obtain a non-resident press visa in a nation run by a dictatorship is to be taken around by government lackeys and shown exactly what they want you to see. Considering I already had to bribe the ferry captain just to get here on an innocuous tourist visa, I surely wouldn't have been permitted near the island with a journalist visa. Even Robin, back on the mainland, told me that she had to maintain our cover and reassure our driver that I was simply a tourist wanting to see the island, and not a journalist or spy.

So, when the postal clerk asked me why I was there, I answered, "I'd heard about this island from other tourists who said it was one of the most beautiful islands in Vietnam."

"You know there were many people who came here to look for treasure, diamonds and gold." He stopped for a moment, and the commandant said something to the postal clerk, who continued, "Many French, many English, many Americans, all come here looking for this treasure."

"Really?" I said, holding back the urge to correct him: *no diamonds, only jade and gold coins*. "I'm amazed. I'd just heard that there was a beautiful beach. . . When can I get my passport back?" I wondered if they had dug up the other caches, and whatever happened to the first cache. Vietnam was doing much better financially. Was this change partly started by an injection of pirate treasure into the economy, in 1983? The commandante was the only one of the militia left on the island from that night. Was he just left out of the loop?

"Soon, soon," the clerk said without even looking at the commandant.

As I slapped a mosquito, I noticed that the whole village had filtered into the large room. With the fluorescent light having been turned on, it was a finishing touch to my flashback of the night of my capture, elbows bound and smarting head wound aside. And they were just as curious about the outside world as ever. Being there didn't hit me as emotionally as you might think, but the realization that the commandant was actually one of the militia who had dragged me onto the boat that night just floored me—I'm not too good with names, but faces I can remember forever. As the night deepened, I confirmed his identity by my evasively casual questions about how long he had been in the militia on the island.

I could tell by the looks he was giving me that he was getting suspicious, as though he were searching his mind for my identity, and was frustrated because he was so sure that he knew me, but couldn't place me. About every third or fourth question kept revolving around to what I did back in the States. Through my answers, they learned that I had earned my degree at San Francisco State a couple years earlier, and that I worked in the software field as a technical writer.

"Ah," they said, "like Bill Gates!"

"Uh, yeah, like Bill Gates."

As the commandant held his eye on me, I, for the first and only time, thanked my bad work habits of sitting behind a computer for twelve hours a day, and gorging on the rich food available in the Silicon Valley. Because of this, I was fifty pounds overweight and that, along with time, made it pretty difficult for the commandant to recognize who I really was. I couldn't help smiling at him as I realized why he couldn't place me. They got no argument from me when the postal clerk said it was time to go to sleep, other than my asking, again, "When do I get my passport?"

"Soon," he said, just like the old days.

Led back to the captain's house on stilts, the captain and his family invited me to share their meal of fish soup laid out on the floor, the waves crashing below, telegraphing in increasing intensity the incoming storm. After our meal, we went to sleep, and after the monster lightning and thunderstorm that I was sure was going to turn the captain's house into a mass of driftwood, I learned that once you leave Saigon, it's a whole different country, more like the Vietnam that I recalled from 1983 to 1984, a place where I was rudely awakened from my sleep by Hanoi's propaganda news being blasted out on the village speaker system at 5 a.m., just like at the Kien Giang Prison.

After a breakfast of Vietnamese coffee and a baguette, and a haggle by the captain who wanted me to bribe him some more, to which I replied in the way Vietnamese poachers do to game wardens in California—*Toi khong hieu*: I don't understand—he backed down and took me around to the north of the island. As we motored, I reflected on the years since my release and an article I had come across in *The Anchorage Daily News* about Tim Page, the photojournalist "who made war sexy" and his search for his good friend and my idol, Sean Flynn. I learned that within weeks of Flynn's and Dana Stone's disappearance in Cambodia, they were bound and slaughtered like farm animals, shot in the back of the head by a drunken Khmer Rouge and buried in the jungle until Page's discovery in 1990. I had read the article after having gone up to Alaska to get away from the stress of modern living, and to live alone in a cabin, having learned the lessons of introspection afforded me while in solitary in Vietnam. By 1990, I was once again suffering from a really bad case of post-traumatic stress, and this time it wasn't from just being an observer. So, again, I'd had to take care of myself.

I not only confirmed that I had done right by going back through my memories and reframing them from just painful to heartrendingly enlightening strengths, but also, I'd been able to take those lessons back to the Bay Area with me, and provide aid to other PTSD sufferers as a drug and alcohol rehab counselor for Friendship House Association of American Indians in San Francisco.

I smiled as I thought about all that, because a circle is so important in so many societies. There's the circle of life. The family circle. The Native Circle. The circle of healing. The circle a PTSD sufferer must follow in order to heal. Full circle was where I was as I stood on the deck of the ferry boat, looking back at the white sandy beach where Knight and I had first landed. The captain and I waited for a twin-oared boat from shore that moved like a water beetle, just like the one that carried me out to the waiting boat that night of our capture. It would take us into the shallow water and I would then follow the path up from the beach to where I was laying that night when the sky exploded in tracers and muzzle flashes.

While the beach had been deserted the night we were captured, it was now populated by a few bamboo shacks. Where there had been an ivory-white sand beach, there was now litter. Where there was once lush green grass, it had been worn away by a country so representative of other countries: overpopulated and still growing. Up from the beach I walked, full of thoughts. Of how life is never static. The opportunity to change is the opportunity to heal.

We walked through the mini-village, and I made my way down the beach to where I had been forced to sit with my elbows bound. I thought about that asshole who had clipped me in the head with the butt of his AK-47. Immediately, just like the impressions of my old house, everything seemed so much smaller, as though because of the trauma in the past, the memory of it made everything that much larger and intimidating. At the house in Saigon, I thought it was just because I was a small child when I lived there, and the world seemed like a big giant vastness then. But now, as I looked at everything from the clear perspective of presence, everything was that much smaller. Squatting down, I scooped up a handful of sand and my mind wandered to stories of Vietnam veterans who had found returning to Vietnam profoundly healing. As I thought about all that had happened, the initial international notoriety of my story, the following public disbelief, and my own questioning of my personal history, I shook my hand from left to right, grains of sand slipping through my fingers, as though I were panning for gold. With all the sand gone, I smiled, knowing that all had truly happened and, despite the pain, I would never have traded the last thirty-four years with anyone. Brushing my palms against each other, I had a clean slate.

The End

Footnotes

1. A Vietnam-era colloquial for the CIA who often found themselves getting their civilian clothes dirty during a firefight, or such event.

2. American Trading Company

3. Foreign Correspondents Club of Thailand

4. Color slide film

5. It's Maekong in Laos and Thailand, and Mekong in Vietnam.

6. Cowboy Lane.

7. Ahmad Shah Masood, The Lion of Panjsher, was assassinated by the Taliban of Afghanistan in September of 2001.

8. A tuk-tuk is a cross between a motorcycle and a minivan, with a driver up front and bench seats facing each other in the back.

9. United Nations Children's Fund.

10. As more Americans arrived in Singapore, the need to lessen the effects of culture shock on us TCKs resulted in the forming of the Singapore American Community Action Council in 1973, which also started the Singapore American Football Program. It was a Singaporean cousin to the Stateside's Pee-Wee Football, except it began in 5th grade and continued all the way up to 12th, since there was no other school for a high school varsity and junior team to play against.

11. Maid.

12. Ex-patriates.

13. All-purpose Light-weight Individual Carrying Equipment.

14. Landing Zone.

15. Night Vision Goggles.

16. During the war, in a fraternal hazing, newbies would be hit with a barrage of stories of those who contracted the "black gonorrhea" being quarantined on an island off the coast of Vietnam in POW-style, bamboo tiger cages, to make the story that more terrifying. This Vietnam War "urban legend" started with the creative minds of servicemen and very real cases of penicillin-resistant strains of syphilis and gonorrhea.

17. Browning .50 caliber machine gun.

18. Army of the Republic of Korea.

19. Research Among Vietnam Refugees Reveals a Blood Bath, Jacqueline Desbarats and Karl D. Jackson, The Wall Street Journal, Monday, April 22, 1985.

20. The reason there were beggars in the streets of Vietnam was not because Vietnam was poor, but because their government was immensely corrupt, even more corrupt than the expired government of South Vietnam. By 1995, according to a US-Vietnam Trade Council official, the Vietnamese Communist Party (VCP) was considered one of the world's wealthiest billionaires, owning assets of almost $20 billion US. The highest ranking officials of the VCP were one hundred of Vietnam's richest, a few worth at least $300 million US! All while the annual income of the typical Vietnamese citizen remained around $20 to $100. If only I had this bullet of information in 1983, so I could shoot the major in his arrogant Communist heart with it.

21. It wouldn't be until editing this book, almost twenty years after I told reporters that prison wasn't so bad, that it was just part of the job of being a correspondent in a hostile country; that I would really feel the full emotional and psychological effects of my prison experience, and realize how incredibly effective hypnosis had been in making me inured to the pain of that hell-hole!

22. Pi and Ti were fed up with Knight's inability to correctly pronounce their true names, Aht and Leung, so they gave themselves nicknames, Ti and Pi.

23. The Glomar Java Sea was an oil drilling ship owned by Global Marine of Houston, Texas and leased to ARCO. It was hit by Typhoon Lex and went down October 25, 1983 off the SRV. In 1984, of the 81 aboard only 31 of 36 bodies were recovered by divers. As of 1985, of the 46 thought to be alive, 43 were confirmed alive and missing. In his book The Bamboo Cage, Nigel Cawthorne, described reported sightings of these civilian MIAs. Also in 1984, Douglas Pierce, father of one of the

crew, was quoted as telling the US Coast Guard Board of Inquiry that his son and 15 other American men were seen in Vietnamese prisons. No doubt in my mind: they didn't have a chance to send a letter to their parents before capture.

24. Even in 2001, according to the latest annual human rights report offered by the US State Department, "Members of the public security forces committed human rights abuses." No diplomat or foreign journalist was permitted to investigate stories unless chaperoned by representatives of that country's government, which was why most good investigative journalists enter totalitarian states on tourist visas and not journalist visas.

25. Now if only we still had presidents like Teddy Roosevelt, who, in 1904, sent a gunboat and a letter to a North African bandit by the name of Mulai Ahmed er Raisuli. Raisuli was holding hostage the American Ion Hanford Perdicaris. The letter read: "Perdicaris alive, or Raisuli dead." Mr. Perdicaris was on that boat quicker than you could say, "Open sesame."

26. Before Ulu Pandan and right after the independence of Singapore, the primary through middle classes of the Singapore American School were taught at the Alexander Road campus, which had been a base for the British regiment that surrendered during the siege of Singapore, the same that was shipped to Thailand by the Japanese to build the infamous River Kwai Bridge. Out of respect, we even had to whistle the Colonel Bogie March during muster every morning before classes, though not having yet seen the movie, or even knowing the gravity of the song's history.

27. Doi Moi literally means "reconstruction". After almost having starved the population of Vietnam during the late 1970s and early 1980s, the VCP initiated a reform program enabling semi-private ownership of farms in 1986. In following reforms, Vietnam had the potential of becoming the next Asian tiger, just like Korea, Taiwan and Japan before it, with an economy that was growing at a rate of 8.1 percent per year from 1990 to 1995. But, a failure by the VCP to provide a business-friendly environment for outside investment, with solid property laws, a stable government and a decent court system, resulted in economic stagnation with its citizens averaging an annual income of only $220, and the unprecedented public protests of the late 1990s and early 2000s.

In 2000, after reading the e-book version of this story, my younger brother learned of how I felt about this photo— while I was in Central America chasing the combat photographer's bang-bang, he found it while collecting belongings for his sojourn into college and the US Navy. Needless to say, I'm happy to now consider it my own, having thought of it often over the years. And evennow, there's still that calming sense of peace...

PTSD Notes

It all starts with what we expose our children to.

What is Post-Traumatic Stress Disorder (PTSD)?

It is a collection of reactions—feelings, thoughts, behavior—which are experienced following a sudden distressing event which is outside the range of normal everyday human experience. It is the unexpectedness of the incident which seems to evoke the stress because it undermines one's trust in normalcy - one can never quite believe in an ordered existence any more. Incidents that can sometimes lead to post-traumatic stress include such things as burglary, an attack, or an accident.

When does it occur and to whom?

Signs of PTSD, such as those listed below, may not appear for days, weeks or even months and years after the event, and can affect those not directly involved in an incident - e.g. to those who witness an accident, or to rescue workers, or to relatives of those involved.

What are the reasons for its occurrence?

It is the way by which our mind and body 'processes' the event, to try to make sense of it, so that we can eventually react to it in a less distressing way. The processing is often made apparent through physical, emotional and psychological signs.

Indications

- recurrent intrusive recollections of the event
- changes in sleep (e.g. not being able to sleep, or wanting to sleep all the time)
- recurrent vivid dreams about the event
- feeling or behaving as if the event were happening again
- changes in behavior (e.g. short temper)
- changes in feelings about yourself (e.g. feeling useless)
- numbed responses
- changes in work effectiveness (e.g. poor concentration, increased stress during reading, symptoms close to dyslexia)
- reduced interest in the external world (e.g. feelings of detachment and estrangement)
- a sense of always needing to be ultra-alert
- a sense of being vulnerable, leading to a fear of losing control
- avoidance of activities, and, or places which arouse recollections of the event
- forgetting an important aspect of the event
- guilt at surviving, or for things not done
- Post traumatic stress disorder is different from a bereavement reaction (in that it is about a stress reaction to a perceived threat) although the two can occur together and interlink. It is also linked

with depression, in that 30% of those in whom the condition is not recognized and dealt with early go on to develop depression.

How does the body react?

At first you may be numb because your mind will only gradually allow you to feel the experience. So the event may feel unreal, as if it couldn't have happened to you. But as you allow your experiences to become more real in your mind, there is a need to think about the event, to talk about it, and at night to dream about it over and over again.

Some people seek refuge in the numbing quality of a mindless activity, such as exercising past the point of numbness, or being involved in group activities that provide only escape from confronting the effects of PTSD, by avoiding any reminder of the trauma— and so it is never dealt with. In contrast to healthy activities that help a person become more consciously present in their day lives, unhealthy activity is simply any activity that is used as diverting attention from the fact that you might need help in dealing with PTSD.

How to help yourself

Being active, maybe through helping and giving to others may offer some relief, as doing things in a routine, especially activities participated in pre-traumatic event, can give a sense of bringing life back to normal.

Keep in touch with information about the event and any developments. This keeps the trauma 'real'—keeping you in the moment—and helps you come to terms with what has happened and how it has affected you.

It can be a relief to receive other people's physical and emotional support, even though part of you might want to reject it as part of wanting to deny what has happened. Sharing with others who have had similar experiences can feel good, barriers can break down and close relationships can develop.

As well as being with other people, you will sometimes want to be alone in order to deal with your feelings: privacy, as opposed to isolation, is very important. Seven months solitary in Vietnam and a year in the wilds of Alaska (with an opportunity to interact when needed with neighbors over the mountain) was this for me.

The Do's and Don'ts of PTSD

DO

- express your emotions
- take opportunities to review the experience with yourself and others
- take time out to sleep, rest, think, and be with close friends and family
- express your needs clearly and honestly to friends, family, tutors, colleagues etc.
- exercise to relieve immediate stress
- try to keep your life as normal as possible after the experience
- be careful: accidents are more common after experiencing severe stress.

DON'T

- expect the memories to go away: the feelings will stay with you for a considerable time
- let embarrassment stop you from giving others as well as yourself the chance to talk
- avoid talking about what happened
- bottle up feelings
- exercise to distraction

When to seek further help

- if you feel disturbed by intense feelings or body sensations that you can no longer tolerate
- if you think that your emotions are not falling into place, and that you feel very tense, confused, empty, or exhausted
- if after a month you continue to be numb and do not have appropriate feelings, or you have to keep active in order not to feel distressed

- if you continue to have nightmares and poor sleep
- if you have nobody with whom to share your feelings and you feel the need to do so
- if your relationships seem to be suffering, or sexual problems develop
- if you have accidents
- if you smoke, drink or take medication to excess since the event
- if your work performance suffers

Healing qualities of Meditative Physical Training

There's an old saying in the warrior community that goes back thousands of years: *Be in the moment!* One of the ways to do this is through physical exercise. However, anyone dealing with PTSD needs to cautious of disassociation from immediate reality that can occur during heavy exercise and an active lifestyle, defeating the purpose of using physical training to become more connected to the present life experience and dissuade the effects of PTSD that cause affected persons to disconnect emotionally and psychologically from those around them.

This is a two-pronged strategy: using tools of introspection, such as a meditation, and physical exercise to instill the body with new programming and event memory. This is an on-going, life-long process! You don't read stories about old samurais stopping their meditations and sword practice until the day they're ready to die, right?

A few forms of physical training that are excellent for working yourself into the in-the-moment consciousness are: weight-lifting, yoga, tai-chi, walking in nature and tracking, and martial arts that incorporate some form of meditation or introspection. The meditative aspect of physical training—pre, during and post-training—is very important!

If you have PTSD resulting from military experience, I'll assume that you also went through the physical training part of that military service, and are aware of the lack of introspection that was incorporated into it. This is one of the aspects of the modern soldier: all the excellent fighting tactics and strategies of ancient cultures, yet none of the post-battle healing techniques from those cultures.

In many tribal societies there was always some type of ritual that returning warriors had to go through before coming back to the village: smoking the horse and themselves down with sage, living away from the tribe for a certain number of months using the time to pray; going to the spiritual healer's tent to pray for an extended length of time.

During WWI and WWII, returning warriors had the months of sea voyage to cleanse and provide an ear for their comrades in combat. Nowadays combat personnel are back at their 9 to 5 jobs in a week, with a only a quick screening, and a "get back to us if you have anything come up." Unfortunately, this follow-up often doesn't occur, as the macho military culture in the US encourages self-reliance which can be construed to mean, in *all* situations, and that not dealing with the symptoms of PTSD on your own can be interpreted by others in a team as not attending to your own of responsibilities.

The first step is admission that something is not as it was (review indications list), and that there's nothing wrong with that, and "how can I incorporate my memories of the previous traumatic event into my life as an asset, instead of a distraction?"

Information provided by Cambridge University and the National Center for Post-Traumatic Stress Disorder.

Where to start seeking further help

- National Center for PTSD
- Child Trauma Academy
- FEMA for Kids: What you might feel in a disaster

For hypnotherapists who specialize in aiding clients with PTSD, check through the varied, yet effective forms:

- EFT — Emotional Free Techniques: http://www.eftuniverse.com/
- EMDR — Eye Movement Desensitization and Reprocessing: http://www.emdr.com/
- In the UK and Europe: http://emdr-europe.org/
- National Guild of Hypnotists http://www.ngh.net/ P.O. Box 308, Merrimack, NH 03054-0308, tel.(603) 429-9438

Recommended Reading

A Third Culture Kid Bibliography (2nd ed.) Dr. Ruth Hill-Useem, technical assistance by Sonya E Schryer. Order at: Dr. Ruth Hill Useem; ATTN: Sonya Schryer; 227 Chesterfield Parkway, 2nd Floor; E. Lansing, MI 48823-4110 USA

Shadows and Wind: A View of Modern Vietnam. Robert Templer, 1998, Penguin Books.

Following Ho Chi Minh: Memoirs of a North Vietnamese Colonel. Bui Tin, 1995, C. Hurst and Co. Publishers Ltd., London.

A War of Nerves: Soldiers and Psychiatrists in the Twentieth Century. Ben Shephard, 2000, Harvard University Press.

Stolen Valor: How the Vietnam Generation was Robbed of Its Heroes and Its History. Burkett and Whitley, 1998, Dallas.

Professional Hypnotism Manual: A Practical Approach for Modern Times. John G. Kappas, Ph.D., 1987, Panorama.

SEAL! Lt. Cmdr. Michael J. Walsh, USN (Ret.) 1994, Pocket Books.

Dirty Little Secrets of the Vietnam War**.** James F. Dunnigan & Albert A. Nofi, 1999, St. Martin's Press.

Man's Search for Meaning. Viktor E. Frankl, Ph.D., 1959, Washington Square Press.

Hypnosis and Hypnotherapy. Calvin D. Banyan and Gerald F. Klein, 2001, Abbot Publishing House, Inc.

The First Casualty**.** Phillip Knightley, 1975, Harcourt Brace Jovanovich.

The Art of Hypnotherapy**.** C. Roy Hunter, M.S., C.H., 2000, Kendal/Hunt Pub. Co.

The Art of Hypnosis. C. Roy Hunter, M.S., C.H. , 2000, Kendal/Hunt Pub. Co.

Hypnotherapy. Dave Elman, 1964,Westwood Pub. Co.

Requiem: By the Photographers Who Died in Vietnam and Indochina. Host Fass and Tim Page, 1997, Random House.

At Home in Asia. Harold Stephens, 1996, Wolfenden.

Allies in Healing: When the Person You Love Was Sexually Abused as a Child**.** Davis, Laura. HarperPerennial, 1991.

Against All Odds: Holocaust Survivors and the Successful Lives They Made in America. Helmreich, William B. Simon and Schuster, 1992.

American Daughter Gone to War: On the Front Lines with an Army Nurse in Vietnam. Smith, Winnie. William Morrow, 1992.

The Battered Woman. Walker, Lenore Harper & Row, 1979.

The Best Kept Secret: Sexual Abuse of Children. Rush, Florence. Prentice Hall, 1980.

Bloods: An Oral History of the Viet Nam War by Black Vet*erans*. Terry, W. Ballantine, 1985.
Child Sexual Abuse: New Theory & Research. Finkelhor, David. The Free Press, 1984.

Highly recommended:

The Vietnam Center; Texas Tech University, Math Rm. 4, Lubbock, TX 79409-1045; telephone: (806) 742-3742; website: http://www.vietnam.ttu.edu/

TCK World http://www.tckworld.com

The Reading Group Guide

Reading Group Questions and Topics for Discussion

1.   Describe the relationship between Fred and his father and why he was estranged from his father. How did the memories of Vietnam create such a stranglehold on their relationship?

2.   Why do you think Fred decided to go to Thailand instead of Pakistan or Central America, hotter areas for press coverage, to start his photojournalism career? Describe the differences between his conscious and subconscious decisions for going to Southeast Asia to begin his career.

3.   Upon leaving the FCCT, Fred returns a salute offered by the night watchman at the mall. What is the significance of Fred's salute?

4.   Fred displayed at least three prominent indications of post-traumatic stress disorder before he went back to Southeast Asia. What were these? Discuss possible reasons for his parents ignoring the signs. Could Fred's low self-esteem, indicated by his refusal to believe he suffered from PTSD, actually have been another symptom of PTSD? Please explain.

5.   Describe the prophetic events of the book, beginning with the film *Midnight Express,* and including the visit to the fortuneteller. Discuss the cycles of events, how one event led to the other, and how they indicated the future.

6.   At what point in the story does Fred begin the actual process of healing? Describe and discuss the main events that led to the healing of memories of Vietnam and reparations in Fred's thoughts about his father.

7.   After Lor's death and Fred's return to Bangkok, what first event indicated that Fred was beginning to experience PTSD symptoms related to the traumatic events of that night?

8. When Fred and Robin arrived in Vietnam, how did Fred know that he had actually found his old home? What was surreal about the experience of being back in the very home of his childhood?

9. While Fred had recognized his captor on Grand Pirate Island, why was it that the commandant didn't recognize him?

10. Describe the differences Fred noticed in the Vietnam of his imprisonment and the Vietnam of 1999. What changed and what remained the same?

11. What were the similarities Fred noticed between himself and Knight, and why did it scare Fred so much? What were the life lessons Fred had learned in this coming-of-age voyage? How did his self-discovery led to the healing between Fred and his father?

The Reading Group Guide to *The Bamboo Chest* is also available at
www.bamboochest.com

The History Club Guide

History Club Questions and Topics for Discussion

1. Most of the public defines the Vietnam War as having started with either the Gulf of Tonkin Incident in 1964, or the landing of 3,500 US Marines at Danang in 1965. Review historical documents at your local library and check the dates of the first American advisor's arrival in Vietnam after the end of World War II. Who was the first American advisor killed in Vietnam?

2. What countries other than China, Russia, North Korea, South Korea, United States, New Zealand and Australia had military personnel stationed in Indochina during the war in Vietnam? In what capacity were these men and women serving? (For example, some of the pilots shot down in MIGs were actually North Korean military advisors.)

3. How many foreign civilians were in Vietnam during the war? Which nation was most represented by this collection of expatriates?

4. During the war in Vietnam, many public personalities stated that the US had no experience fighting insurgency wars. Review materials on the Philippine Insurrection of 1899, the Banana Wars of 1912 to 1934, and Philippine and American guerrilla wars against the Japanese in WWII, along with minor participation in Malaysia and Greece after WWII, and compare the events and how the wars were fought in these two sets of countries: Laos, Cambodia, and Vietnam; and Nicaragua, El Salvador, Honduras, and Guatemala. If the US had fought in Vietnam with the same tactics it had perfected in Central America, do you think the war in Vietnam would have instead resulted in the same type of victory, unknown and unrecognized?

1. Consider the press coverage of the Tet offensive, the amount of military support pumped into Vietnam by China and the Soviet Union, and the US's militarily winning of every battle in Vietnam, but losing every one of them politically. Contrast it with the press coverage and lack of Soviet support during the failed FMLN (Farabundo Marti Liberacion Nacional) Tet II of 1989-which was

suggested by the original architect of the 1968 Tet, General Giap, in a November 11, 1989 meeting with Sandinista President Daniel Ortega--and make a case for why Vietnam would still have been a political loss for the US, or would it have resulted in a surrender by North Vietnam? Would Communist forces have won in El Salvador had they had the same conditions and support as they had in Vietnam? Explain.

5. Research the history of captain William Kidd, especially the map found in Kidd's hidden strong box that was included in this book. Study the history of *Grand Pirate Islands (Iles Des Pirates)*. Discuss the likelihood that Kidd could or couldn't have been in Southeast Asia.

6. Consider the ugliness of war. Would WWII have been won by the Allies, or instead by the Axis powers, had the press corps had the same free-for-all, televised coverage as experienced in Vietnam?

7. Research William Randolph Hearst and stories in *The San Francisco Examiner* during the Spanish-American War. Also, review articles and photo features in the *New York Times*, *The Washington Post*, and *Life* magazine during the war in Vietnam and discuss why Vietnam was labeled the "journalist's war."

8. Many look at the fighting in Iraq and see a lack of cohesion between the White House, State Department and Pentagon. Review information on the Spanish American War, WWII, Vietnam, Korea and Central America to find similarities and differences that either support or disprove this view.

9. Knowing when to get out: review the events in the US's present wars, and compare them to previous conflicts such as WWI, WWII, Korea, Vietnam, and Central America, and state your reasons for when a nation is served by getting into a war, and when it's time to complete that nation's involvement. When does a military identity shift from *defending* to *occupational* (UN and local forces): which is necessary and when?

10. What is too little force and what is too much? One example to consider is the bombing of North Vietnam during the peace talks, and review the comments made by Kissinger, Nixon and General Giap about how Vietnam reacted to the bombing after having first left the peace talks table in Paris. Another example of discussion could be the comparison of numbers of US troops in Vietnam during the Eisenhower years and later during the Johnson years,

and how the incoming mass of US troops in 1965 made it easier for Hanoi's propaganda mill to label them as invaders. Consider the cultural effects on different nations in the wars over the last sixty years, with regards to how military force is applied, for example, in: Germany, Great Britain, Vietnam, Cambodia, Laos, El Salvador, Afghanistan, Bosnia, and Iraq.

The History Club Guide to *The Bamboo Chest* is also available at www.bamboochest.com

AWARD WINNING JOURNALIST AND AUTHOR, CORK GRAHAM has been a guest speaker since 1984, when at the Age Of 19, he enthralled the international media with his coming of age story of having just experienced eleven months in the Socialist Republic of Vietnam as their first American political prisoner held since the fall of Saigon.

After a four-year odyssey in Central America, where he continued his work as a foreign correspondent, and Alaska, where he conducted anthropological studies on the psychological, spiritual, and medical techniques of the area's native healers, Cork returned to California, working as a drug and rehab counselor for the Native American community and beginning a career in motivational public speaking to crowds interested in learning how to use the mind to reach full potential.

"What's special about Cork Graham is that he talks about these tools from life experience, heavy life experience." — Sandra James, Arizona.

A trained specialist in Neuro-Linguistic Programming (NLP), hypnosis, and other esoteric mind change techniques, some of which he uniquely created in order to survive the challenge of a Communist re-education prison, and guerrilla warfare in Central America, Cork Graham has become a public speaker noted for not only a wide range of wildly entertaining and enthralling stories, but also having a skill for using those stories to help a large audience make profound personal and professional changes for the better!

"Thank you for helping me make changes to my life that I couldn't before, even with all those NLP courses I'd taken!"— Cameron, New York, NY.

His story and appearance credits include:
- ABC Good Morning America

- CBS Morning News
- CBS News
- ABC News
- NBC News
- San Francisco Chronicle
- The Times of London
- Washington Post
- National Review
- Bangkok Post
- LA Times
- San Francisco Examiner
- KPIX Bay Sunday
- O'Loughlin Trade Shows
- International Sportsmen's Exposition
- The Times of San Mateo
- Playboy
- Game and Fish Magazine
- National Public Radio

Speaking Engagement Topics of Interest:

- Combat Journalism
- Outrageously Effective Sales Copy: The keys to writing it and strategically using it for profound effect!
- Solitary: Life fortifying lessons learned through the ordeal of political imprisonment
- PTSD: Healing the memory of trauma from childhood through adulthood
- Ex-Patriation: Living and working in a foreign country
- Sifting Dirt: How to scrutinize media content for the complete facts
- How the Media Hypnotizes the Public and How You Can Protect Yourself!

- Cross Cultural Marketing Strategies: How to design and how to implement
- Phobias: The Master Guide
- Secrets of the Profoundly Successful: How to push yourself outside of your borders!
- Hypnosis: Practical uses outside of the clinical environment
- Survival Training: Becoming comfortable in the wilds
- Eye of the Hunter: Lessons from the woods applied to the business world.
- Guerrilla Fighter in the Boardroom: How to implement the strategic mind of a guerrilla fighter in your marketing plan!
- Beyond the Mirage: How to effectively use ancient shamanic techniques in modern times
- Infopreneur: Success as an entrepreneur in the information field!

To schedule Cork Graham for your next TV/ radio show, seminar, or conference visit:

www.corkgraham.com

www.ingramcontent.com/pod-product-compliance
Lightning Source LLC
LaVergne TN
LVHW051543070426
835507LV00021B/2378